Complete quotes from the book jacket

"I do think this is a very stimulating book that will make people think. It will make some of them mad.

"Societies do change over time through very complex processes, and I think the author puts his finger on a very important process in possible changes in child rearing.

"The fundamental question which this book raises, on the nature of the effect of family and child rearing on the history of the economy, is very real and has received far too little attention from social scientists. The critical question here is: How do we encourage, through our ethical standards and even through government policy, the development of a culture of learning, both in which the field of human knowledge is constantly widened and in which error becomes unstable?"

KENNETH E. BOULDING
Distinguished Professor of Economics, Emeritus
Insitute of Behavioral Science
The University of Colorado at Boulder
author of *Ecodynamics* and *Three Faces of Power*

"I found it necessary to read Guy Odom's book twice. My first reading left me so disturbed. My second reading was intended to allay my fears but they were intensified.

"Odom has described with clarity why we Americans feel uneasy about our nation. He argues persuasively it will not get better if we don't effect changes. He does not leave us without hope or direction but he warns us that the time is short.

"This is must reading for all of us but it is especially pertinent for persons who are engaged in human services and for persons who work with and develop social policies."

ALONZO A. CRIM, Ed.D.
Professor of Educational Administration, Benjamin E. Mays Chair
Georgia State University
former Superintendent, Atlanta, Georgia, School District

"As I am, by Guy Odom's definition, a 'dominant woman,' I can personally identify with parts of *Mothers, Leadership, and Success*. His conclusions are not always mine, but he raises issues that are critical to modern-day American culture. The work is not only thoughtful but thought-provoking. Guy Odom exhibits remarkable knowledge, as well as appreciation, of the influence of history on current problems facing us as a nation. He obviously cares a good deal about our future."

THE HONORABLE GERALDINE FERRARO

"I have read *Mothers, Leadership, and Success* in its entirety and portions of it several times. It is stimulating and provocative. I admire you for producing such a learned work with such clearly presented convictions.

"As the son of non-believing immigrant Jews, I was especially interested in your provocative observations on Jews and on the kibbutz."

VICTOR GOERTZEL, Ph.D.
retired Research and Clinical Psychologist
author of *Cradles of Eminence* and *300 Eminent Personalities*

"Guy Odom is a brave man. Seeking to understand what it is that leads some people but not others to achieve success in their lives, he has delved into the circumstances of early childhood and, following promising leads, come to a number of conclusions that many will find outrageous. Knowing this, he yet dares to share his findings with us. This book will be highly controversial for in addition to the critics there will also be many who, like myself, applaud Odom, not least for his intellectual honesty.

"I am personally fascinated by this book because of the close parallels that can be drawn between Odom's analysis of the importance of the mother (or other primary caretaker) in the development of human character and desire for success and my own belief in the equally crucial part played by a chimpanzee, mother in determining the eventual social rank of her offspring. (Similarities should not surprise us in view of the fact that our genetic material differs from that of the chimps by only just over 1%.)

"*Mothers, Leadership, and Success* is an important and powerful book with a chilling message that we would do well to heed."

JANE GOODALL, Ph.D.
Scientific Director, Gombe Stream Research Centre

"Guy Odom has amassed an impressive array of evidence supporting his thesis that maternal dominance is of crucial importance in the rearing of high-achieving individuals. His concept of maternal dominance as an overlooked influence on individual leadership and success is both original and brilliant.

"At once scholarly and provocative, Odom's analysis and interpretation should stimulate wide debate regarding the rise (and fall?) of American society."

WAYNE H. HOLTZMAN, Ph.D.
President, Hogg Foundation for Mental Health
Hogg Professor of Psychology and Education
The University of Texas at Austin

"No nation in the history of the world has ever survived the ravages of success. All great nations rise and fall, and we'd better understand why. Guy Odom has given us his intriguing theory which should be of great interest to all who care about the future of America."

RICHARD D. LAMM
former Governor of Colorado
Director, Center for Public Policy and Contemporary Issues
The University of Denver

"This book represents a tremendous scholarly enterprise. I found it fascinating.

"In the main I agree with Guy Odom's major thesis and the way in which he sees psychological factors as the major determinants of everything from the rise and fall of civilizations to the reasons for race prejudice and the balance of trade between two countries. He has been very imaginative in thinking of consequences of his major thesis and energetic in checking out those consequences.

"Needless to say I thought the treatment of the hereditarians' arguments excellent."

DAVID C. McCLELLAND, Ph.D.
Professor Emeritus, Harvard University
Distinguished Professor, Boston University
author of *The Achieving Society* and *Power: The Inner Experience*

Additional quotes

"*Mothers, Leadership, and Success* is a book you'll read, put down and pick up again. The reader will experience a great range of emotions from anger, frustration, disappointment, enchantment to exaltation. The greatest effort on the reader is the mental stimulation, thought provoking, analytical thinking created by the text. It's tough."

HENRIETTE L. ALLEN, Ph.D.
Administrative Assistant to the Superintendent
Jackson Public School District, Jackson, Mississippi

"History, psychology, political science all wrapped around a central theme—the dominant woman! Career women must not miss this insightful analysis of the role they have played in the emergence of world powers.

"As an early childhood education specialist, I applaud Guy Odom's book. He brings into perspective the importance of early intervention to prevent school failure. His arguments are compelling and worthy of consideration."

LILLIAN C. BARNA, Ed.D.
Superintendent of Schools
Tacoma Public Schools, Tacoma, Washington

"Many authors write books that expose problems and pose questions. In *Mothers, Leadership, and Success,* Guy Odom delivers answers. This book should be required reading for parents, educators, and aspiring young adults who care deeply about the future of this nation. Guy Odom addresses forthrightly the societal conditions that must change to ensure our future."

RONALD E. ETHERIDGE, Ed.D.
Superintendent of Schools
Columbus Public Schools, Columbus, Ohio

"Guy Odom's well-written book gives us real insight into the make-up of leadership and success—and is especially relevant to those of us involved in politics. His ideas on what breeds strong, effective leaders should be read by anyone in political life. As a campaign consultant to male *and* female candidates, I see first hand how Guy Odom's theories are translated into reality."

PETER FENN
Political Consultant

"Guy Odom has determined the underlying factor for predicting human success. This knowledge has the power to change the course of education and the fate of nations."

MILTON K. NEGUS, Ed.D.
Superintendent of Schools
Roswell Independent School District, Roswell, New Mexico

"The history of the United States of America is replete with major crises. This same history also records that the leadership of America has effected solutions, in part by developing in-depth understanding of the reasons these crises exist. America's crises today—in education, productivity, and related economic issues—can be solved once again by having a fundamental understanding of the reasons for that particular crisis.

"Guy Odom's book provides the leadership of America and its concerned citizens with new insights that can aid in comprehending the complexities of these issues. This in turn can lead to a consensus on actions that must be taken if America is to regain its position as the world economic leader and maintain its humanitarian pursuits."

BILLY R. REAGAN, Ed.D.
Educational Consultant
former Superintendent, Houston, Texas, School District

"Since the beginning of time, society has worked hard to create a perfect formula for success. Guy Odom's book provides interesting research that brings us back to the realization that the home was our first classroom; and that our parents were our first teachers.

"Leaders in the education community should read this research while searching for the ingredients for the perfect formula.

"Strong, positive, effective, intelligent leadership, plus personality traits, is paramount if a high quality of education in this nation is going to increase the quality of life and education for our fellow man.

"If for no other reason than to reinforce what many already believe, all of us should read this book."

VINCENT E. REED, Ed.D.
Vice President for Communications, *The Washington Post*
former Assistant Secretary for Elementary and Secondary Schools
United States Department of Education
former Superintendent, District of Columbia Public Schools

"As our country grapples with education reform and searches for the key to producing successful citizens, Guy Odom's provocative ideas in *Mothers, Leadership, and Success* provide a fascinating insight. It is my belief that his ideas will stimulate debate and provide tools that enhance the quest for solutions and strategies in this important moment in our history."

RICHARD W. RILEY
former Governor of South Carolina

"A provocative book. It should be read by all who care about our children and our nation. It will please some, alienate others, but it assuredly will stimulate everyone who reads it. This book can positively influence the direction of history."

M. DONALD THOMAS, Ed.D.
Educational Consultant
former Superintendent, Salt Lake City, Utah, School District

"Many women will read this book and be dismayed; others will be delighted. Guy Odom has managed to write a book that will evoke these, and many other reactions. But this remarkable book not only arouses our emotions, it makes us think—an even rarer commodity these days."

CAROLYN WARNER
President, Carolyn Warner and Associates
former Superintendent of Public Instruction, State of Arizona
1986 Democratic Party Nominee, Governor of Arizona

"This book confirms a thesis I have long held—that quality Marines generally come from stable homes with a strong degree of maternal love, guidance, and support. I recommend this book to all aspiring leaders who seek by inspiration and persuasion to motivate others toward achievement of a common goal."

LOUIS H. WILSON
General U. S. Marine Corps (Ret.)
26th Commandant of the U. S. Marine Corps

Mothers, Leadership, and Success

Mothers, Leadership, and Success

GUY R. ODOM

with the assistance of

Leona Rita Osfield

Foreword by TERREL H. BELL
former United States Secretary of Education

POLYBIUS PRESS   HOUSTON   1990

Acknowledgment is made to the following for permission to reprint previously published material:

From THE FATE OF EMPIRES by Sir John Glubb. Copyright © 1976 by J.B.G. Ltd. Reprinted by permission of The Estate of Sir John Glubb.

From LYNDON JOHNSON AND THE AMERICAN DREAM by Doris Kearns. Copyright © 1976 by Doris Kearns. Reprinted by permission of Harper & Row.

From THE POWER BROKER: ROBERT MOSES AND THE FALL OF NEW YORK by Robert A. Caro. Copyright © 1974 by Robert A. Caro. Reprinted by permission of Alfred A. Knopf, Inc.

Direct inquiries to: Polybius Press, P.O. Box 20209, Houston, Texas 77225

This book is printed on acid-free paper, and its binding materials have been chosen for strength and durability.

Library of Congress Cataloging-in-Publication Data

Odom, Guy R., 1931-
Mothers, Leadership, and Success

Includes bibliographical references.
1. United States—Social policy—1980- 2. Social history—Modern,
1500- 3. Leadership. 4. Sex role. 5. Dominance (Psychology).
6. Child rearing. 7. Cycles. 8. United States—Economic
policy—1981- I. Osfield, Leona Rita, 1949- II. Title.
HN65.O514   1990   649'.1—dc20   89-23027
ISBN 0-9624006-0-2

In memory of
Dr. John Wesley Smith

[S]cientific training is not well designed to produce the man who will easily discover a fresh approach.

Thomas S. Kuhn
The Structure of Scientific Revolutions

They are to dedicate the statue of my mother to Demeter in Nemea or wherever seems best.

Aristotle's Will

We are our mothers.
They are their mothers.
We are all our mothers.

Mordecai
April 8, 1976

Contents

BOOK TWO

TABLES

FIGURES

Acknowledgments

I wish to thank Rita L. Atkinson, Ph.D.; Gerald P. Bodey, M.D.; Donald E. Buford; John L. Colonghi; Vicki d'Hemecourt; Nancy Hadley; Governor Richard D. Lamm; Charles A. LeMaistre, M.D.; Karen S. Odom; Wanda J. Odom; Carolina Pruneda; J. William Sorensen; and Virginia Lee Underwood, who provided advice, encouragement, and suggestions during the development of this book. And later, several who contributed endorsements also provided suggestions.

I thank all of you for your counsel and wisdom from which I benefited greatly. You will recognize your thoughts in the book.

Especial gratitude is extended to Wayne H. Holtzman, Ph.D.; Billy R. Reagan, Ed.D.; and M. Donald Thomas, Ed.D.; for the untold hours they committed to many aspects of this book. Dr. Holtzman's manuscript criticisms were sorely needed and greatly appreciated.

I am greatly indebted to Ted Bell. I know no person more credible, just, honorable, and dedicated in the field of education than Dr. Terrel H. Bell, author and former United States Secretary of Education. Considering the book's provocative theme, Dr. Bell exhibits in the Foreword a willingness to confront new ideas with an openmindedness seldom found today in Americans of his stature.

September, 1989   Guy R. Odom

Foreword

In the process of becoming chairman and chief executive officer of the nation's largest and most profitable home construction company, Guy R. Odom found what he believes to be the wellspring of success and power for the United States: strong-willed, dominant, achievement-oriented leaders. His book contains a powerful message for all who recognize that the strength and vitality of our country rest upon the leadership qualities, the will, and the character of our people.

Mothers, Leadership, and Success answers some difficult questions. In this era of nationwide disquiet about our future capacity to effectively lead the free world, what will be the source of new generations of strong and dominant men and women? How can we help produce the thousands of talented, strong-willed people our nation will need in the future? Can leadership traits be established early in life? What can schools do to develop future leaders for our country?

Guy Odom has sought answers to these questions for many years. After extensive research, continuous reading, and careful thought, Odom presents his responses to these crucial concerns. The message is clear: intelligent and energetic men and women over the past two centuries have provided the power and impetus that constituted the greatness of America throughout its history. More importantly, *Mothers, Leadership, and Success* can be the basis for our producing the leaders needed to keep the United States in a position of world leadership.

Odom grew up in the small town of Groveton, Texas. He developed a strong interest in reading, was encouraged to achieve, and worked hard at whatever he did. Intelligent, energetic, and determined, he soon exhibited the qualities of leadership. He became chief executive officer of Norwood Homes, Inc., a small Houston, Texas, homebuilding firm, in 1967. There he began trying to identify people who had the potential to achieve success. As a successful entrepreneur, Odom made Norwood Homes the largest homebuilding company in Houston. He sold Norwood Homes to U.S. Home Corporation in 1971. In 1973 he built a new company, Homecraft Corporation, into the twentieth largest homebuilding company in the United States. He sold the company to U.S. Home Corporation and assumed the duties of chief executive officer of that firm from February 1977 to August 1984.

During this period of his career, Odom began to conduct research on personality and intelligence, and how to apply these characteristics to quickly increase organization size, dollar volume, and profits. In conjunction with personality and intelligence screening, Odom instituted a management development program to prepare new managers to take on vastly increased responsibilities. His program was extremely successful. U.S. Home became the largest homebuilding company in the United States with annual sales in excess of $1 billion.

As chairman and chief executive officer of U.S. Home Corporation, Guy Odom was constantly in need of effective, highly motivated, achievement-minded individuals. He probed for human traits that could predict success and leadership behavior. Through insight and wisdom, he developed a system for selecting "the best people" for his corporation—those who would accomplish what many believed to be impossible.

Prior to their selection, Odom's management trainees were interviewed, given intelligence tests and personality surveys, and thoroughly evaluated. He utilized a thoughtfully developed procedure that allowed him to identify the energetic, intelligent managers who helped him lead his corporation to the zenith of the nation's home construction industry. His management philosophy was relatively simple: "Get the best people. Give them direction and room to grow. Provide the right incentives and growth will follow."

Odom's management development program was recognized on a national level. *Fortune* ran a feature story about his personnel selection and management programs in its December 4, 1978, issue. In 1980 Odom was selected Builder of the Year for 1979 by *Professional Builder*. In January 1982 *The Practicing CPA*, published by the American Institute of Certified Public Accountants, had its lead article on Guy Odom and his management development program. Similar articles have appeared in other national and international publications.

Odom's selection process and development programs have been cited in books within and outside the homebuilding industry. Ned Eichler, a visiting professor of business administration at the University of California, Berkeley, included Guy Odom's selection and development programs in *The Merchant Builders*, published by MIT Press. Odom was profiled in *Contemporary Business* (third edition) by Louis E. Boone, University of Central Florida, and David L. Kurtz, Seattle University. The book was published by CBS College Publishing, a division of Holt, Rinehart, and Winston. Odom was also featured in the "Epilogue" of *The Classic Touch: Lessons in Leadership from Homer to Hemingway* by John K. Clemens and Douglas F. Mayer, both of Hartwick College, Oneonta, New York (published by Dow Jones-Irwin).

Odom's selection and development programs were designed to build intellectual competence and further foster the relentless, driving energies that were crucial to building a profitable, highly successful company. Odom studied the classics and requested his leadership people to do the same. They met to discuss the lives of history's highest achievers and to learn all they could that would build qualities of strength and wisdom, and prompt the insightful expenditure of human energy.

In all these efforts to build a great company by establishing qualities of excellence in the minds and wills of his managers, Odom studied the lives of exceptionally high-achieving persons in and out of his company. What builds character, determination, and a relentless will to achieve in some people? Why is it present in a few and absent in so many? What are the antecedents of leadership and success?

Guy Odom has advanced some very persuasive theories that shed light on these questions. The theories appeal to common sense and have been validated through the lives of the hundreds of individuals whom he has studied. *Mothers, Leadership, and Success* is not a study of Guy Odom and his personal achievement. Rather, it is an exploration of a fundamental question: whether heredity or environment is the primary determinant of intelligence and achievement.

This question has been debated for decades. From the beginning one side and then the other has gained in popularity and acceptance. In the 1960s environment held sway. In the 1980s it appears that inheritance has gained greater recognition. The ongoing controversy has intensified, polarizing segments of American society.

Psychologists continue to be divided on this issue. According to biological determinists, if a child is predetermined to be intelligent, then he can respond to education. The opposite is true if a child is considered to be lacking in intelligence because of heredity. Education then can do little to help him, thereby leaving little hope for the future success of millions of Americans as adults.

One of the most complex facets of this divisiveness involves testing for intelligence. It appears that many psychologists who believe that inheritance is the primary source of intelligence also believe strongly in IQ testing. Others who adhere to the belief that environment maximizes intelligence are opposed to such testing. At the same time, educators administer tests of all descriptions, yet hold differing views on the validity of such tests as the Scholastic Aptitude Test—and so the debate continues.

These diverse views spill over into the debate over early childhood education, whether it is beneficial or detrimental. My own position was expressed in 1973 in my book *Your Child's Intellect: A Guide to Home-Based Preschool Education*: "Early childhood, indeed, infant development in the learning processes is therefore desirable for all children, regardless of background or ability." It is a position that is supported by *Mothers, Leadership, and Success*.

Odom's book begins with a simple and unusual idea of the childhood origin of success. It continues with descriptions of marriage combinations never before explored. Odom brings to light child-rearing practices of different marriage combinations to provide a different perspective about adult actions.

This perspective is applied to several fields of study involving the social consequences in adulthood of different child-rearing practices. This exploration is more than thought provoking; it is provocative.

His canvas becomes larger as he proposes a natural law for the cyclical rise and decline of past empires and places the present stage of the United States in its cycle. Since his belief in recurring cycles is rooted in a common theme, he places blame on no political party or political leader. The realistic summary of facts in the later chapters, "Age of Affluence," "Age of Intellect" and "Age of Decadence," could be viewed as chilling or frightening. Yet, optimism leaps forth in his final chapter, "Considerations." Further, he believes that chapter to be only the merest beginning of the process of finding a new educational direction for the United States.

Guy Odom is the product of a demanding and loving mother who trained him for excellence from early childhood, coupled with the forceful elementary and secondary schooling of the educational system of the 1930s and 1940s. His success came in business enterprises, yet this book could affect the thoughts and actions of people to a far greater degree than his past endeavors. Should Odom's theory be correct, those who have a life's work invested on the side of biological determinism may, even though they find themselves influenced by this book, be concerned that their reputations will be endangered.

This book should be of particular interest to educators; to those who believe in the importance of early childhood training; to assertive, dominant, achieving women (especially those electing not to bear children); to investors; and to anyone concerned with the present weakening of our democratic and capitalistic society. High achievers in the United States, especially those of the Jewish faith, should find this work extremely enlightening. I also believe that Guy Odom's book will have strong appeal in other countries, particularly Germany and Japan.

Mothers, Leadership, and Success comes at the right time—a time in history when there is a desperate need for leadership and a compelling need to improve education and to prepare potential leaders. This is an important book. It will be provocative, stimulating, and controversial. It should be read and debated in corporate, government, and educational circles.

Guy R. Odom has a powerful and significant message, one that can profoundly influence decisions in raising up future generations of competitively successful leaders for our nation at a time when we so desperately need them.

Terrel H. Bell
former United States Secretary of Education

According to E. B. White in the third edition of *The Elements of Style* by Strunk and White, "The use of *he* as pronoun for nouns embracing both genders is a simple, practical convention rooted in the beginnings of the English language. *He* has lost all suggestion of maleness in these circumstances." I followed the conventional use of the *he* pronoun throughout this book to facilitate a smooth flow of ideas. Well before they reach the midpoint of this book readers will have no doubts whatsoever as to where I stand in regard to gender differences.

Introduction

Twenty-five hundred years ago, *Know thyself* was inscribed above the lintel of the Temple of Apollo at Delphi. Understanding one's self is a prerequisite for understanding the motives of others. Although psychology provides solutions to many puzzles of the mind, it has not yet wholly yielded the key to the ancient Greek admonition. Unanswered questions about individual behavior remain. This book attempts to give new insight into behavior, its origins, and its relationship to success.

Some people seem driven to strive for success; others appear to be content with lesser goals. Highly successful individuals all seem to be dominant, energetic, and intelligent. Are these characteristics necessary for success and, if so, what are their origins? Lacking these traits, will an individual be unsuccessful or attain only limited success?

Some mothers rear their children in a demanding, structured environment whereas other mothers are permissive. In certain families all the children achieve success whereas in others none of the children are successful. In still other families, some of the children succeed but others do not. Do child-rearing practices directly affect and even predict adult successes?

Data suggest that children of highly successful fathers rarely equal the fathers' successes, yet children of unsuccessful fathers often become successful. Can one parent alone influence a child's future? If neither parent has strong needs to achieve, will that affect the attitudes toward success of their offspring? Are there social consequences when ambitious, successful women elect not to have children?

In the middle and upper classes, men and women who have different ambitions and needs for success frequently marry one another. When both work, one spouse often earns a considerably larger income than the other. Few marriages include two highly ambitious partners. Do differing ambitions and achievement needs influence the selection of a marriage partner?

1

Jews have been an identifiable group for over four thousand years. During that period, they have been successful and persecuted. Can a specific personality characteristic contribute to their successes and perhaps to their persecutions as well?

Many have noted that all great empires rise and fall, and some speculate that the United States is following the same path. No great city-state, country, nation, or empire has retained its dominant world position indefinitely. Historically, all great empires begin with conquest and end with corruption and decadence. No general theory has been accepted to account for why great countries rise and subsequently decline, and few solutions have been offered to prevent their failures. Can identifiable personality traits contribute to individual, group, and national successes and failures?

This book proposes fresh ideas on what underlies achievement and success, ideas applicable across a broad range from individuals to entire nations, past and present. I recognize that neither these ideas nor their applications are susceptible to the conventions and constraints of traditional scholarship, since hard data supporting my theses are difficult or literally impossible to find. I am unable to validate many of my assumptions and conclusions by methods more rigorous than extensive reading, thoughtful observation, practical reasoning, and deductions based on these processes.

However, it should be noted that for eighteen years (1967-1984) as a corporate chief executive officer, I personally studied and applied the results of personality surveys and intelligence tests for executive, managerial, and sales personnel selection in business enterprises. These businesses were composed of managerial and sales executives with administrative support staffs. Labor was subcontracted.

Fairly early in my tenure as chief executive officer, I realized that I wanted to be associated with a large firm. Enlarging the current company as quickly as possible seemed the best approach. But how? Technical knowledge is readily available and so is information on how to develop and make the most of employee talents. But there are no books to tell us how to find the right people. To grow at the rate I desired, we needed people who could grow at the same pace, taking on newer, more demanding, and difficult responsibilities, and taking them on in an expeditious manner.

Business literature and lengthy discussions with psychologists all pointed in the same direction; they named intelligence the indispensable ingredient in a growing enterprise. Smart people, so conventional wisdom went, could keep pace with a growth company.

Following this path, psychologists administered IQ tests to the company executives and evaluated the results. Intelligence became the primary focus for selecting individuals. I implemented a testing program using the services of several psychologists.

From the inception of the company's testing program, we used the Wechsler Adult Intelligence Scale (WAIS), administered by outside psychologists. Even though expensive compared to more conventional paper and pencil tests, the one-to-one WAIS always proved helpful and was well worth its price. Beyond the overall score, its subtests provided valuable information to correlate with on-the-job tasks. This held true for executive, managerial, sales, and administrative levels. Among psychologists the WAIS is still considered one of the best, if not the best available measure of adult intelligence.

The earliest program, intelligence testing with a personality analysis aimed only at avoiding employment of people with identifiable psychological problems, did not work. By 1969 the company was swollen with highly intelligent managerial, sales, and administrative personnel. But many of these employees were thinkers rather than doers. Intelligence as the primary focus did not produce the anticipated results.

We now recognized that intelligence, even with protection from specific psychological problems, was not enough. Though the first results were disappointing, the problems were not insurmountable. We began to study personality. We placed greater emphasis on identifying and understanding the interactions of personality traits and their influences on job success. We refined the selection process by studying the personality patterns of the most successful employees.

Learning about personality traits and their influence on success when combined with intellectual ability was the most difficult and the most rewarding aspect of my personality studies. We tried, compared, and refined different personality surveys, drawing new conclusions as to how best to match individuals to particular jobs.

From 1967 through 1984, we administered several thousand Wechsler Adult Intelligence Scale tests and an equal number of personality surveys of various types. We evaluated each person for executive potential on the basis of intelligence, personality, and job history.

For eighteen years in ongoing, expanding businesses, I had an excellent living laboratory. As understanding of the program improved and we saw employees we had identified as potentially successful achieving as predicted, we continued refining our views about intelligence, personality, and achievement. Few psychologists have had a like opportunity to study correspondingly large numbers of individuals, to correlate intelligence and personality with age, ethnic group, sex, and education, and to evaluate these variables with individual business success on a year-to-year basis.

As with all tests and surveys, interpretation is critical. In 1971 we evaluated the successes and failures that occurred during 1967 through 1971 and remedied misinterpretations of data. The 1972-1984 period produced rewards for the enterprise and for the employees hired using intelligence tests and personality surveys. Detractors (primarily competitors) were plentiful, but the results spoke for themselves. In each location, our company became the training ground for the industry. In time many competitors attempted similar testing programs.

Now we could hire people and predict on-the-job performance based on intellectual and personality variables in conjunction with work background. We observed and measured individual success and capitalized on predictable strengths in deploying valuable human resources. We knew what to look for and found it in goodly numbers of people from a cross section of America.

Understanding of an individual's strongest psychological needs combined with knowledge of his intellectual strengths permitted the companies with which I was involved to limit risks and still allow employees without prior related work experiences to manage new tasks and people. In most cases, substantial rewards ensued to both the company and the employee.

I was gratified to see people, particularly women and ethnic minorities, achieve success in an area never considered because they had lacked experience in that field. Our firm was one of the first in our industry and stood almost alone for many years in hiring and training women superintendents, managers, and executives. The company developed a reputation, according to *Everybody's Business: An Almanac,* as "a good place for women to get ahead."

We sought management trainees based on potential and did not limit our hiring practices to knowledge of the job. Using the hiring program, we identified highly intelligent minorities with striving personalities who had not been considered before for corporate management positions. Because of their mintority status some had gravitated to civil service; this provided a fertile field for solitication of minorities for our company.

During 1976-1984 some spouses of successful company executives and some of their teen-age and older children became the subjects of personality surveys. Publicity on the program piqued the interest of successful individuals outside the company, who used the surveys primarily to make personal evaluations and sometimes to gauge the success potential of their young adult children. Their curiosity added to our statistics several hundred additional personality surveys unrelated to business applications. Other information given to me in 1976 provided me with the key to partially predict success—not only for individuals but for their children.

Even though it is still common to focus on intelligence as the most important factor in determining executive success, one of my most important findings was that personality traits are equally significant and in many cases more important to success than high intelligence. There are too many examples of highly intelligent individuals never achieving the success seemingly forecast by the intellectual capability shown in their childhood and adolescence. My coming to realize the significance of an individual's personality traits was a major contributor to my economic success.

Through the years many people worked for the companies with which I was involved and contributed to the development of viable intelligence and personality programs. Though there are too many to list here, I thank them for their important contributions.

Any generalist covering a variety of subjects and territories uses generalizations, and those can be criticized with ease. Still, everyone who reads of necessity goes beyond personal experience; many analyses of psychology, anthropology, history, politics, economics, or any other discipline go beyond the personal experience of a particular analyst. As one who in this book is summarizing and simplifying large amounts of data, I know to expect critical dissection by the experts in the many fields I have touched upon. This is the fate of the synthesist.

I recognize that new ideas are not readily accepted. Over time, people have stubbornly rejected new ideas even when they provided answers. However, rejection of a simple idea is difficult after it becomes evident through the observations and personal experiences of a great many people.

New ideas usually go through three stages before acceptance. They are labeled absurd. Next, it's maybe. And finally, that's obvious, I knew it all the time. The thesis of this book is one of those large, "simple" ideas that will make almost everyone wonder why he did not see it for himself a long time ago.

Because my basic belief is simple, I believe eclectic readers will discover, as I did, that it is possible to link seemingly unrelated subjects and to draw logical conclusions that go beyond personal experiences. The idea was given to me and, in this book, I offer it to you.

This is not a book for scholars or academicians with a single-field interest or those with a deep-rooted, unshakable belief in biological determinism. The new viewpoint in the book's first section may trouble a few; my applying this perspective to different fields in later chapters will trouble many. Nonetheless I hope that readers with open, inquisitive minds who do not fear change will find that the content appeals to their intellect and their common sense. Its objective is to provoke thoughtful evaluation and new insights. I believe that it can be valuable to innovators and doers, useful in social, political, and money-making situations, and perhaps can also provide a stimulus for rethinking the educational process.

I believe that all knowledge is good; only the ways in which it is used or abused can be bad. It is this belief that permits this book to be written. Each reader has a frame of reference based on his experiences, personal beliefs, values, prejudices, and judgments. The book may provoke anger in some, regret in others, or simple disbelief. It is my hope that it will offer recognition and answers for many, and with these the impetus for change.

BOOK ONE

PART I
Origins of Individual Success

Chapter I

Dominance and Nondominance

The world is made up of all manner of people. There is one great group of humans who have good moral values, are tolerant of their fellow men, compassionate, helpful, and hard working. They have no high aspirations and are content to get along as best they can, trying to be happy and, usually, trying to make other people happy too. They are, in many ways, the salt of the earth, the backbone of a nation. There are more of them than any other group, I think. Sometimes they are led astray under the wrong leadership.

There are the misfits, who contribute nothing and merely take.

And then, there are the dominant types—bright, go-ahead, and successful. Many are also aggressive, inconsiderate, ruthless, and even dishonest. They give business its bad reputation. And politics too.

They are often workaholics, sparing but little time for family and friends, becoming increasingly short-tempered and hard to get along with as they get older. But they are the ones who, by and large, cause change in the world. And while change is by no means always good, it quite often is. The world might be a nicer and gentler and more peaceful place without them. But, in many ways, we need them. And, indeed, many are good people who have changed things for the better.

How do these different individuals develop? And what does this mean for families, groups, societies, and even nations? This leads us to personality.

The term *personality* is ambiguous and has many definitions. The statement that someone has a "pleasing personality" naturally draws the question, pleasing to whom? A pleasing personality is not necessarily pleasing to everyone. The expression can describe either a successful diplomat or an individual who has difficulty saying no and who may be referred to as a "yes-man."

I use *personality* as the organized pattern of an individual's behavioral characteristics; each personality manifests itself in recognizable behavioral traits. To describe a personality accurately, specific traits must be used. For example, to describe a person as having a "masculine personality," can be misleading since the phrase denotes only a small cluster of traits evidenced by the person. He may be masculine and at the same time lethargic, hostile, and critical or he may be masculine, energetic, agreeable, and accepting.

The complexity of individual personality and behavior is demonstrated in *Trait-Names: A Psycho-lexical Study* (1936) by Gordon W. Allport, Ph.D., and Henry S. Odbert, Ph.D. The study, made while Allport was at Harvard University and Odbert was at Dartmouth College, encompassed 17,953 words characterizing personal behavior and personality, and comprising 4.5 percent of entry-words in *Webster's New International Dictionary* of 1925. The criterion they used for selecting each word was its capacity to distinguish the behavior of one human being from that of another. The study also addressed the difficulties involved in using specific traits as pertaining to individuals, and the problems incurred by labeling individuals through the use of personality trait-names.

One problem in defining a personality trait is that one trait very often overlaps or shades into another. Traits also become hard to define discretely because each individual has a personal frame of reference when he or she defines and uses a particular trait descriptively. This personal frame of reference applies whether describing one's self or others. The difficulty can be seen in Allport and Odbert's assertion that, "One man may characterize a friend as *cautious*, a second may consider him *timid*, a third thinks he is *cowardly*. . . . One of these designations may in point of fact be more apt than the others, or conceivably all three may be inexact. The empirical discovery of traits in individual lives is one problem, that of selecting the most appropriate names for the traits thus discovered is another."

The difficulties with using traits to describe human beings are no less troublesome today than they were a half century ago when Allport and Odbert published their study. People still assume that traits applied to individuals represent actual components of their personalities. If not used carefully, specific names for personality traits can be traps, completely misleading so far as psychological definitions are concerned. Each personality trait represents a range of behavioral characteristics changing from person to person.

Recognizing the difference between trait-names and the personality traits themselves is the first obstacle to be overcome in explaining personality characteristics. It is necessary to convey in understandable language that personality traits are real and obvious to the discerning observer and that the degree or intensity with which they manifest themselves in an individual can be measured and comparisons made by using various psychologically developed personality surveys.

Each individual has a unique personality and manifests the traits of that personality in ways special to him; that does not mean, however, that traits cannot be defined in ways applicable to many. Although most personality characteristics overlap, some are more common and therefore more easily understood than others. For example, the traits of amiability and hostility are rarely seen as overlapping in a person.

Since personality measurements are not concise, it may help to think in shadings rather than absolutes when considering a particular personality trait that an individual exhibits. An elementary example is the designations average, above average, and below average. By using gradations, it is easier to grasp to what degree an individual's behavior evinces a certain trait.

The concept of hot and cold provides a concrete example of thinking in shadings. The temperature differences between the absolute extremes of heat and cold, the points at the lowest and highest ends of the scale, are so far removed from everyday experience that it is impossible to perceive what they actually are. Temperature is usually gauged within a narrower range. A particular personality trait can also be viewed as ranging in degrees instead of as an extreme or an absolute.

Sociability, for example, is a personality trait individuals discern easily in themselves and in others. The extremes of sociability would find the anti-social hermit at one end of the spectrum, and at the other the gregarious individual who always appears surrounded by people. But even the hermit has occasional contact with others as a necessity of life, and the most gregarious individual requires some time alone other than for sleeping. Consequently, it is difficult to conceive of a mentally healthy individual as absolutely shy or absolutely sociable.

Most needs to socialize lie between the extremes, and vary from one situation to another. It is too easy to label one person sociable and another unsociable; when one thinks in black and white, one may be semantically inaccurate. One should more accurately think in degrees, viewing the person as very sociable, sociable, somewhat sociable, somewhat shy, shy, or reclusive, with many additional degrees of sociability possible.

Similarly the trait of dominance, the primary subject of this book, varies by degree in each individual. Dominance is one of the least understood and most complex of all personality traits. No one is totally dominant or totally passive. For simplicity's sake, persons may be referred to as dominant or nondominant, or the trait itself be called dominance and its absence nondominance, but these terms should always be recognized as aspects of a *range*—not as absolutes. Some individuals are extraordinarily submissive and others extraordinarily domineering but, as with any other personality trait within the range of normal behavior, dominance generally lies between these extremes.

This book concentrates on the individual, social, and national ramifications of success or failure as a consequence of personal dominance levels. It should be emphasized that much of this subject matter relates to individuals with a relatively rare amount of high dominance and omits the vast middle ground where in most situations individuals are not particularly dominant or submissive.

Dominance is defined by the dictionary as "rule; control; authority; ascendancy." Synonyms for dominant include prevailing, principal, predominant, paramount, and preeminent. Numerous terms are used to describe dominance, some with positive and others with negative connotations. Among these are ascendant, ambitious, assertive, authoritative, controlling, domineering, overbearing, and dictatorial.

Dominant people are not necessarily—or even usually—domineering (defined as "inclined to rule arbitrarily or despotically; overbearing; tyrannical"). Most highly dominant individuals are persuasive. The degree of dominance in one individual compared to another is seen in the degree of inner need to influence, usually in a positive manner, the behavior of others.

I will use the terms dominance and dominant to describe those individuals who exhibit great needs to be in control, to lead, and to take charge in any field with which they become involved. Highly dominant people have a greater need for personal freedom, entrepreneurship, and achievement than less dominant people do. Dominance is reflected in one's need to mentally coerce the behavior of others, whether overtly through the exercise of authority or subtly with finesse.

Dominant people have psychological needs to control their future and to avoid being controlled by others. Depending on their dominance levels, men and women desire to manage in varying degrees the events and people in their lives. They believe that they can master their environment and manipulate and control what happens around them. Dominant people are not determinists. They believe that success and failure are unrelated to fate.

For dominant people, success means using their skills, knowledge, and control of others to mold their world according to their desires. A comedian wishes to control an audience, to make others laugh on his demand. Some are successful in eliciting laughter from audiences of fifty, others from fifty million. Successful corporate leaders shape positively the behavior of employees and customers to increase the well-being and profitability of a corporation. Successful scientists persuade others to support their efforts to control the forces or properties of the natural world. A diplomat manipulates other dominant leaders into adopting his viewpoint and suggestions.

I believe that dominance and leadership are synonymous, that every leader of consequence was or is dominant, and that anyone lacking high dominance never has been or will become a great leader. Mahatma Gandhi and Martin Luther King, Jr., advocated and practiced nonviolence, but who would view either as a nondominant leader? Regardless of the field, a high degree of dominance surfaces in the leaders of great endeavors and high achievements.

There are, of course, highly dominant people who never attain outstanding success. Some desire to control those with whom they come into immediate contact, yet have no desire to be successful in the eyes of society. Others strive for worldly success, but never acquire it.

The term nondominant describes individuals who have far fewer needs to achieve, to be in control, to lead, or to take charge than do highly dominant individuals. Many nondominant persons are more amiable and cooperative than their more dominant counterparts. Acknowledged as followers rather than leaders, they usually have a much greater need for security and for accepting and maintaining the status quo. Some reared in permissive environments show little regard for rules and dislike structured surroundings.

The need to dominate is rarely totally lacking in anyone; almost everyone has, at some time, been successful in the persuasion of others. Dominance and nondominance involve degrees, not absolutes.

Dominant individuals do not act with the same degree of dominance in all situations. Deference is given based on the position of one person in relation to another according to the circumstances encountered. A dominant person, for example, may assume a nondominant, subordinate role with his supervisor or the company's chief executive officer or a celebrity. The same person can comfortably take a dominant, superior position with other employees, business associates, friends, or family members. In Japan business cards are exchanged; each person then knows his rank compared to the other. In many instances, after exchanging cards, the higher ranking person will talk more and louder while the other lowers his voice and speaks less often. Both may be highly dominant, yet they observe social amenities predicated on the business status of each.

A person's need to alter his surroundings to his desire, the extent of the environment he attempts to control, and the frequency with which he wishes to exert that control can be considered measures of that person's level of dominance.

The interaction of all the traits of an individual's personality often clouds the issue when one is trying to assess a single trait, such as dominance. Depending on the observer's interpretation, an individual's actions may seem to indicate dominance when actually they express a very different trait. The trait of being critical provides a vivid example of how one personality characteristic becomes confused with another. To be critical is to be "inclined to find fault or to judge with severity, often too readily." Synonyms for critical include captious, censorious, carping, and faultfinding. Consequently, a very critical person's relationships with others frequently appear dominating. Although it can simulate dominance, criticalness is a specific personality trait in itself.

Criticalness can be described as a continual dissatisfaction with the way things are; the overly critical person has a limited ability to see good in things, events, or people. But dissatisfaction with things as they exist is not the same as a desire for dominance, which involves changing things. Unless the critical individual also has a high level of dominance, he is not motivated to effect change. Any individual, dominant or nondominant, can be critical.

Unfriendliness is another personality trait easily mistaken for dominance. An unfriendly person is defined as "not amicable; without indications of friendly or kindly disposition; unsympathetic; aloof; hostile; antagonistic." Unfriendliness is yet another independent trait found in both dominant and nondominant people. By being argumentative or antagonistic in speech and actions, the unfriendly, nondominant person is frequently viewed as attempting to dominate. Rather, he is expressing his higher-than-average levels of dissatisfaction and hostility. His antagonism may even stem from his perception of being unable to control his life. His lack of high dominance limits the meaningful actions he can take to effect change because his hostility cannot translate into the need to change and control others.

Many factors, including personality traits and personal attributes such as good health, combine with dominance to affect directly or indirectly the individual's efforts to achieve success. Like dominance, they are manifested in a wide range of intensities and are best measured in degrees. Two of the most important traits are energy and intelligence. The combination of dominance, intelligence, and energy shows up in leaders throughout history, although different words described these characteristics during different eras. Each is separate but, in this book, dominance is viewed as a catalyst for intelligence and energy. In addition, dominance is presented as the primary source of achievement.

The trait of high energy appears frequently in individuals described as workaholics; they never seem to become fatigued or burned out. Energetic people require less-than-average amounts of sleep. They often have large stores of nervous energy as revealed in mannerisms like feet-tapping, finger-drumming, and speed in eating. The behavior of energetic people is reflected in their impatience; they generally appear to be in a hurry.

High energy magnifies other personality traits including dominance. Because of the activity his energy generates, a dominant, sociable person with a high energy level appears considerably more dominant and more sociable than one with similar needs to control and socialize but with a lower energy level.

A low energy level limits a dominant individual's success. Conversely, greater-than-average success can be achieved with a high energy level without a correspondingly high dominance level. A combination of high dominance and high energy substantially offsets a lack of other traits that are positive for achieving individual success.

Superior intelligence is a distinct advantage but it alone does not furnish the drive for achieving great success. The same holds true for high levels of dominance and energy. However, dominance coupled with energy even without high intelligence can provide the propellant to enable an individual to achieve considerably more-than-average success. A combination of high intelligence, high dominance, and high energy ensures a greater degree of success than when only one of these traits is prominent.

As reflected by their actions and achievements, the most visibly successful people, past and present, exhibit the combined traits of dominance, energy, and intelligence in far greater degree than is found in the average person. Individuals at the next lower level of success also have these traits but to a lesser degree. So it continues down the ladder until the degree of intelligence combined with the degrees of dominance and energy becomes average and then below the average of individuals in a particular society. At that point, failure by an individual having less than the population average of these three traits becomes inevitable and visible not only to him but to his family, friends, and associates.

Job comparisons provide concrete examples of the interplay of dominance, energy, and intelligence. Let us say a sociable individual working on a commissioned sales basis has high dominance and high energy but lacks superior intelligence. Such a person could achieve high levels of success in direct sales and, because of that success, seek and be promoted to a managerial position making substantial demands on judgment. This individual probably will have risen quickly in sales because of his sales ability, much of which could be attributable to his levels of dominance, energy, and sociability. Yet on reaching a high managerial position requiring strong logic and reasoning ability (intelligence) in decision making, his shortcomings become evident in faulty decisions that cause failure in the position. Returning to direct sales, possibly with a different firm, he might again be successful only to be subjected to the same process of promotion followed by apparent failure.

In his lifetime, this individual achieves greater-than-average success. However, his high levels of dominance and energy cause him to develop greater expectations than someone less dominant and energetic, so that he often considers himself a failure. This internal conviction of failure comes from his lack of accomplishment as he judges it by his frame of reference, since the combination of high dominance and high energy is almost impossible to satisfy at any achievement level. Even though he attains outstanding success in one area, this person is dissatisfied because he did not succeed in everything he attempted.

Naturally, there are many individuals in the direct sales field who have high intelligence, high dominance, and high energy. These are the best, the superstars, in their chosen field. These professionals are rewarded handsomely with money and status, and many feel little desire to enter the ranks of management.

A counterpart to the sales-managerial individual is an unpublished college professor having superior intelligence but lacking high dominance and high energy. Consistency and continuity in this individual's career eliminate the ups and downs experienced by the sales-managerial person. The professor should attain a higher-than-average success level. Although believing privately that he could accomplish more, and observing the successes of others apparently less intelligent than himself, the professor probably does not perceive himself as having failed. The lack of high dominance and high energy helps keep his expectations below the point at which he would consider anything less than high achievement to be personal failure.

Individual personality traits attract people to certain endeavors. There is a job closely fitting every personality; the task is finding the fit. The aggregation and meshing of traits that comprise an individual's personality create the occupational attraction. If an individual misjudges his personality or the appropriateness of occupation, he usually rectifies the error by a job change. If unable to make a change, the individual suffers since that position is not right for his personality.

The trait of emotional stability or instability provides an example of personality and occupational fit. Severe mood swings are one sign of emotional instability. They manifest the ups and downs of emotional feelings, which an individual cannot conceal by will power alone, particularly over an extended time. The tendency to react the same way under most conditions most of the time characterizes emotional stability. Such a person has a psychological need to appear consistent in mood even though it limits the expression of feelings.

A high level of emotional well-being visible in mood consistency combined with optimism might contribute to the success of a wartime general or a head of state. However, the same psychologically controlled behavior would severely limit his success in an artistic field such as acting. To be psychologically comfortable with expressing a wide range of emotions would be an asset for a great actor. Conversely, a highly acclaimed actor would not gain the same success if his field of endeavor were that of a national leader or wartime general.

Both emotional stability and instability stem from childhood training. Mood consistency, born of a strong reluctance to show emotion, results from training that discourages demonstrations of feeling. Openness regarding emotional feelings stems from training that encourages the display of a wide range of emotions.

Demonstration of job-fit and potential success in less obviously disparate fields might compare a public relations executive of a large corporation and a purchasing executive in the same corporation charged with procurement for the construction of a forty-story office building. Assume their compensation packages are equal and their intelligence, energy, and dominance are in the same general ranges. The public relations executive should be agreeable and accepting; the purchasing executive must be skeptical. If these individuals changed positions, each would fail. Who has ever known a successful hostile public relations executive or a successful agreeable purchasing executive?

Elite segments of the Armed Forces contain individuals who are different from the average serviceperson. Agents for the Federal Bureau of Investigation and the Central Intelligence Agency differ from their counterparts at equivalent government levels in the Department of Health and Human Services. The typical accountant is not attracted to direct selling, and the typical salesperson is not interested in accountancy.

Judgments of success and failure are linked to the era and the specific society in which an individual lives. The society's structure, values, and goals determine such judgments; what would be considered a high level of success in one time and place might be seen as failure in another. History is replete with examples. Dominant, energetic, and intelligent Royalists lost their lives on the guillotine in France in 1792 while around the world, notably in the United States and Great Britain, their counterparts reaped rewards for possessing the same qualities. In the 1930s and 1940s, dominant, energetic, and intelligent Jews were murdered in Germany and Eastern Europe while their counterparts in the United States and Brazil prospered.

Right or wrong, the United States measures outstanding success by three broad categories: wealth, fame, and power, singularly or in some combination of the three. Democracy and capitalism provide the cultural framework for such measurement. Success can be achieved through individual effort or with the effective use of an inheritance. Without individual achievement, inheritance alone gives only the illusion of success.

Successful leaders are easily identified. Because they are conspicuously rewarded, we can judge their individual efforts and contributions in their chosen fields (for example, the arts, sciences, medicine, government, or business) by the amounts of wealth or fame or power they garner. Less visible are the key people in these areas who make sizable, although sometimes indirect, contributions—with credit for their endeavors often given to the team leader. They are well rewarded even though their accomplishments are considered the result of team rather than individual efforts.

Naturally, there are exceptions. United States presidential cabinet members are team players, but they also hold power and prestige through their individual posts. Although team members, as cabinet heads they are highly visible.

Although high achievement creates high success, it does not inevitably instill inner self-content, a rarity among high achievers as well as failures. Both dominant and nondominant individuals can deny themselves contentment by developing false expectations that create false perceptions.

The way each person views himself tends to shape his assessment of others and his vision of the world around him. False expectations and perceptions distort reality. As Thomas Sowell states in *Civil Rights: Rhetoric or Reality?*, "People do not change their vision of the world the way they change clothes or replace old light bulbs. But change they must if they mean to survive. No individual (or group) is going to capture all of reality in his vision."

In *Toward a Psychology of Being*, Abraham Maslow sets forth thirteen milestones in achieving individual "self-actualization." The first and perhaps the most important but hardest to achieve is a "superior perception of reality." Striving to attain Maslow's "superior perception of reality" can help diminish false expectations.

Very dominant individuals generate distortions of reality internally as evidenced by their unwillingness to accept a specific level of success. Often their expectations exceed any actual successes they attain. The reality of success already achieved becomes distorted in the minds of dominant individuals by a constant need for further successes. This limits the emotional satisfaction of achievement and contributes to an inability to be content at any level of attainment.

In nondominant individuals, distortions of reality normally are generated externally by society and its prevailing cultural expectations. Socially induced expectations, when forced on the nondominant individual, cause any success he achieves relative to his capabilities to fall short of society's false standards. He may see himself as a failure, unable to reach the contentment level his endeavors warrant.

Individuals, men in particular, who have considerably lower amounts of dominance, energy, and intelligence than the population average cannot possibly meet the expectations set by society in the United States. Judged by these standards alone, they are destined to fail, but this is failure only as defined and measured by the society in which they live. With different societal expectations, they could well be productive and content. It would then be possible to eliminate the stigma of failure and accompanying loss of dignity to themselves, their family, peers, and society as a whole.

It is my conviction that, although differences in cultures affect the nature of what is seen as success or failure, success (other than in contact sports) and failure in all societies result from combinations of dominance, energy, and intelligence. It is my conviction further that, though they differ in particulars, child-rearing practices are the root of adult successes and failures, and that a successful future role or an unsuccessful one is not only established during childhood but is established specifically by mothers.

Chapter II

Dominance and the Individual

Once the relationships among females were studied in a number of species, it became clear that not only are female Cercopithecine monkeys as potentially obsessed with status as are males, but their rankings are clearly hierarchical and are usually inherited from the mother according to birth order.

Jane B. Lancaster
Female Primates

In the Savanna species, DeVore has observed that the dominance of the mother in the female hierarchy affects the social status of her child, just as Imanishi discovered among Japanese Rhesus and Crab-eating macaques.

Julie Macdonald
Almost Human: The Baboon

From the scanty knowledge available at present it seems at least probable that the status of the mother will shape the social position of her offspring within the clan [of hyenas]. Miss Hyena, for instance, is already a high-ranking individual in her own right, even in the absence of Lady Astor.

Hugo and Jane van Lawick-Goodall
Innocent Killers

Figan's dominant mother may have influenced interactions during his earlier years of development.

David Riss and Jane Goodall
"The Recent Rise to the Alpha-Rank in a
Population of Free-Living Chimpanzees"

Males with very dominant mothers apparently can enter the dominance hierarchy earlier and attain a higher position more easily than other males.

Claud Bramblett
Patterns of Primate Behavior

A few determined individuals devote lifetimes to research on the animal world, and their discoveries continue to enlighten mankind. However, much of the world's population sees hardly any psychological resemblance between humans and animals and assumes that man shares few if any child-rearing practices with other species. Yet many similarities exist between chimpanzees and humans relating to mother-child bonding. Are we really too far removed from such "unintelligent" sources to gain any insight into human behavior? I believe the foregoing quotes to be relevant to humans in regard to the dominance trait.

Many believe that a child is born with personality traits such as a tendency toward assertiveness or passivity, timidity or intrepidity, or a cheerful or unhappy disposition. They do not see the child as an infinitely moldable creature lacking a personality substructure of its own. Others believe that a newborn infant is a *tabula rasa*, a blank slate on which anything may be written.

How then does an individual in any culture or society become highly dominant, dominant, average in dominance, submissive, or highly submissive? Why do different individuals exhibit high, average, or low energy? Why does an individual possess superior, average, or below average intelligence? Are these differences attributable primarily to heredity or to environment?

Many psychologists attribute personality traits to a combination of inherited characteristics and environmental influences; few believe that traits are developed almost exclusively through environmental factors experienced after birth. Freud postulated that there are definite stages in human psychological development in which certain experiences lead to fixations that affect adult character. Regardless of their stance on the heredity-environment question, psychologists and psychiatrists recognize that a wide range of personality traits and behavioral patterns tend to recur in a family, either directly copied or reversed from one generation to the next.

Culture, as related to child rearing, is the total of living patterns built up by a group of human beings and transmitted from one generation to another. A baby is born without culture; culture comes into play after birth, when the mother transmits culture as she perceives it to her child. The mother's enculturation, in turn, came from her mother's perception of culture. Cultural transmission began in mankind's past. Experience, whether based on logic or superstition, produced the first culture. In each society, children learn the sum of these experiences (culture) through maternal agency (the primary caretaker), generation after generation.

Babies are responsive to the outside world from the moment of birth. Infants exhibit some survival instincts such as rooting for the nipple, swiping at a cloth placed over the nose and mouth, and avoiding the edge of a precipice. However, these instincts are minimal when compared with those displayed by nonhuman species.

In any population, averages can be established for the stages of development of normal, healthy children. About sixty days from birth, a child is noticeably more aware and pays more attention to his surroundings. During the same sixty days, his vocalization increases dramatically. With support, he can sit for a moment or two at three months. At eight months, he can sit without support; by eleven months he is crawling well. He is usually walking at fourteen months. Averages are also available for other accomplishments a child exhibits between his birth and the day he walks.

A baby cannot do anything he is not physiologically and mentally ready to do; he requires specific levels of muscular, nervous system, and brain maturation for each new action or skill. He will perform these activities at some time without encouragement, demands, or praise. But at what age? Why do some babies master specific activities much sooner or much later than the average? Can encouragement influence infants to accomplish a skill earlier rather than later? Can acquiring abilities early be a consequence of meeting the mother's expectations?

The period beginning with birth and extending through the age of five has the most sensitive and profound influence of any period on a child's behavior in adulthood. Through the age of five, attitudes, needs, fears, and behavior that govern the child's later life are instilled in him by the person directly responsible for his day-to-day nurture and rearing, usually the mother. For his first five years, she serves as model and mediator. She instructs, praises, rewards, and punishes. It is she who demands responses and actions. These are the years that most influence one's achievements as an adult. Dominant or nondominant, the mother, as the person who rears the child, molds her child's personality.

Psychological needs arise in part from fears or phobias. (A phobia is a fear or anxiety that has no basis in reality.) Phobias that exert a compelling influence on an adult begin with powerful childhood fears. These phobias create psychological needs. When adult needs are strong and evident, past childhood fears that created them can be identified; when childhood fears are extensive and recognizable, future adult needs become predictable. An overwhelming childhood fear of punishment contributes to an adult need to punish; a strong childhood fear of failure causes an adult need to achieve.

The child who develops a fear of not meeting his mother's expectations and demands for energetic behavior is likely to develop psychological energy, identifiable through individual mannerisms, tightly organized living habits, strong work patterns, and fewer hours allocated for sleep. An average energy level characterizes the adult whose mother had average expectations of energy for her child. The child whose mother made few demands for energetic activity may grow up to be lethargic. A lethargic person has little need to exhibit energetic behavior, since he had little fear of sluggishness in childhood; demands were not made nor praise given for energetic activity.

Discipline is not a euphemism for punishment. A disciplined environment is one in which a disciplined mother exercises her will to limit and restrict unrestrained behavior by the child and guide it in controlled channels. The product of such a mother's organized behavior is an organized, self-controlled adult. An undisciplined mother exhibits little self-control and makes few demands on the child to restrain or regulate uncontrolled behavior. Her permissive child-rearing practices produce an undisciplined adult who has few needs for self-control.

Similarly, transmission of the dominance trait depends on demand or lack of demand. A dominant mother has the need to assert herself and have her way in molding her child. She controls him in varying degrees from birth, the degree of dominance evident in the level of her expectations and the demands she makes and continues to make over the years of childhood. As he meets each set of expectations, the mother may impose new goals. She may make even greater demands in the areas in which she sets the highest value.

By making greater-than-average demands on a child at an early age, the mother stimulates learning, pushes the child to know success, and establishes dominance as a characteristic of his personality. Because the child of a dominant mother was stimulated to meet each stage of achievement earlier than average, as an adult he places greater-than-average demands for achievement on himself.

Comparatively, if the child's accomplishments equal the average, he may become an average adult, and if they take longer than those of an average child, his needs for achievement as an adult may be less than average. Less-than-average expectations and demands by a non-dominant mother produce a nondominant adult.

Each child's dominance level is determined by the mother. The child becomes dominant or nondominant to the degree that the mother makes and enforces her demands of the child.

The dominant mother's expectations begin early with such things as walking, talking, and toilet-training. She uses her will to force obedience, and exercises authority over the child with little regard for what others may think about her child-training tactics. She may appear to her child as too often critical of his efforts because of her insistence on the best. But at the same time he also views her as loving and supportive, if she praises his successes.

In *Nicomachean Ethics* Aristotle states, "in educating the young we steer them by the rudders of pleasure and pain." Demands are the pain; praise is the pleasure. As demands made by the dominant mother create dominant behavior in the child, the mother's use of praise heightens the child's desire to achieve.

Love and understanding are great gifts a mother can bestow on her child. Indifference and a lack of love can become lifetime handicaps. Love, tenderness, and understanding of the infant's needs by a dominant, demanding, encouraging mother produce an adult with needs for achievement. An equal amount of love, tenderness, and understanding given without demands and encouragement for early accomplishments produces an adult with lower achievement needs.

A dominating mother is not necessarily or even usually a domineering mother. Dominating is used in the sense in which the mother exercises her will over that of the child. When in conflict with a child's wishes, having her way is more important to a dominant mother than to a less dominant mother. Methods used by dominant mothers in exercising their wills vary greatly. They include many variations of control: excessive punishment without praise, for example, or excessive praise with minimal punishment, or manipulation with the finesse and skill of a polished diplomat. A strong-willed mother bends the child's will to hers to obtain the results she desires.

The dominated child does not necessarily become a domineering youth or adult. Some do, but a vast number of dominant individuals exercise their will and have their way by achieving. Within the laws of each country, achievement is a socially acceptable manifestation of dominant behavior.

The mother's style of dominance correlates to the child's pattern of dominance when an adult. More clearly seen in daughters, it is sometimes masked in the maleness of sons. As a child, John D. Rockefeller received little compassion from his mother, Eliza Davison Rockefeller. According to Anthony Sampson, "his mother, a devout Baptist, would tie him to a post and beat him when he was disobedient." The sometimes ruthless business decisions of John D. Rockefeller are well documented. The templet did not change; the only difference was in those who were beaten and how the punishment was meted out. Margaret Carnegie's dominance with compassion produced Andrew Carnegie, cast in a similar mold but tempered with a different alloy. After fulfilling a promise to make his mother rich, his gifts to libraries, research projects, and world peace totaled $330 million. His essay "The Gospel of Wealth," describing the social responsibilities of rich men, was widely read in the United States and Europe.

The period from age five until puberty is a sensitive period, almost as important as the child's first five years. During this time, outside relationships and influences as well as the relationship with the mother affect the child. When away from home, the child is most touched by school experiences—interaction with the teachers and other students.

Working mothers and day-care centers are a cause and effect of recent societal changes. Both are increasing year to year, creating a new dimension in child-rearing practices. Spending most of the day away from the mother undoubtedly affects a child. But how? A child of a nondominant mother may be little changed, but the extended time away from a dominant mother during the sensitive period through age five could dramatically dilute demands for childhood accomplishments. Future studies of child-care centers could evaluate the dominance trait so that we may draw conclusions as to the merit or the harm wrought by these widespread changes.

Mothers who encourage and make early demands for learning on an infant usually continue to do so throughout elementary and high school. This continual reinforcement sets one child on a course of achievement far different from that of a child of an indifferent mother or a mother who made few infant demands.

The school years test the effects on each child of being reared by a dominant or by a less dominant mother. In the extreme, her influence can be so pervasive that the child interprets interactions with teachers as an extension of the mother's teachings. A child of a demanding and encouraging mother perceives a teacher in the mother's role and responds to instructions as he would at home. A child of a more passive mother tends to benefit less from or to be indifferent to instruction.

"Peer pressure" is a recent term applied to students. Its implication is usually negative and is blamed for drug use, rule breaking, and unwillingness to conform to laws and traditions among preteens, teens, and young adults. Its effects differ among young people according to their individual dominance levels.

Dominant students are motivated primarily by achievement needs and are apt to compete with their dominant peers to perform and win. Any "peer pressure" brought to bear on these pupils is likely to be marginal and unsuccessful. The more dominant the student, the more independent he is, and the more he concerns himself with accomplishment. Attempts at control by others his age evoke his fear of domination and limit the effectiveness of "peer pressure."

The lower a student's dominance level, the more susceptible he becomes to "peer pressure." If his friends, his peers, are involved with drugs, have little regard for laws, and are generally nonconformists, he is more apt to follow their example.

"Peer pressure" could be described as conforming to mores one shares with friends. It is perhaps less "pressure," as many adults stigmatize it, and more a case of shared inclinations.

After puberty, socially detrimental behavior such as juvenile delinquency or later criminal activity caused by poor child-rearing practices can be modified, but only at a psychological cost to the individual and a financial cost to society. Conversely, with positive child-rearing practices, behavior after age twelve can be enhanced, for example, through rewards for achievement, to the benefit of society.

One thing well learned by a child with a dominant upbringing will last throughout his life—he wants to have his way, he wants to be in control of his life. He does not want anyone to dominate him as his mother did. The need to dominate others is a defense mechanism to prevent others from dominating him.

A highly dominant individual will go to astonishing lengths in business, politics, or a profession to place himself in a position where few can dominate him. Freedom from domination allows him to become to a high degree the master of his time. Being the master of one's time, beholden to few and dominated by no one, becomes one of the subconscious goals of a highly dominant individual, because in this way he frees himself from the domination his mother exerted during those sensitive childhood years. Extraordinary work efforts, even though subconsciously motivated to avoid domination, usually result in success. When combined with high intelligence and high energy, they can reap conspicuous rewards of wealth, fame, power, or some combination of the three—particularly in a democratic, capitalistic society.

The pattern of a dominant mother who generates needs for achievement in her offspring has existed over the centuries. Success or failure followed depending upon the social and political environments that existed which accommodated or rejected such needs. When in the past we have read of high achievers being honored, glorified, even hailed as world heroes, it is interesting to think that the rewards these individuals gained were only a consequence of actions inevitably set in motion by a dominant mother in an environment fortuitously amenable to their psychological needs.

Psychiatrists, psychologists, and sociologists have made extensive inquiries into the derivations of leadership. Many of their studies focus on the individual's parents, separately or—more often—together. You can judge the interest in the subject by the enormous amount of literature on child rearing; however, most books and papers do not directly advocate molding dominant children through specific child-rearing practices.

In his engrossing work *The Achieving Society*, David C. McClelland acknowledges that domination of a child produces differences in future adult achievements depending on whether the domination comes originally from the father or the mother. When such domination originates with a powerful father, McClelland notes that the son exhibits lower achievement. McClelland makes no reference to the personality of the wife of such a dominating man. However, he discloses that fathers of high-achieving sons show less dominating behavior than do fathers of low-achieving sons. McClelland does not compare the differences in dominant behavior between mothers of high achievers and mothers of low achievers.

McClelland suggests that males with powerful (dominant?) fathers are low achievers because they become dependent on their fathers when making decisions. On the other hand, McClelland points out that dominating behavior does not interfere with the development of achievement if such domination comes from the mother. McClelland refers to Marian R. Winterbottom's work in the area of achievement motivation in children.

Marian Winterbottom's insightful doctoral dissertation at the University of Michigan, *The Relation of Childhood Training in Independence to Achievement Motivation*, acknowledges Freud's contributions in his assumptions that motivation is the key to understanding behavior and that childhood experiences are the key to understanding individual differences in motivation. Even though Winterbottom notes that she has no personality data on the mothers, she considers conditions in childhood that lead to the development of achievement motivation. In detailing the motives for achievement, she recognizes the problem of why some individuals respond intensely to achievement and others less or not at all. Winterbottom's first hypothesis is, "The more demands a mother makes upon her child for individual accomplishment and successful independent behavior, the stronger his achievement motivation will be."

Winterbottom believes it unlikely that extreme differences in intelligence or school achievement scores determine the degree of motivation of children. However, by keeping the intelligence of the children surveyed within the normal range, she thus acknowledges that there could be some relationship between intelligence and the development of achievement motivation. The mother's influence on the child's achievement motivation might have been more obvious had Winterbottom's study focused on the mothers of those with considerably higher-than-average intelligence. This could have furthered Winterbottom's second hypothesis, "The earlier the mother makes her demands in the life of the child, the stronger the child's achievement motivation will be."

"Achievement," writes Winterbottom, "is the only way of avoiding failure."

A dominant mother usually expects and demands more of her child than a nondominant mother. Failure becomes a real possibility in the child's mind. If the child resists her demands, the dominant mother often uses everything at her disposal including direct or subtle threats of rejection and ridicule to make the child conform to her expectations. She does not allow her child to fail her. She forces him to succeed by encouraging him to try again and again until he fulfills her expectations.

In adulthood, long after the mother's domination ceases, the subconscious retains its fear of failure. It is translated into extraordinary endeavors to prevent failure from materializing. Through extensive work and effort, and the resulting accomplishments and rewards, the phobia is alleviated somewhat.

Fear of failure is popularly confused with the need for security and a fear of taking risks. Dominant people are forced to take risks because of their fundamental need to achieve long-term success. Risk-taking is an often misunderstood action because all of us, both dominant and nondominant, must take some risks. Crossing a busy street is a risk; driving an automobile is a risk. However, the risks taken to achieve, accomplish, and win are distinctly different for dominant than for nondominant individuals.

The word entrepreneur is much used, but its definition as "a person who organizes and manages any enterprise, especially a business, usually with considerable initiative and risk" does not address the element of success. Therefore, many persons with outstanding business attainments are referred to as successful entrepreneurs. McClelland defined a full-time entrepreneur as "someone who received 75 per cent or more of his income from entrepreneurial activities." There are wide differences in success among entrepreneurs: from annual incomes of $10 million to $10 thousand to failure in every entrepreneurial undertaking.

Highly successful entrepreneurs sometimes experience failures early in their careers, but their later successes are greater than any early setbacks. Although their risk-taking and successes are viewed as phenomenal, they regard the risks and subsequent rewards differently than do many of their less dominant counterparts. The dominant individual may perceive his odds for success as so favorable that in his mind little risk-taking is involved in starting a new business. This person considers most of his business decisions to be conservative even though to others they appear speculative. He gives little thought to the possibility of failure; his need for achievement becomes an all-consuming drive that generally leads to success.

Many nondominant people regard starting a new business as a high risk. If the venture fails, that can be taken in stride, as the possibility of failure is not totally unexpected. For such people starting a new enterprise may be similar to gambling; it can be looked on as betting against unfavorable odds but with the possibility of large winnings. The risk of beginning a new business or expanding an inherited family business might be considered a long shot; in that light, failure becomes acceptable.

To varying degrees everyone dislikes rejection and failure. Dominant individuals are more disturbed by them than nondominant people. These phobias, originating from a dominant mother, were first perceived by the child only as relating to the demands his mother made of him.

The efforts a dominant mother expends in dominating her child are subconscious. She rears the child in virtually the same way that she was reared, namely, by domination by her mother. She knows no other way. Continual demands were made on her as a child, little different from those she makes on her child, and those demands she strained to meet. In sum, the child of a dominant mother is the recipient of the upbringing handed down through the maternal side of the family from earlier generations, whatever the culturally oriented differences may have been.

There can be great differences of dominance among the children of one family, depending on what demands their mother places on them. The most dominant child is frequently the mother's favorite. Often this is the one for whom the mother has the greatest expectations; she generally makes the greatest demands for excellence on this child. This child may also be the recipient of the greatest amounts of the mother's love and praise.

Birth order is important, particularly for the first born and especially if male. In many instances, the second born is not as dominated as the first and consequently is less dominant as an adult. This pattern often continues through the birth order. There are, of course, instances of highly dominant mothers who spend almost equal time with a large number of children, make almost equal demands on them, and have almost equal expectations for each child; as a result they rear a whole family of highly dominant and successful children.

Other circumstances besides favoritism and birth order may cause a dominant mother to be unable to spend equal time with all her children during their formative years, circumstances, for instance, relating to health, or economics. Those on whom she makes fewer demands will have lower levels of dominance, energy, and intelligence.

To the degree the child is dominated by the mother, he will as a youth and as an adult exercise a similar degree of dominance over others, within the boundaries set by society. This psychological need to dominate and control others is based on the individual's childhood fear that becomes in adulthood a phobia of being dominated and controlled.

Because training for dominance in childhood is a crucial element in rearing a successful adult, it is highly doubtful that this can become a learned ability after the fact for a nondominant adult. Each person is to a great extent a product of his or her mother's upbringing, little more and little less.

Still, if you are a nondominant mother with young children, do not be upset. There are ways that you can move your children toward achieving contentment, the rarest achievement of all. You can also make the most of outside influences that can contribute to your child's future well-being.

۞ ۞ ۞ ۞ ۞ ۞

An attempt to change one's personality is almost always fruitless; trying to change the personalities of others is a fool's errand. However, attempting to *know thyself*, at least to the extent of guarding against one's weaknesses and building on one's strengths, is attainable.

Chapter III

Recognition of Mothers

There are people who recognize the mother's importance in instilling the desire to succeed in her children; some of history's most famous high achievers credited their mothers with helping them attain success. They publicly expressed respect and gratitude for their mothers' efforts on their behalf. There are numberless written acknowledgments of the role of mothers in their children's successes. For example:

Thou hast never in thy life
Showed thy dear mother any courtesy,
When she, poor hen, fond of no second brood,
Has clucked thee to the wars, and safely home
Loaden with honor.

William Shakespeare
The Tragedy of Coriolanus,
V, iii, 176

A noble mother must have bred
So brave a son.

Thomas Campbell
"Napoleon and the British Sailor"

Men are what their mothers made them.

Ralph Waldo Emerson
The Conduct of Life: Fate

The future destiny of the child is always the work of the mother.

Napoleon Bonaparte
Sayings of Napoleon

All that I am, my mother made me.

John Quincy Adams

Her life gave the lie to every libel on her sex that was ever written.

John Quincy Adams
After his mother's death

A man is mostly what his mother makes him.

Sir Richard Burton

All that I am or hope to be, I owe to my angel mother.

Attributed to Abraham Lincoln

He is all the mother's, from the top to toe.

William Shakespeare
The Tragedy of Richard III,
III, i, 175

God could not be everywhere, so he created mothers.

Unknown
A Jewish proverb

The greatest battle that ever was fought—
Shall I tell you where and when?

On the maps of the world you will find it not:
   It was fought by the Mothers of Men.

Joaquin Miller
"The Greatest Battle That Ever Was Fought"

And say to mothers what a holy charge
Is theirs—with what a kingly power their love
Might rule the fountains of the new-born mind.

Lydia Huntley Sigourney
"The Mother of Washington"

We can probably say with confidence that most of the great men in history owed their characters to their splendid mothers, rather than to the example of their fathers.

Sir John Glubb

It is the general rule that all superior men inherit the elements of their superiority from their mothers.

Jules Michelet

They say that man is mighty,
   He governs land and sea,
He wields a mighty scepter
   O'er lesser powers that be;
But a mightier power and stronger
   Man from his throne has hurled,
For the hand that rocks the cradle
   Is the hand that rules the world.

William Ross Wallace
"What Rules the World"

Successful adults who evaluate their parents' influence on their accomplishments are affected by their personal memories and differing perceptions of reality. They are also influenced by societal assumptions of proper parental roles in child rearing. In any historical period, society's expectations and influences tend to color, shade, and bias individual perceptions about the relative dominance level of each parent. If society assumes that a strong "father figure" is the principal factor in individual success, a successful adult is likely to remember his father as being more dominant than his mother although this may not have been the case. In such societies, owing to enculturation, any credit given the mother for a child's success is usually somewhat (and, depending on the particular time, often greatly) diminished and dominant qualities are ascribed to the father even though he achieved little. The term "mother figure" is rarely used in the context of achievement. This in itself contributes to the diminution of some attributions of success to mothers.

The mother's influence on a child has long been recognized in those highly successful individuals whose parents' dominance levels were widely disparate, cases in which the mother was considerably more dominant than the father and where his influence was clearly minimal or nonexistent. In these instances contemporary writers and historians concur that the mother's influence was the larger parental contributor to the child's later success.

Victor and Mildred G. Goertzel discuss the characteristics of both parents in *Cradles of Eminence.* This eye-opening book contains brief histories of the parentage, early environment, childhood, and education of four hundred thirteen famous twentieth century men and women. The Goertzels categorize one hundred nine mothers of the eminent four hundred thirteen as dominant; however, they believe only twenty-one of the fathers fit that description. They found the adjectives most commonly used to describe this trait for both men and women were "dominating, overwhelming, adamant, strong-willed and determined."

Although the Goertzels specifically identify one hundred nine mothers (26 percent) as dominating and sixty-four (15 percent) as smothering, of the remaining two hundred forty (58 percent), many are referred to as opinionated, possessive, and aggressive. None are designated failure-prone or submissive, and only one is noted to be lazy. Only twenty-one (5 percent) of the fathers are referred to as dominating and eight (2 percent) as smothering; many of the remaining three hundred eighty-four (93 percent) are described as failure-prone, improvident, family deserters, alcoholic, abusive, or gentle.

What about other successful people? Many credit their successes to the father, to both parents, to the paternal or maternal grandmother or grandfather, or both. In some instances, the successful individual credits his achievements to someone outside the family who reared him from early childhood. Others may be credited with having helped the individual in specific accomplishments.

Some high achievers take personal credit for their successes. Sometimes described as egotists for refusing to credit anyone other than themselves, such individuals maintain that no one helped them while they were striving and that they attained success through their efforts alone.

Still, most successful people share credit for their achievements with others. The distribution of credit among many sources has been a major factor in disguising—and often completely hiding—the primary source of success and achievement.

In instances in which the father was dominant and successful and the mother, also dominant, was at home rearing the children, the mother's influence has commonly been overlooked.

The source of success is further hidden in the high levels of success and achievement attained by those both of whose parents during their childhood were dominant and both individually successful outside the home. An easily recognizable modern example, because highly visible, involves marriages between actors and actresses, both of whom are famous. Since both are successful, as parents they are both dominant. Although these marriages often end in divorce, their high-achieving children have two successful parents to share any credit for their achievements.

I am convinced that research on each individual living today who has achieved high success, and whose leadership and dominance is thereby recognizable, would show that in varying degrees his or her mother is the root of such achievement. Some may ask for more evidence. History is rich in examples of the connection between dominant figures and the early shaping they underwent by their mothers. Candid interviews with highly successful men and women will reveal the same connection.

It must be remembered that only a few decades ago most dominant women did not work outside the home. Many times daughters were dominated to the same degree as sons, but the demands differed because of gender. Thus some dominant mothers programed dominant daughters to fulfill themselves as homemakers and mothers and, at the same time, demanded that sons achieve success outside the home.

Each reader may also find the proof in himself. Even though the conclusions may be disquieting, you can find the existence or lack of existence of high dominance in your maternal grandmother, your mother, your spouse, and yourself. Analyzing the success of siblings, particularly males, is another simple exercise. Are your brothers successful? Are the brothers of your spouse more successful? Were your uncles—your mother's brothers—successful, and what success came to your maternal grandmother's brothers?

With few exceptions, a dominant mother is necessary if a child is to become a highly successful adult in a society that measures success by the acquisition of wealth, fame, or power—and most large societies judge success in these terms. If one accedes to this definition of success—and it is a reality not a construct—then it must be recognized that dominance is an inexorable factor in achieving this success.

Parental records exist (with patrilineal more readily available than matrilineal) for almost all famous historical figures. By studying their biographies, one can identify common threads in the childhood training of the successful man or woman.

rlz rlz rlz sh sh sh

The histories of two successful men with dissimilar geographic, religious, and social backgrounds demonstrate the passage of the dominance trait through the maternal line to a son who achieved highly visible success. Doris Kearns, as excerpted from Chapter 1, "Growing Up," of *Lyndon Johnson and the American Dream*, describes the child-rearing practices of a highly dominant mother directed toward a favored son:

However concocted, Rebekah's family portrait, the types and conceptions she delineated, nonetheless affected Lyndon Johnson for the rest of his life, forcing divisions between intellect, morality, and action, shaping ideals of the proper politician and the good life. . . .

. . . "My mother," Johnson said, "soon discovered that my daddy was not a man to discuss higher things. To her mind his life was vulgar and ignorant. . . . she felt very much alone. . . . Then I came along and suddenly everything was all right again. I could do all the things she never did."

Remembering his early years, Johnson spoke almost exclusively of his mother. When he mentioned his father, it was to enumerate his liabilities as a husband and explain what he did to Rebekah.

. . . There was no room in Rebekah's Protestant ethic for uncontrolled and frivolous behavior. . . .

. . . She seemed under a compulsion to renew on her son's behalf all the plans and projects she had given up for herself. The son would fulfill the wishful dreams she had never carried out, he would become the important person she had failed to be.

. . . He learned the alphabet before he was two, learned to read and spell before he was four, and at three could recite long passages of poetry from Longfellow and Tennyson. "I'll never forget how much my mother loved me when I recited those poems. The minute I finished she'd take me in her arms and hug me so hard I sometimes thought I'd be strangled to death."

But . . . one gets the impression Lyndon never experienced her love as a steady or reliable force, but as a conditional reward, alternately given and taken away. When he failed to satisfy her desires . . . he experienced not simply criticism but a complete withdrawal of affection. . . .

So close was the boy to his mother, as Johnson recalled, that one imagines him as an only child when in fact he had four siblings . . .

. . . Though Johnson City was hardly more than a village, it had a high school, in which she [Rebekah] soon taught debating, a newspaper, for which she wrote a weekly column, and an opera house, in which local plays, directed by Rebekah, were performed. Rebekah organized a Browning Society. She gave private lessons in elocution and she taught a class in "Old Bible." She joined a temperance society.

In school, Johnson became something of a troublemaker. . . . He often failed to complete his lessons. But Rebekah refused to give up. Every morning at breakfast, holding his lesson book in her hand, she would read aloud to Sam the lesson of Lyndon's that was due that day. Forced to listen, Johnson would learn. If it took longer to read the lesson than to eat breakfast, Rebekah would walk him to school, reciting from the primer all the way. . . .

"Mother was interested in national politics, not local." . . .

. . . She had her own way of showing her displeasure—not to yell or even to scold, but to greet her son at all times with an impassive stare. . . . Johnson knew by his mother's withdrawal that he had not lived up to the splendid vision she had held of him as a boy.

When Johnson graduated from high school in May, 1924, Rebekah allowed her quarrel with her son to surface at last. When she spoke, daily taking him to task for his slovenly manner, she had, as Johnson later described it, "a terrible knifelike voice." . . .

. . . "I'll never forget," Johnson later said, "how my mother helped me out on those exams. She came to San Marcos and stayed up with me the entire night before the math exam, drilling me over and over until it finally got into my head." From the breakfast table in Johnson City to a student room at San Marcos College, she was always his coach. . . .

. . . From the world of work and the conquest of ever-widening circles of men, Johnson hoped to obtain the steady love he had lacked as a child. The problem was that each successful performance led only to the need for more. There was no place to rest so long as love and the self-esteem based on love depended upon another's approbation. . . .

Lyndon Johnson was driven to achieve by the strong need to control others instilled in him by his dominant mother. He was elected a United States congressman at age twenty-eight. Eleven years later he was a member of the United States Senate where he retained his seat for thirteen years. In 1960 Johnson was elected Vice President, and he became the thirty-sixth President of the United States in 1963 after John F. Kennedy's assassination. He also amassed a fortune.

Even though Kearns writes little about Johnson's maternal grandmother, Ruth Ament Baines, she brings out that the choice of husbands by Johnson's mother and maternal grandmother was strikingly similar. Presumably, Ruth Ament Baines was a dominant woman who handed down the trait of dominance to Rebekah as it was passed from Rebekah to her son Lyndon Baines Johnson.

The biographer Robert A. Caro in The Power Broker: Robert Moses and the Fall of New York gives vivid descriptions of a highly dominant mother and the transference of the dominance trait from the maternal grandmother to the mother to the son. Here, there was no question that the trait of dominance was passed down three generations through the maternal line. In the following excerpts from Chapter 1, "Line of Succession," Caro describes Robert Moses' family background, beginning with his maternal grandparents, Bernhard Cohen and Rosalie Silverman:

[W]ithin the circle of his family, Cohen was almost pitied. . . . what they recalled most vividly about Bernhard Cohen was how unmercifully he was bullied by his wife. "My grandmother had the reputation of being as hard as nails," one says. "She had that reputation because of the way she treated her husband."

Rosalie's bent was intellectual rather than maternal. . . . A sharp mind was coupled with a sharp tongue, which she used on those who disagreed with her opinions. . . .

. . . "The way Grannie Cohen treated Grandfather Cohen was quite striking," the granddaughter recalls, "She absolutely sat on him." . . .

Old age did not change Grannie Cohen. . . . Age certainly did not wither her independence. . . .

. . . Unlike her mother, Bella [Robert's mother] had a quiet, unassuming manner . . . She also possessed a kindliness that is not remembered as one of Rosalie's most noticeable attributes. . . .

Nonetheless, of Rosalie's five children, Bella was the one most like her mother. . . . And if her appearance was that of a quiet and sweet little girl, quite different from her mother, people who bothered to talk to the little girl found that the appearance was deceiving. In discussing her opinions, Bella was mannerly and soft-spoken, but the opinions delivered in that soft voice were direct, forceful—and not particularly susceptible to alteration. . . . "After you had talked to her," recalls an acquaintance, "you began to observe her more closely. And it didn't take you long to realize that under that quiet manner was an astonishing amount of arrogance. She was her mother's daughter."

In 1886, at the age of twenty-six, Bella married Emanuel Moses, a thirty-five-year-old department-store owner from New Haven. . . . [with] a successful business. But he was too slow and quiet for the Cohens; . . . they felt, in fact, that Bella had married beneath her.

. . . Bella disliked New Haven. She felt there was no cultural activity there worth talking about, and she felt she was many cuts above the run of the local matrons. In 1897, the Moses family moved to New York.

Emanuel Moses never let anyone know how he felt. . . . he was forty-six years old, a businessman who had achieved success and who had seemed to be heading for more. . . .

He was to spend the rest of his life in retirement.

In New York, Bella found a cause. It was the Settlement House movement.

In expounding her proposals, Bella was always a lady. She never raised her voice. But veneered only thinly by her excellent manners was a certain aggressiveness—and if there was a prolonged disagreement with her proposals, the veneer could wear thin indeed. When discussing a project in which she was especially interested, Bella had always displayed impatience with other people's ideas, but in her later years on the Madison House board she seemed more and more unwilling even to consider such ideas—or, in fact, to listen to them. Says one House staffer who sat in on board meetings: "In a quiet way, Mrs. Moses could really be quite . . . impatient. She knew what she wanted and she intended to have it." Says another: "She liked to get things done. And if she had to step on toes to get them done, she'd step on toes."

. . . "The relationship between Mother and Father was simple," Paul Moses would recall. "Father did what Mother directed."

Bella was strict with her children. . . . she ordered every aspect of their lives. Their advice was not solicited . . .

Bella was particularly interested in the boys' education. . . .

. . . And she furnished still other instruction herself, assigning them books . . . Casually reading a passage, she would suddenly turn to one of the children and ask, "What's that mean?" "And when she asked that," Paul would recall more than half a century later, "you had better know." Even while the children were playing, they were reminded of the importance of good English. If one of them mispronounced a word, down the stairs would come their mother's voice saying, "What was that? What was that?"

. . . Teachers at the schools they attended told Bella with a unanimity that must have become almost monotonous that her sons were brilliant. . . .

. . . The father, of course, was the outsider. It was not that anyone was actually rude to him, relatives and friends would recall. His family's attitude was, rather, amiably patronizing. In the words of one visitor, "It was the kind of thing where, when Emanuel said something, the kids would say good-naturedly, 'Oh, Dad! Oh, Father!' And then they'd go right on with what they had been saying. It was as if everyone, including him, had sort of accepted the fact that he had nothing to contribute." . . .

Relatives and friends began to notice that within this family circle, an inner circle was forming. . . . More and more, it became apparent that

Robert was his mother's favorite. This favoritism was expressed with the intensity that characterized everything Bella did. . . . Increasingly, Bella Moses began to cater to her younger son's every whim. "You would never think of this word in connection with Bella," one relative says. "But the only word you could use to describe her treatment of Robert was 'doting.' "

No one was sure of the explanation. Relatives speculated that it was because Bella's slashing, incisive mind had found in Robert a mind with like qualities. Perhaps this was part of the explanation, but it ignored the fact that her other son possessed the same qualities. Perhaps another part of the explanation was that when the family discussions grew especially lively, Robert knew where to stop. On issues about which Bella felt especially strongly, Paul would often disagree with his mother. Robert never did. And Bella Moses, after all, was not a woman who liked to be disagreed with.

. . . If Bella cherished the ideal of public service, public service conceived of in idealistic, almost Platonic terms, this ideal was becoming the theme of more and more of Robert's conversation, too. More and more, . . . Robert began to talk about dedicating his life to "helping people."

The imitation went beyond enunciation of ideals. People who had classified as a manifestation of supreme and deep-rooted arrogance Bella's refusal to be swayed by—or, in later years, even to listen at length to—the opinions of others, now began to notice this same arrogance in Robert. They noticed also that, increasingly, the rhythms of Robert's voice echoed the sharpness of his mother's sallies. The tall, handsome young man even adopted—consciously or unconsciously—a distinctive pose favored by the graying, bespectacled, plain little woman, an unusual tilt of the head. When a person disagreed with Bella, she had a way of leaning her head back on her neck and staring at the disagreer through the bottom of her spectacles with her eyes half closed, quizzical and skeptical. People began to notice that, while Robert Moses did not wear glasses, he was beginning to adopt, in arguments, the same tilt of the head.

In later decades, when Robert Moses was famous almost as much for his personality as for his achievements, observers would marvel at the depth and degree of his outspokenness, stubbornness, aggressiveness and arrogance. They would wonder at the origin of the mold in which he had been formed in so hard a cast. But relatives and friends of the Moses family never wondered. Whatever it was that made Robert Moses the way he was, they knew, whatever the quality that had shaped an unusual—in some ways unique—personality, the quality was one that they had watched being passed, like a family heirloom, from Robert Moses' grandmother to his mother to him. . . .

This is the stock from which Robert Moses sprang. He went on to become, as Caro states, "America's greatest builder." He shaped New York and its suburbs during more than forty years in public service. He constructed seven bridges connecting the island boroughs to the mainland: the Triborough, the Verrazano, the Throgs Neck, the Marine, the Henry Hudson, the Cross Bay, and the Bronx-Whitestone. He built Lincoln Center, the New York Coliseum, and Shea Stadium. Moses was involved in public housing constructed by the New York City Housing Authority between 1945 and 1958, and the United Nations headquarters buildings. He controlled the construction of city parks and zoos, skating rinks, bridle paths, golf courses, tennis courts, and baseball diamonds. He built a system of state parks, parkways from New York into its suburbs, and beaches—including Jones Beach. When Moses resigned, New York state had over 2.5 million acres of parks, 44 percent of state parks nationwide. Robert Moses was a formative force in the creation of parks and highways, and in urban renewal in the United States.

Lyndon Johnson and Robert Moses were sons of highly dominant mothers. Each was his mother's favorite. Although they came from entirely different backgrounds, they were subjected to the same demanding child-rearing practices. Their mothers expected them to accomplish at an early age, demanded achievement, and rewarded their sons when they met their expectations.

Moses grew up in a cultural center, New York, was reared in an affluent family, and attended the best schools. Since his background was Jewish and there is a perception in the United States that Jewish mothers are "different," his mother and his maternal grandmother were readily recognized as the sources of the dominance trait that had passed from grandmother to mother to son.

There seems to be less willingness to recognize the same descent of dominance in Lyndon Johnson's case. His background was the conventional male Protestant background, and his birthplace, the southern United States, was an area still culturally inclined to believe in paternal influence on success. Johnson came from a poor family; he had no social or financial advantages. It was a struggle to make ends meet. Yet, like Robert Moses, he was reared by a highly dominant mother. Both became successful adults owing to the influence exerted on them by their mothers. The passage of the dominance trait from mother to son is the same in spite of the social and cultural differences that existed during their childhoods.

Lyndon Johnson was not the only President of the United States with a highly dominant mother. Where information is available on the personalities of mothers of American presidents, the dominance trait is easily discernible.

The same trait is conspicuously absent in almost all of the Presidents' wives and children. One stellar exception is the dominance of Abigail Smith Adams, the wife of President John Adams and the mother of President John Quincy Adams.

Although now more common, it was historically atypical for fathers to have direct day-to-day responsibility for child rearing. However, a dramatically different situation occurred in the case of John Stuart Mill, considered by some to be the most intelligent person who ever lived. High dominance was transmitted from the father, James Mill (a well-known philosopher, journalist, head of India House, and author of *History of India*), to his son John. James shunted his wife aside and lavished his energy and attention on making his infant son a genius. Despite his tyrannical methods, he succeeded. John began learning Greek at age three. He could read Greek and transpose it to English before he could understand its meaning. By age six, John was a Greek and Latin scholar, a historian, and a logician.

Research shows that Isobel Fenton Milne, the mother of James Mill, was a highly dominant woman. In this case, high dominance passed from grandmother to father to son. The practices by which John Stuart Mill was reared represent one of the most unusual cases ever recorded.

With rare exceptions, the transmittal of the dominance trait goes through the maternal line, mother to child. The highly dominant daughter is usually the carrier of dominance but, because of the country's socio-political climate, the highly dominant son is more often the one to achieve success. This transmittal from mother to child, generation after generation, century after century, has gone relatively unnoticed and unrecorded.

Chapter IV

Parallel Worlds

Ours is a world of health and sickness, sound and music, heat and cold, work and play, laws, rules, religion, learning, shelter, food, and sleep. All mankind occupies that world, but each individual's perceptions of and expectations from life are different. Geographic, social, and political environments shape our worlds, but within each world one's life is dramatically affected by his degree of dominance, level of intelligence, and the income category in which he was born, reared, and occupies as an adult.

Because of differing levels of dominance, individuals look at the possibilities affecting their lives from different perspectives. A disparity of perceptions of reality exists between dominant and nondominant individuals. Despite living in the same physical world, hearing and seeing the same concrete manifestations of that world, each lives in a somewhat different psychological world. These worlds are parallel; the individuals living in them have the same beginning (birth), the same course of physical growth, and the same eventual end (death) but, in part because of the dominance trait, they follow divergent life paths. They have separate and uniquely different expectations, perceptions, and perspectives. Consequently, those with widely dissimilar dominance levels have been unable to truly understand and share each other's psychological worlds. Like parallel lines, their worlds never converge.

"Beauty in things," according to David Hume, "exists in the mind which contemplates them." And Margaret Wolfe Hungerford said, "Beauty is in the eye of the beholder." These maxims hold true also for other of the varying perceptions people have of their environment. Through the eyes of the beholder, that is, through one's personal frame of reference, each of us perceives reality with his own unique vision.

"Oh wad some power the giftie gie us to see oursels as others see us!" wrote Robert Burns in "To a Louse." Each individual views himself not as others see him but as he perceives himself. Each person evaluates his strengths and weaknesses primarily from within rather than without. The observations, comments, advice, and opinions of others influence him, but he tempers them to fit his mental perception of himself.

Human beings who exhibit a difference in the dominance trait, coupled with their individual differences in intelligence and energy, do not live in the same psychological world. Rather, they live in parallel worlds of thought and action. Highly dominant mothers live in a world psychologically parallel to that of mothers with lower dominance levels. Their children also live in different but parallel worlds, worlds programed subconsciously by the mother and dictating subconsciously each child's future life. Each of the parallel worlds is consistent lineally mother to child, generation to generation.

The expectations, demands, and praise transmitted to the child by the mother are, in effect, a program. They are a map imprinted on the child's mind that guide him through life. Adult successes and failures vary based on the degree of dominance exerted by the mother over her child.

A significant effect on the United States dominance ratios has occurred since the second World War. As women moved into the post-World War II work force, they began achieving in male-dominated areas. In 1948 Margaret Chase Smith was elected a Senator from Maine. In 1949 twelve women became the first women graduates from Harvard Medical School, and Georgia Neese Clark of Kansas became the first woman Treasurer of the United States. In 1953 Alfred Charles Kinsey published *Sexual Behavior in the Human Female*. In 1955 Marian Anderson became the first black to sing at the Metropolitan Opera, and ordination of women ministers was approved by the Presbyterian Church.

These breakthroughs by dominant women outside the traditional fields of teaching and nursing into business, finance, and politics, although small, inspired other dominant women to forego or limit childbearing and to devote more time and energy to fulfillment outside the home.

The discovery of the birth-control pill, first marketed nationally in the early 1960s, gave women almost error-free personal control over decisions of how many, if any, children to have and when to have them. Highly dominant women were probably among the earliest users of the pill. In 1987 there were some ten million users of the pill in the childbearing age group.

Legalization of abortion in 1973 by the United States Supreme Court provided yet another vehicle for the withholding of children. The use of artificial birth-control devices and abortions by dominant women is expected to continue. Conversely, the under-utilization of these options by many nondominant women is also probable. No matter the reasons, dominant women are having fewer or no children. This is changing the nation's child dominance levels in an exceedingly short time. Presumably, for the near future, the imbalance of dominance levels in birth generations will continue.

The phrase from the Declaration of Independence, "all men are created equal," is perhaps one of the most quoted and misleading statements ever made. If created means born, then taken literally the statement is true. But its interpretation causes misunderstandings. Some assume that if all are born equal, equality is thereby extended throughout a person's lifetime. That assumption generates false hopes and expectations in some people and makes them susceptible to false promises. For those born with sound mind and good health, the proposition is roughly true at the moment of birth. However, from birth forward, equality of man cannot exist and has never existed.

Two first-born children of the same sex, born at the same instant to parents in identical income categories, both mentally and physically healthy, but whose singular difference is that one was reared by a highly dominant mother and the other by a submissive mother, will, upon reaching adulthood, view themselves, the people around them, and their environment from dissimilar perspectives. Each will react differently from the other throughout his life. Inequality between the two widens as time passes primarily because one individual is dominant (owing to his dominant mother) while the other is nondominant (owing to his nondominant mother). The two individuals will live in parallel but disparate worlds because of the level of the dominance trait they carry within themselves. Such a disparity will manifest itself differently in each society and in various periods.

Parallel worlds can be found in descriptions and studies related to Type A and Type B behavior. According to *Type A Behavior and Your Heart*, published in 1974, Meyer Friedman, M.D., and Ray H. Rosenman, M.D., were the first to have "discovered and dubbed Type A Behavior Pattern." They described it as "a particular complex of personality traits, including excessive competitive drive, aggressiveness, impatience, and a harrying sense of time urgency." They named as Type B "men who felt no sense of time urgency, exhibited no excessive competitive drive or free-floating hostility." Their studies on the predictability of Type A behavior and coronary heart disease contributed to medical knowledge.

Perhaps Friedman and Rosenman can be classified as Type A; possibly that led them to focus on the physical and psychological characteristics of Type A behavior—twenty-five categories ranging from "acquisitive nature" to "serum cholesterol level." They considered only three categories of Type B behavior. Friedman and Rosenman believed that Type B behavior was healthy and something to which Type A people should aspire. In any case, they recognized great differences in each type's attitudes and behaviors.

"The Relationship Between Wives' Social and Psychologic Status and Their Husbands' Coronary Heart Disease" by Dorit Carmelli, Gary E. Swan, and Ray H. Rosenman was published in the *American*

Journal of Epidemiology in 1985. This study used the Thurstone Temperament Schedule in surveying Type A and Type B individuals. Individual behavioral traits analyzed included activity, vigor, impulsiveness, dominance, emotional stability, sociability, and reflectiveness. Of significance in considering parallel worlds is their observation that "An educated, active, and dominant wife heightens the risk of coronary disease for Type A men, whereas the highly educated and stable [dominant?] wife is protective for Type B men."

From the standpoint of dominance, four marriage combinations are evident: dominant husband/nondominant wife, dominant wife/nondominant husband, nondominant wife/nondominant husband, and dominant husband/dominant wife. These combinations have not previously been analyzed.

The dominance levels of the partners contribute to the success or failure of the union and to its material gains. Perhaps a more important consideration is the future advantages or handicaps children of the various marriage combinations will face.

Chapter V

Dominant Husband - Nondominant Wife

A marriage between a dominant man and a nondominant woman can be considered an excellent match. It reflects a patriarchal society's most treasured ideal of marriage—the husband as provider and the wife as nurturer. This family is headed by a successful husband who earns increasing financial rewards.

The marriage should be relatively free of strife. There is rarely any question either in or outside the marriage about the husband's leadership or the wife as a team player. Until recent years, the husband as sole breadwinner was proud that his wife never needed to work outside the home; the dominant husband preferred that the wife remain at home—he had little desire for a competitive wife in the work force. The nondominant wife with minimal needs for achievement outside the home had little desire to join the labor force. Although each marriage partner's reasons for the wife's not working were different, the results coincided.

A dominant husband has an underlying fear of being dominated, especially by a woman. The nondominant wife poses few threats to him because she has no psychological needs to dominate or control her husband. Because of her lower dominance, the wife has no great fear of being a follower.

The husband's world is based primarily on achievement and success; his greatest concerns are work and accomplishment. His dominant mother programed him to strive for success; he wants to achieve.

The wife is motivated primarily by needs for security. She is dependent on the husband for leadership and security. She, in turn, provides support. If she works outside the home, she still lives in semidependence. Her income is probably considered by both as only supplemental. At home or at work, the wife's world revolves around the husband and his needs, the children, and the home.

If the husband is successful, such marriages are usually long-lasting; divorces are rare during their first twenty-five years. In America today, a preponderance of the most successful, achievement-oriented, dominant men in all fields where high success can be measured have long-lasting marriages with nondominant women.

Although these wives compete for their husbands' time, they seldom compete with their husbands outside the home. In their view, they allow the husbands to spend the time necessary to achieve success in the work force. By being married to dominant men, these wives achieve material prosperity through the husband's financial rewards.

This marriage describes the majority of those in the top five income categories. (Table 1 sets out the 1987 family income categories for the United States used throughout the book.) Although presently rare, a marriage between a dominant man and a non-dominant woman in the lowest two income categories should result in a rapid income rise to a higher category. This marriage seldom occurs in the lowest two categories, since the numbers of dominant men found there are relatively small. Yet such marriages were common in the United States in past generations, as discussed in Chapter XI, Migrations and Immigrations.

Table 1. Family Income Categories, United States - 1987

			Percent of Families
1.	Super Rich - Net Worth	Over $100,000,000	
2.	Very Rich - Net Worth	50,000,000 to 100,000,000	
3.	Rich - Net Worth	25,000,000 to 50,000,000	
4.	Wealthy - Net Worth	5,000,000 to 25,000,000	22.9
5.	High Income	75,000 and up	
6.	High Upper Income	50,000 to 75,000	
7.	Upper Income	35,000 to 50,000	20.2
8.	Intermediate Income	20,000 to 35,000	26.6
9.	Low Income	10,000 to 20,000	18.6
10.	Poor	Under 10,000	11.7

Median Income - $30,853

Children of marriages between a dominant husband and nondominant wife will be nondominant (because it is the mother who is nondominant) and will live in her world. A nondominant mother usually makes fewer demands on the child in his early years than does a more dominant mother; in addition she is considerably more aware of the baby's demands for attention and, whenever possible, attempts to satisfy the baby's desires. She rears the children with practices similar to those her mother used.

When the nondominant mother meets resistance to her training attempts, as in encouraging her baby to walk, the baby often wins. He walks when he is ready to walk. In like fashion other levels of achievement are reached when the baby is ready. The mother finds it hard to make many demands on her child.

Toilet-training and weaning are often postponed. (Although Japanese mothers wean their children later and cater to their demands, early childhood training includes imparting the fear of shame and ridicule, a basic social control in Japan.) Training time is usually longer than for the child of a dominant mother. The nondominant mother is comfortable in letting the child develop at his speed. She has no great needs to force the child to meet goals within any specific time span.

A nondominant mother has no phobia of being dominated. Not having been dominated by her mother, she consequently has no great need to dominate her children. Expectations of obedience by the child are flexible since she does not strongly demand or enforce them. To obtain obedience, she may use rewards—before having actually been obeyed—more often than enforce demands.

As with dominant mothers, the nondominant mother requests of the child the things that are important to her. However, since the mother rarely forces compliance or maintains pressure for accomplishment, the child feels little compulsion to meet her demands. If the child falls short of the mother's expectations, she often accepts effort in lieu of achievement.

For the most part, the nondominant mother is more susceptible than the dominant mother to outside influences—of family members, in-laws, relatives, and friends. For example, education is usually important to the nondominant mother if she grew up in a family in the first seven income categories or if she and her husband are members of these income groups. She will probably provide learning stimuli, by reading to the child at an early age, for instance, or providing educational toys. This early stimulation to learn establishes a child's intelligence level. Thus, a child can attain high intelligence without being highly dominant.

Observers have contradictory views of this mother. To many, she appears a loving, caring person who dotes on her children and tries to give them everything they want to make them happy. She seems to provide great opportunities for her children to grow and develop their talents. To others, this mother appears undisciplined and undemanding of the children (especially of a son, thereby creating a "mama's boy"). Some believe she does not control her children's behavior but lets them run over her. These contradictory perceptions could all be true. The results of the mother's child-rearing practices will manifest themselves when the children reach adulthood.

Lack of confidence is shared by everyone to varying degrees. Everyone is born insecure. We gain self-confidence (self-esteem) through accomplishment; no other path leads to its development.

In childhood and adolescence, the son of a nondominant mother often appears more self-confident and less insecure than a more dominant peer. By winning many of his childhood battles with his mother, he may have accomplished more at an early age than his dominant counterpart. This individual, however, is hampered in achieving outstanding success as an adult. Having had few demands for early accomplishments made on him by his mother, few fears of failure were set in motion. Without an adult phobia of failure, he has no strong psychological need for high achievement. In some instances, even unemployment does not trigger a sense of guilt. Absenteeism and tardiness may evoke less anxiety or concern than a more dominant counterpart would feel.

Children of either sex who receive the same nondominant upbringing show no difference with respect to the dominance trait other than what enculturation assumes and society rewards. Except for physical differences, every psychological fear and need related to dominance is the same in both sexes. Assuming that the amount and focus of time and energy the mother expends on each child are comparable, she programs all children in the family in the same manner.

The fathers' expectations of children in these marriages are often unrealistic, since the children are nondominant like their mothers. These fathers sometimes unwittingly alienate their children, particularly sons, by demanding achievement, and bring grief to the entire family. These fathers do not understand the dominance trait and its ramifications; since they attained some success, they see no reason why their sons should not do even better—particularly if a father is more successful than his father was.

The dominant father's influence on his children's dominance is in conflict with the mother's nondominance. He negatively reinforces the children's achievement needs, except possibly in the area of education. If the parents' interests in education are compatible and quality schools are available, this sometimes fuels the children's academic success. However, even with the efforts of both parents, the children of this marriage combination often fail to respond to education owing to their lesser dominance levels and consequent lower needs for achievement.

The successful father, whose upbringing shaped him, may believe that his wife is not rearing their son correctly. He may rationalize during the child's early years that times and child-rearing techniques have changed. The mother may view any criticism of her child-rearing practices as a personal affront. The nondominant mother is rearing her children by the only method she knows, the way that she was reared. She will interpret and apply any books about child rearing to her specific child-rearing frame of reference, her own upbringing.

Neither parent really understands the significance of the different way the other was brought up. The father, using examples from his childhood, may advise the mother as to how to rear their son. If the father is sufficiently immersed in his work, however, the mother rears the son as she wants without much interference or criticism from her husband.

The husband's mother, dominant like her son, may criticize the wife's child-rearing techniques. Since the mother-in-law understands only her own methods of rearing children, she believes the grandchild should be reared as she and her son were. Rarely will a nondominant wife and a dominant mother-in-law agree on any aspect of child training. Even if the husband supports his wife against his mother, his expectations for the son rarely diminish, but are likely to increase in proportion to the son's age. As the son matures, the husband's criticisms of the wife's child-rearing methods may multiply; the wife then may become more firm and obdurate. The dominant father often rechannels his criticism from the mother to the child.

Often expectations and resulting demands on a teen-age son by the father escalate. The father may stop rationalizing the differences between his expectations and his son's actual achievements in school grades, choice of friends, and in some cases lack of belief or interest in the work ethic. Rather the need accelerates to try to change him because he fears failure, not only in his own eyes but in the opinion of others, in not having a successful son. He believes incorrectly that if he quickly changes the son's attitudes to match his expectations, he can become a greater success through the son's hoped for successes.

The son becomes resentful. Nondominant, he does not understand why his father is pressuring him. He may realize correctly that he cannot meet his father's expectations even though he knows his father believes the opposite. Predictably, the father continues to exert pressure on his son to achieve, for example, by intensifying his efforts to force the son to improve his school grades. He may spend more time with his son trying to persuade him to excel and attempting to show him how to change. The son might then regard these encounters as unwarranted lecturing and find it impossible to relate to or be comfortable with his father. Many times they are unable to communicate or to share ideas, as they have little in common.

If tension and stress continue between them, the son looks to others, especially nondominant friends, with whom he can feel at ease. Depending on the degrees of the father's dominance and the son's nondominance and the false expectations of both, their relationship deteriorates into the flinging of derogatory remarks by the father about the son's choice of friends and his lack of interest in work and achievement.

Living in one psychological world, the father in this scenario is disappointed in what he sees as his son's lack of ambition. He suffers pain and guilt, and views himself as a failure at fatherhood. Living in a parallel world, the son resents and is wounded by the father's attitudes and actions that he cannot relate to or even understand. He views himself as a failure for not meeting his father's expectations.

The mother finds herself caught in the middle. She believes both that her husband is too demanding and that her son should try harder. She may blame herself for the son's failure to meet his father's expectations. If she chooses sides, no matter which one she chooses, she will lose.

Outside forces, especially public education systems, fail to differentiate between nondominant and dominant boys. School curriculum requirements are the same for all regardless of dominance levels. Children of families in the upper, high upper, and high income categories not attending private schools usually attend the more exacting public schools. Curriculum demands on the nondominant son may worsen family problems.

On the other hand if the son excels at sports, he commonly draws praise from his dominant father, which alleviates some of the pressure he feels coming from him and from the school system.

However sports, although providing some relief, do not really solve the nondominant son's problems at home and at school, especially if because his family falls in the higher income categories much is expected of him.

The combination of the father's direct and indirect pressures on the son sometimes results in the son leaving home in his teens. Perhaps he runs away or lives with friends. The situation frequently becomes so unbearable that, in increasing numbers, these sons—and daughters under similar circumstances—choose far more dramatic methods of escape such as suicide.

Upper and high upper income families are most susceptible to society's expectations in child-rearing practices. Both the nondominant mother and the dominant father may believe that they have failed or are failing to rear their son properly.

If unhampered by societal expectations, this son is capable of a high level of contentment with lower achievement than his dominant counterpart. He is not a driven person; he was not programed for high success. He does not understand those who have strong needs to achieve and who strive so hard to create wealth, power, or fame for themselves. He may well view them as foolish and unable to enjoy the fruits of their labors.

The needs for security and maintenance of the status quo prevail for much of the nondominant man's adult life. Having had security and lack of pressure as a child, as an adult he cannot understand or accept society's expectations for him to excel. It is unfair to tag him an underachiever.

The successful, dominant father with a nondominant wife and son could consider two possibilities to improve the tenor of their family life. First, he could love his son with the same understanding that sustains the love he has for his wife and, second, he could ask his son to achieve only in those areas where he could be successful. If the father were able to do this, he might come to understand to some extent the son's parallel world in which his psychological needs for security, equality, and acceptance, though unlike his own, are similar to those of his wife. He might then be able to see in his son many of the qualities he finds endearing in his wife. Moreover, this new insight might enable him, even without complete understanding, to accept and enjoy the son as an individual rather than to expect a replica of himself. If the father is able to recognize that the son has a different perception of reality than his own and that both have strengths and weaknesses, perhaps their stresses and tensions will lessen.

The successful, dominant father can immeasurably assist his non-dominant son in the job market. The father's contacts, if used in the true best interests of the son, can benefit and help shape a potentially rewarding future for him. The father can guide his son to employment areas in which he will not be expected to be a high achiever or to duplicate his father's success. The son can then be happy in a career geared to his capabilities.

Additionally, particularly in the top six income categories, the father can look ahead; it may be only a matter of time until the son marries a dominant woman. (This possibility diminishes each year, since the ratio of dominant women is declining.) If this occurs, his grandchildren—especially the first born—by having a dominant mother, can be expected to be dominant just as he is.

Society normally does not impose the same hardships on a non-dominant daughter born to a family in the upper and high upper income categories as are placed on a son. As these income categories are the most susceptible to society's ideas of a woman's proper role, being a homemaker wins social approval. However, social roles in these groups are undergoing a rapid, dramatic change.

To maintain the family's status in the upper and high upper income categories, many wives are choosing or being forced to work to supplement the family's income. In light of economic reality the working wife is becoming accepted and valued. This is especially true when the woman's position is not executive or at least not threatening to the husband. Society's acceptance of working wives is being extended even to working mothers, as a second income becomes necessary to allow many families to sustain their economic status.

A nondominant daughter often faces demands to excel from a successful, dominant father if she is an only child or the first born of all female children. He may demand that she be a high achiever in the business or professional world. We can posit that the results of his demands will be identical to what occurs with a nondominant son: She will be unable to fulfill her father's expectations and will suffer the same tensions and stresses as a nondominant son. Again, the dominant father of a nondominant daughter should use the same tactics of love and understanding as described for a nondominant son to resolve the impasse between them.

A daughter of a dominant father and nondominant mother will be nondominant like her mother. In the highest seven income categories, she could be courted by high-achieving, dominant men just as her mother was. She attracts dominant men because she has few psychological needs to dominate or control others and so does not constitute a threat. Eventually, the daughter may marry a dominant man, although this prospect dims each year as their ratios decline. Her husband then could become successful just as her father did.

A son of a dominant father and nondominant mother born in the top five income categories may be treated differently from one born to a couple with similar dominance levels in the lower income categories. The same parallel worlds of dominance and nondominance exist; similar tensions, stresses, and resentments are experienced by the son; and the same fatherly demands may well be made on the son to excel and achieve. However, there is enough wealth in the highest five income categories to mitigate the enculturation for achievement, and often as time passes the father lessens his demands on the son.

Many children in the upper five income categories are educated in private schools, where teachers are influenced more directly than in public schools by the family's money not only as tuition but as potential future school support. Since teachers in private schools are likely to pay more attention to individual students, a son may suffer less school-induced stress and tension than a son in the next two income categories who more often attends public schools. Equally or possibly more important, the nondominant mother probably received and sets a high value on a good education. If so, she may focus her strongest efforts on educational training in the home during the sensitive early years.

The son of a dominant father and nondominant mother in the top five income categories usually receives a better-than-average education and often is spoiled by his family, even to the point that he is seen as a playboy. Eventually, he may marry a dominant woman. With a diminishing number of dominant women of his age and social class, he may well marry beneath his income category. The dominant wife often takes charge in the marriage. Any grandchildren, especially the first born, will probably be dominant like the son's wife. If the family fortune erodes because of the son's spending habits, it could be rebuilt by the third generation. Many times the poor, dominant grandfather makes the original fortune, only to see his nondominant sons exhaust their inheritance. The dominant grandson, unaffluent because of his parents' excesses, rebuilds the family wealth, fulfilling Andrew Carnegie's "three generations from shirtsleeves to shirtsleeves."

Inheritance tax advantages can now alter this sequence. If the first grandchild is a boy, his adult success may be heavily favored by laws designed to transfer wealth through elaborately structured trusts, especially the complex "generation-skipping" type. This enables the dominant grandfather, who originally made the money, to bypass the second generation and move some inheritance directly to the third generation. With this inheritance, the third generation, if dominant, will be most fortunate, for coupling financial inheritance with the dominance trait spells outstanding success. Many family histories are replete with examples of inheritance used with dramatic results by a dominant third-generation man or woman.

The daughter of a dominant father and nondominant mother in the highest five income categories is usually fortunate. She is likely to receive a superior education, learn the appropriate social graces and, if attractive, be the belle of the ball. She may marry a dominant, high-achieving man as her mother did. The dominant husband may become the successful son-in-law consistently found in business and politics. With high needs to achieve now coupled with access to capital and his wife's family contacts, he often attains extraordinary success.

The son or daughter of a dominant father and nondominant mother in the low and poor income categories will be nondominant like their mother. They will have a difficult time achieving success as measured by power, fame, or wealth. Since these categories presently contain lower percentages of dominant individuals of either sex than do other income categories, there are few marriages of dominant men and nondominant women.

In the low and poor income categories a vicious cycle is more visible now than several generations ago. Earlier in this century, members of these groups, inspired by seeing the financial growth of others, could anticipate escaping upward. Now, primarily because of the preponderance of low dominance levels, few escape into higher income categories. Consequently, the numbers of those in the two lowest income categories increase annually as does the defeatist attitude that there is no hope for improvement.

Chapter VI

Dominant Wife - Nondominant Husband

Under American society's value system, the marriage of a dominant woman and nondominant man has been perhaps the least understood combination of partners, although these unions have been with us throughout history. Numerous articles in recent years refer to *changing lifestyles, role reversal,* and *mothering by men* to describe such marriages. The increasing percentages of women executives give these marriages greater visibility. Today women's accomplishments are no longer isolated occurrences, and comparisons of these marriage partners are more frequent yet no better understood.

These unions fly in the face of a patriarchal society's ideal of marriage. The husband is expected to be the family provider or at least its major provider while the wife devotes herself primarily to the children and home. If she has outside employment, her income is expected to be only supplemental to the husband's. Patriarchal social values preclude the wife's being employed solely to gain personal satisfaction through work-related achievement and success. Society's attitude has been that a wife should work only as long as necessary or until the first child is born. She should then leave the work force to care for the children, maintain a home, and encourage the husband's work endeavors.

There are doubts in this marriage as to who is the leader; many times the wife makes major decisions. For the sake of social conformity, the wife often, consciously or subconsciously, minimizes her leadership role. Such a downplaying of importance fits leadership assumptions in patriarchal societies.

Until recently, marriages between dominant women and nondominant men were fairly long lasting, comparable in mutual compatibility to marriages between dominant men and nondominant women. Once women began accomplishing outside the home in fields other than the traditional teaching and nursing, and increasing their financial independence, divorces multiplied. (Five million American wives now earn more than their husbands.) The differences in accomplishments and the often marked disparity in income between these husbands and wives produce strains making divorce more common.

These marriages usually produce smaller material rewards than the dominant husband, nondominant wife combination. In the past even more than now, the successes of their children, particularly sons, were counted among their rewards.

A nondominant man has strong security needs and minimal entrepreneurial risk-taking needs. Except in wartime, the most secure jobs available for individuals in the low to intermediate income categories have been as enlisted men in the Armed Forces. Children of military personnel are often called military brats. Even when used in a derogatory manner, this term highlights the phenomenon of dominance in a large percentage of white enlisted men's children, many of whom achieve success as adults. Observers look no further to account for their successes than their easily identifiable, extensive childhood travel with its consequent gains in new experiences. Few realize that these children had dominant mothers and nondominant fathers and that their adult successes were actually a result of the mother's influence and expectations, just as with any dominant child raised by a dominant mother. The opportunity for extensive travel is a benefit little different from the opportunity to attend an intellectually challenging school; neither alone causes a person to be successful.

For several generations, the same phenomenon has been discernible in the successes achieved by many children of Protestant ministers. Could it be that the majority of Protestant ministers are nondominant and usually marry dominant women who normally rear the children to be dominant? I propose that this is true except in the case of Protestant ministers who have acquired power, fame, or wealth. I submit that the overwhelming majority of those ministers, because of their successes, are dominant and marry nondominant women; any nondominant children of such marriages are unlikely to achieve the success levels of their fathers.

Marriages between dominant women and nondominant men work well in the top seven income categories. They occur less often in the lowest two categories, which now contain fewer dominant women. Today, a marriage between a dominant woman and a nondominant man in the lowest two categories results in a family income rise to a higher category through the efforts of the dominant wife. However, since a dominant woman's successes are somewhat limited by discrimination, the income level does not increase as dramatically as is possible for a dominant man under the same circumstances.

Although having a dominant mother does not guarantee dominance, children of a marriage between a dominant woman and nondominant man are likely to be dominant. The first-born child, particularly if male, usually receives the most attention and time from the mother and is frequently the main repository for the mother's expectations.

Each step of a child's life takes on above-average importance for the dominant mother. She wants her child to do better than other children. She often toilet-trains the child at an early age, and weans him early. Even his walking at an earlier age than his peers is important to her; many successful men remember at what age they first walked as repeated to them by their mothers. In the eyes of the dominant mother, normal childhood developmental timetables become challenges for her child to best.

Whatever the mother believes important she translates into demands on the child. If intelligence and education are important to the dominant mother, grades from elementary school forward become her measure of her child's ability to excel. If she is interested in sports, she begins training him to outperform others at an early age. In whatever area of competition she regards as important she will call for early and unceasing effort to achieve excellence on the part of her child. One of the most important things in this mother's life is that her child excel; the highly dominant mother wants the child to surpass all others. Many times she uses punishment as well as praise to that end. She may even use her strongest weapon, withdrawal of her love, if that is necessary to force the child to achieve her goals.

As described in Chapter II, Dominance and the Individual, in discussing nondominant mothers, observers assess mother-child relationships differently, an indication of how difficult it is to see through to the essentials of personal situations. To some, this mother seems a loving, caring person who dotes on her child and who is doing her best to help him become a success. To others, this mother seems overly disciplined, making too many demands on the child and, if a son, creating a "mama's boy." Still others believe that she leaves little opportunity for the child to develop his personality, thereby creating an insecure individual who may be haunted throughout his life by the specter of failure. Strangely enough, all these contradictions could be true, and many become recognizable later.

To repeat an essential element of my thesis, this mother's expectations, translated into demands on the child, raise his threshold of potential. Sons and daughters of highly dominant mothers often spend their lives working and achieving success after success.

For many successful individuals, each new conquest merely opens new vistas of potential achievement and diminishes past successes. One of the harshest measures a dominant individual can use to judge himself is what he believes could have been achieved as opposed to what he has accomplished. Often driven people, these individuals continue to pursue new goals all their lives, long after having apparently "proved" themselves. Some never feel the sense of achievement and satisfaction that should accompany their successes.

Subconsciously they feel unable to fulfill the expectations their mothers set during childhood.

These dominant people cannot understand others who have few needs to show initiative, to work prodigiously, to better themselves, or to demonstrate spectacular success. Some driven, successful people view nondominant individuals as lacking in ambition or simply lazy.

The overriding feelings that are likely to affect the adult life of the son of a highly dominant mother are a phobia of being dominated and a need to be in control. Risk-taking, the hallmark of an entrepreneur, is one manifestation of the need to be in control. To the successful entrepreneur, taking a risk is of small consequence compared to the alternative of being controlled by others.

A daughter given the same dominant upbringing by a dominant mother is no different in this trait from a son. Allowing for physical differences and the ability to bear children, every psychological fear and resulting dominance need is the same for a daughter as for a son.

According to the time she spends with each of them, a dominant mother will program all her children for dominance in the same way. If the dominant mother makes fewer demands on some than others, they will be less dominant as adults than those on whom she makes greater demands.

In most cases, the nondominant father's influence has a minimal effect on the future dominance of the children. This is not true of some children now being reared by a nondominant father who fulfills the homemaking role while a dominant, more successful mother competes in the business world. In these cases, the children will probably be nondominant like their father, as he is filling the traditional shoes of the mother.

In the highest four income categories—wealthy, rich, very rich, and super rich—the nondominant husband, because of his wealth (for the most part inherited), is able to disguise his nondominance except from his family and close friends. Because of his wealth, his opinions are solicited, and he may wield influence as an extension of his wealth. As a passive investor, as an appointee to a governmental body, or—in recent years—as an elected official to high office, his money disguises his lack of leadership ability. People customarily associate the ownership of wealth, whether earned or inherited, with intelligence, ambition, and leadership.

The dominant wife in these income categories often chooses not to compete in the work force. If she elects to work, it probably will be in the arts, the media, or politics.

With the protection of wealth, neither marriage partner's life truly revolves around the other's needs: achievement for the dominant partner and security for the nondominant partner. The husband's limited needs for achievement present no problem as his inheritance provides material well-being and status, satisfying society's view of him and his view of himself as a successful man. Having access to the same wealth, the wife rarely views acquiring more wealth as a worthy goal.

The son lives in his mother's world and so is similar to her in dominance. The mother's expectations for him and her child-rearing methods generally are acceptable to the father who has the prevailing cultural bias in favor of male achievement. However, some dissension may occur deriving from the father's memories of his childhood. He may believe the son is being pushed too hard, too fast. The dominant mother usually wins and controls her son's upbringing. If the mother's attention focuses on education as a worthy achievement, the son's ability to excel in school may meet with his father's approbation and cause him to concur in the wife's child-training methods. Consequently, most parental arguments about the mother's child-rearing methods diminish when the son enters school.

Although the father and son live in parallel worlds, the father is unlikely to resent his son's successes. Because society admires success, the nondominant father usually takes immense pride in the son's achievements. Even though he does not understand his father's apparent lack of ambition, the son ordinarily accepts or ignores it.

This son has the potential to be highly successful. He is dominant, achievement-oriented, and probably educated at the best schools. In addition, he most likely has access to large amounts of capital and family contacts with which to fuel his early adult ambitions.

The son usually marries a nondominant woman in his income class. Daughters of dominant fathers and nondominant mothers are readily available in these four income categories. This marriage fits the "money marrying money" designation, and most are long-lasting.

The daughter of a dominant wife and nondominant husband

within the highest four income categories will probably be dominant like her mother. Since the majority of the population views the wealthy, rich, very rich, and super rich as unique, the dominant daughter's outward manifestations of her needs to excel and to accomplish are generally accepted.

School leadership is ceded as this daughter's due, although based more on the family's money than her dominance. This young woman is frequently attracted to free-thinking, liberal universities. In college it may be important to her to lead causes for social change. As real leadership is seldom needed to maintain the status quo, she frequently gravitates to areas of change where leaders are needed, recognized, and acknowledged. Even though the causes are sometimes superficially damaging to the family's income status, involvement provides an opportunity for her to exercise dominance and authority.

For the dominant daughter of the upper and high upper family income categories, a dramatic difference emerges. Society's views and enculturation are most severely imposed on her. She lives in her mother's world with its needs for achievement and recognition. She and her mother may rationalize the father's inability to achieve outstanding success; since the father is nondominant, his work ordinarily is less financially rewarding than that of a dominant father.

As he accepts without understanding his dominant wife, the father accepts his daughter because she is female and has psychological needs similar to those of her mother. Until adolescence, the different perspectives of the father's and daughter's parallel worlds may not greatly disturb their relationship, since he can exercise parental control. From adolescence forward, the daughter will strive to have her way.

The relationship between mother and daughter differs from that of father and daughter. The dominant daughter usually obeys her mother and achieves in whatever areas the mother chooses. If the mother's focus is education, the daughter is expected to make good grades; if in sports, she is duty-bound to excel. The same applies to any field of endeavor.

Conflicts between dominant mothers and their dominant daughters do occur, especially during the daughter's teen-age years. They are relatively short-lived and rarely escalate into long-range struggles with serious consequences.

Dominant boys are reluctant to accept her leadership in high school. She is too reminiscent of their dominant mothers. Her friendships with dominant boys usually have a utilitarian purpose beneficial to both. Dating is another matter. As if by prearranged pact, the highest achieving boys in her class do not usually date her; if they do, it probably happens only once. This feeling is mutual because the dominant girl seldom enjoys dating dominant boys. Although the reason is rarely recognized, each is too threatened by the other's dominance to enjoy the other.

When a dominant daughter enters the work force, she finds confirmation of society's discriminatory attitudes toward women based on sex. A highly intelligent, highly dominant, and energetic woman quickly has it borne in upon her that she is not being treated evenhandedly. A dominant woman believes that her contributions to a firm are at least equal to those of her male counterparts, yet she often finds that she must work twice as hard to receive half as much recognition.

When an intelligent, energetic, dominant woman at the junior executive level first meets her male peer group's wives socially, she realizes that she has little in common with them. They act differently, talk about subjects unrelated to job performance, and even dress differently. In an upwardly mobile work environment, the dominant woman comes face to face with the parallel world of her male peer group's wives. The married junior executive's nondominant husband differs from her male peer group. At social functions, he does not fit comfortably with either his wife's dominant peer group because of the dominance trait or with the wives because of their "femininity."

Society's expectation that every woman should bear children creates conflicting emotional tugs on the dominant woman in the upper and high upper income groups. She wants to compete and achieve, but society's mores about motherhood also affect her. Few people understand her needs to lead and to achieve, most importantly in competition with men. The dominant woman lives in a world parallel to nondominant women and nondominant men, neither of whom understand her needs.

The "establishment" exists and is male controlled. Dominant men live in the same psychological world as dominant women, but they rarely acknowledge that both have the same achievement needs. Dominant men commonly perceive dominant women as threatening, the same perception they had as children of their mothers. They have little desire to relive a childhood in which they were dominated by their mothers. These men have power and opportunity; few feel any need to share them with women. This leaves only other dominant women to understand her and share her psychological needs.

Another social imbalance, especially in the intermediate, upper, and high upper income categories, shows up in the dominant woman's usual selection of a nondominant husband. With fewer needs to achieve, his contribution to a two-income family frequently places the total income well below that of a dominant husband and nondominant wife team. If the dominant wife chooses not to enter the work force (a rarity today), the family income is greatly diminished since the sole breadwinner is nondominant. The husband, because of his lower dominance, is handicapped in obtaining and holding the high-paying jobs usually held by dominant men and dominant women.

A far more positive future awaits the dominant son. He epitomizes society's expectations. He upholds the tradition of success in the United States, since he will probably achieve greater success than his father. In most instances he is obedient at least to his mother, usually makes good grades in school (if this is a major focus of the mother), and is a high achiever. Rarely does this son consider running away from home, much less take such a step. Of their 413 famous twentieth century men and women, Goertzel and Goertzel note that when children, "The boys and girls who rebelled against parents were few—twenty-four—and their rebellions were often short-lived."

The son usually is dominant like his mother and lives in her psychological world. Although living in a parallel world, the father supports the middle-class view of success and concurs with the mother's desires in rearing their child. When the mother is far more dominant than the father and the son agrees with the mother's achievement values, the son may have little respect for what he perceives as his father's lack of ambition.

If dominance in this son is accompanied by high levels of intelligence and energy, his adult rewards normally include copious amounts of power or fame or wealth or a combination of the three. His achievement of high success is the hallmark of democracy and capitalism. He can move from any income category to the wealthy and even to the rich, very rich, and super rich categories. He is then praised as a living example of what can be accomplished in the United States by hard work.

Yet hard work plays only a part in this man's success. More crucial are the achievement needs programed in him by his mother from birth through childhood and adolescence; he simply follows the blueprint established for him by his dominant mother.

Chapter VII

Nondominant Wife - Nondominant Husband

This couple does not exist in separate, parallel worlds. Having been reared similarly, by nondominant mothers, the partners live in essentially the same psychological world, at least as concerns the dominance trait.

Nevertheless the marriage could result in a stormy relationship. Each partner may appear to the other unwilling to take the family leadership role, whereas actually neither may be capable of doing so. Decision making and problem solving are apt to be minimal. Each may be tempted to blame the reluctance to make decisions on the other. Any semblance of dominance, assertiveness, or leadership by one over the other is a consequence of other things: hostility overcoming friendliness, an advantage of larger physical size or larger personal income, or the contentment of one versus the discontent of the other.

Until recently some marriages between nondominant individuals in the highest six income categories were short and ended in divorce. Even with sizable child support responsibilities, the family's financial position prevented the divorce from being monetarily traumatic for either spouse. Each would wish to remarry a dominant individual, since nondominant people tend to marry individuals with contrasting dominance levels, and vice-versa. Today, marriages between nondominant people in these income categories last longer, as the diminishing supply of men and women with high dominance limits those available for remarriage and so becomes one reason that inhibits divorce.

Children of a nondominant marriage combination become nondominant like their mother. In the highest seven income categories, they face a future similar to that of the children of nondominant women married to dominant men, as previously outlined.

In the intermediate income category, children of nondominant parents face a different future. In today's environment, both marriage partners usually work; they realize that two incomes are necessary to maintain their position in the middle class. Outside activities or family ties help sustain these marriages especially if neither partner has a parent from a higher income category. Nevertheless divorce is common unless a religion that restricts divorce plays a major part in their lives. If divorced each chooses a dominant person, if available, when remarrying.

Children of these unions lack the advantages and protection money provides in the upper seven income categories. The parents are rarely able to leave an estate of consequence, so there is little money to inherit.

If a divorce occurs, the mother normally receives custody of the children. Child support may be minimal because of the father's income bracket. In addition, increasingly large numbers of fathers do not make court-ordered support payments.

Should the mother remarry quickly and restore the family to its predivorce income category, the children will grow up in the circumstances described for nondominant children in the intermediate income category.

If the mother does not remarry, she must work to support the family. Her net income less the cost of day-care supervision for the children could eventually place them in the low or possibly the poor income category. The drastic income drop on losing one of the family's wage earners forces a corresponding reduction in the standard of living. This change is most evident in the neighborhood to which the family may be forced to move.

People usually accept the income category in which they grow up, whether it is high or low. In the intermediate and low income categories, one can hope to earn his way up to a higher income stratum and to have better housing in a better neighborhood. But when an individual drops rapidly from the intermediate to the low income category, the drop is traumatic. There is little to console one for dramatically reduced housing and neighborhood standards.

The number of low and poor income families comprised 30 percent of all American families in 1987. A profound plurality of marriages in these two income groups were between nondominant partners. Furthermore, because of sheer numbers, these marriages exceeded all such alliances in the highest five income categories combined.

The children of nondominant parents in the low and poor income categories are nondominant like their mother; indeed the non-dominant father's influence strengthens their nondominance. Living in the same psychological world as the mother and children, the father concurs with the mother in her child-rearing practices, since they are similar to the way he was brought up. In contrast to the top seven income categories, little monetary protection through inheritance or income exists for these children. Many dismiss this population segment with the expression, "For ye have the poor always with you . . ." (Matthew, 26:11).

Couples in the lowest two income groups continually face unemployment, underemployment, and low earning capability when employed. The loss of a week's pay by either partner places immediate financial strain on the marriage. Money problems are easily recognized and consequently are usually identified as the primary cause of the marriage's dissolution, but perhaps the major handicap is that neither partner provides leadership in the marriage.

Often the husband abandons his wife and children, temporarily alleviating his financial burden. For the abandoned or divorced mother with children, financial frustration increases with dramatic, negative effect. With minimal or nonexistent child support, the double burden of earning a living and rearing the children falls on her. Earning potential is so limited that in many cases she must accept welfare assistance, even though she may feel a loss of personal dignity by doing so. She cannot afford them, but the mother keeps her children and tries to maintain the family unit. Frequently the grandparents, usually on the maternal side, take the children. Sometimes the mother and children live with her parents indefinitely, "waiting for things to get better."

Many children of abandoned and divorced wives in the lowest two income categories become grade-school or high-school dropouts. They also comprise a high percentage of state correctional system inmates. Though "born equal," these children's circumstances will have become dramatically unequal long before adulthood.

The lowest two income categories have a higher birth rate than any other two income categories of the population. Fertility is a consistent factor in all income categories, but it can be altered by individual choice. Many women in the highest seven income categories choose to suppress their potential fertility, lowering the birth rate for these categories. Some people mistakenly believe the same choice is available to the low and poor income groups.

For nondominant marriage partners within these groups, the most prevalent force affecting the birth rate is the perpetuation of family attitudes. If a mother did not use artificial birth-control methods, her daughter is unlikely to do so. Her natural fertility then prevails.

Another force is the desire for and love of children on the part of many women. They have children to fulfill themselves and hope that somehow everything will work out—that in some way life will get better.

Politics is also a factor: denial of government-funded abortions for women in the lowest two income categories who want but cannot afford abortions. Without judging the concept of abortion, one can find the words and actions of politicians opposing governmental abortion funding for the poor to be ironic. The most prominent politicians are children of dominant mothers and have much higher earnings than members of the low and poor income categories. They are in the same income categories as many dominant women who have secured abortions regardless of legal constraints.

By not supporting federal abortion expenditures, politicians help ensure that birth rates for women in the lowest income groups continue to be much greater than those of more dominant women in higher income groups. By increasing the imbalance of births in favor of nondominant women, these politicians contribute to a force that will affect future generations. In the not-too-distant future of the United States, just as has happened throughout history, dominant individuals stand to be treated as pariahs by the nondominant masses.

Because of the nondominant mother, the dominance characteristics —needs for achievement, accomplishment, leadership, and control— are missing in the children of nondominant unions. In the lowest two income groups, lower dominance levels show up during the school years in poor attendance, low grades, and early dropping out, and later in a lack of marketable job skills.

In the past, lower dominance levels effectively isolated this now large segment of the American population from the country's mainstream. Some families have been isolated for generations, but their suffering went unremedied because of their relatively low population percentage. It was hidden also because many earlier members of the low and poor income categories with higher dominance levels moved up and out of those groups. Today the increased birth rate of nondominant parents with the resultant nondominance of the children and grandchildren has increased the distinctiveness of these groups as a population percentage and in raw numbers. In addition, the increased acquisition of wealth by the more dominant segment in the United States has called attention to the disparities among income groups.

This group, that of the lowest two income categories, comprises a large and rapidly increasing percentage of our population. It will increase because of the cycle of nondominant children duplicating their parents' existence, and because it has few paths by which it can become upwardly mobile.

History gives the poor many names: helots, peasants, serfs, peons, the masses. Two names prevail, the *have-nots* and the *exploited*. Historically, these classes are exploited by dominant leaders who use them to overthrow other dominant leaders.

Chapter VIII

Dominant Husband - Dominant Wife

No parallel worlds exist for this husband and wife; they live in the same psychological world with respect to dominance. Nevertheless, when the partners are in the same age group, this marriage often results in a turbulent relationship. Each needs to be in control and will make demands on the other. Each has intense needs to achieve. If the wife is not employed, her lack of involvement outside the home becomes a major contributor to a stormy marriage.

With the upward mobility currently possible in the work force, many dominant wives achieve career success. Accomplishments outside the home greatly diminish the stress and tension caused by two dominant people living together.

This pairing in the United States represents a minuscule percentage of marriages within the same age group, since a dominant man or woman most often chooses a nondominant marriage partner. Marriages of dominant and nondominant individuals ensure less tension and stress. Additionally, more nondominant potential marriage partners are available than in the past because the birthrate among dominant women has been diminishing over several decades.

Although currently comprising only a small percentage of total marriages, those between dominant individuals occur more frequently in the highest · six income categories. The combination of two dominant partners is virtually nonexistent in the low and poor categories, where only a few individuals have high dominance levels.

In the United States both partners of a marriage have freely chosen whom they wished to marry. Arranged marriages for family, financial, or political reasons have never been an influential force as they were in historical monarchies. There are no active marriage brokers as in some foreign cultures such as India, Ireland until very recently, or Japan where some 60 percent of all marriages are arranged, usually by families or family friends. The strength of the middle class preserves American freedom of choice.

That people are free to choose their marriage partners in the United States helps explain why few marriages here occur between dominant individuals from the same age group. They find it exceedingly hard to get along under one roof. Arguments proliferate over the unwillingness of either to give up any amount of control or to compromise, and the determination of each to win. Often tensions come to light during courtship and the engagement is canceled, the couple attributing their problems to personality differences rather than realizing that their similar dominance levels cause the conflict.

Dominant partners in first marriages are psychologically threatening to one another. Each has needs to achieve, to be in control, and to compete; these can be construed by the other partner as being hard to please, domineering, or uncompromising. Only by developing a level of confidence and respect through accomplishment, especially in different areas, are highly dominant individuals ever likely to become compatible.

Language barriers contributed to marriages between dominant individuals among early immigrants, since their choices were limited to a circle of people who spoke a common language. As the immigrants learned English, their circle enlarged and their marital choices expanded. Since many immigrants were dominant (see Chapter XI, Migrations and Immigrations) and the percentages of dominant people in the United States one or two hundred years ago were greater, it was harder to find a nondominant marriage partner than it is today.

In the country's past, marriages between dominant individuals took place in all income categories. Divorce remained socially unacceptable and relatively uncommon from America's formation until 1945. Social attitudes, economic considerations, and the proscription of divorce by almost all religious faiths tended to restrain divorce except in the then top five income categories. Although often filled with bitter arguments, the marriages lasted.

A static wealthy class appears to be forming in the United States, but it has not yet become a major factor in the marriage selection process. Marriages within class confines for the highest three income categories will probably increase. However, it is anticipated that such marriages will include few in which both partners from the same age group are dominant.

Through much of America's earlier history, no real or imagined permanent disparity existed between the *haves* and *have-nots*. The rich were there and were usually admired unless dishonest; even then, they were often tolerated. Although there were poor people, they were viewed as unfortunate, temporary *have-nots*. The poor expected to rise above their station, and a majority did. Members of the poor and low income categories expected their children, if not themselves, to move up to the middle class and, if they did not, believed that their grandchildren would certainly accomplish that feat. In any case the very rich and the very poor represented small portions of the population, both numerically and as percentages of the whole.

Upward mobility was expected and striven for, and marriages between dominant men of a lower income category and dominant women of a slightly higher one occurred frequently. Potential problems stemming from the dominance trait in these marriages were tempered to some extent, since the woman from a slightly higher station represented a prize for the man from a lesser class. In the woman's case, a husband from a lower income category was not regarded as a humiliation, since she usually had a higher social position that protected her feeling of self-worth, and a man trying to "better himself" was respected.

Today, with a greater acceptance of divorce by society and religion, marriages between highly dominant individuals of the same age group are often quickly terminated. When remarrying they frequently choose nondominant partners and remember their first marriages as brief, acrimonious periods in their lives.

Second marriages between very dominant individuals occur most often with a significant age difference between the partners; the highly successful, dominant man remarries a considerably younger, dominant woman. The age disparity favors this couple. The husband probably has attained a high level of self-confidence, allowing him to tolerate high dominance in someone many years his junior, provided it is channeled into areas not in direct competition with those in which he has achieved. The dominant, younger wife respects his accomplishments and accepts, at least in the early years of the marriage, his position as the leader. In most cases, children of this marriage are dominant.

Remarriage also occurs between a successful, dominant woman and a dominant, young man many years her junior. This combination is less common, possibly because of social bias.

Religion is still a factor in preserving unions between highly dominant individuals of the same age group. One religion, Judaism, has prevailed in its positions on marriage and divorce longer than any other faith. The Jewish faith has continued for more than four thousand years, and a high percentage of its followers are dominant.

On the other hand, the dominance trait is the single largest factor causing Jews to marry outside their faith. This is reflected in marriages of dominant Jews of both sexes to nondominant persons of other religions. Interfaith marriages increase during times of affluence or relative peace for Jews.

For most members of the Jewish religion, however, the marriage pool is within the narrow circle of their faith. Most Jewish marriages are between dominant and nondominant partners. Still, since most are dominant and, in keeping with the tenets of their faith, marry within the religious community, a number of Jewish marriages occur between dominant individuals. By living within their faith, many such partners see that their marriages endure.

Regardless of religious affiliation, children of dominant parents are expected to be dominant. Since parents and children all live in essentially the same psychological world, not only are they programed by the mother for success, but the father's influence strengthens their dominance.

The son is dominant like his mother. Since both his parents were reared by dominant mothers and experienced similar child-rearing methods, his father, also dominant, concurs with the mother's child-rearing goals and practices. This magnifies the mother's pressure on the son to succeed. In addition, the dominant son has access to family capital and contacts through his dominant father or dominant mother, which can accelerate his accomplishments, especially in business and politics. (Children from a marriage of a dominant mother and a nondominant father usually spend an inordinate number of years either making money or building a political base.) When both parents are dominant, money is assured and little time is diverted from the attempting of large goals earlier in life.

Given the same upbringing as a son, a daughter of dominant parents has the same basic psychological needs to achieve. She also will be dominant and programed for success in whatever field she selects. The two greatest handicaps this daughter is likely to face are society's view of a woman's proper place in life and having to achieve in a male-oriented society. Nevertheless she will probably succeed, since the income category occupied by two dominant parents is substantially greater than average. Her chances of success will probably be enhanced by a superior education and her family contacts. In addition, she will have had the childhood experience of being exposed to a dominant father while being reared by a dominant mother.

Perhaps within these four marriage combinations within different income groups lie answers to unresolved, centuries-old debates. If intelligence is largely inherited, why does the overall intelligence of a successful society initially rise and subsequently fall? What are the roots of discrimination? Could the descendants of different marriage combinations, with their different dominance levels, affect intellectual levels, discrimination, worldwide migrations, and political regimes?

PART II
Social Consequences
of Dominance

Chapter IX

Intelligence and Achievement

. . . genetic theory predicts, and experiment verifies, that physical and mental traits, including intelligence, show regression to the mean. This fact poses enormous difficulties for any environmentalist explanation of individual differences in IQ, because it is the children born to the most able and successful who regress *downwards* towards the mean, in spite of the environmental advantages their family offer, while it is the children of the dullest and least successful who regress *upwards*, in spite of their deprived upbringing. I know of no attempt to explain this phenomenon in environmental terms. . . .

H. J. Eysenck
The Intelligence Controversy

Dr. Eysenck, author and professor at the University of London, is an outspoken advocate of the heritability of intelligence. He believes it likely that, in modern Western countries, such IQ heritability is not lower than 70 percent or higher than 85 percent.

Those who believe that a major portion of intellectual achievement is inherited must explain away large amounts of data. The focus of this chapter, as in the discussion of dominance and child-rearing practices, is: first, to dispel the notion that intelligence is primarily inherited; second, to show how intelligence and achievement levels in individuals and social groups result from early stimuli in child-rearing practices; and third, to explain why, because of family formations, this idea has been overlooked.

The word intelligence, which comes from the Latin *inter-legentia*, was coined about two thousand years ago by the Roman writer Cicero. He used it in reference to the selective and discriminatory powers of thought and reason. The word intelligence is still associated with a person's reasoning ability.

No systematic study of intelligence was attempted until the advent of experimental psychology late in the nineteenth century. The earliest modern writers to attempt an objective analysis of intelligence and to consider the possibility of its measurement were Sir Francis Galton of England, Alfred Binet of France, and C. Lloyd Morgan of the United States.

In 1904 the French government asked Alfred Binet to devise a simple test for the school system. It wanted something teachers could use to identify children who were too dull to benefit from ordinary teaching methods. Binet began with a rather revolutionary assumption that seems fairly obvious today. He believed that a dull child would be much the same as a normal child except that he would be retarded in his mental growth. Consequently, a dull child would behave on any test like a normal child of a younger age. Binet confirmed the concept in experimental tests and coined the phrase "mental age."

To better understand specific educational systems, past and present, as well as their intended results, one must first acknowledge intelligence—that intelligence exists, that disparity in intelligence exists among individuals and groups, and that intellectual ability can be measured with a high degree of accuracy. Once these ideas are accepted, the age-old question arises as to the cause or causes of intellectual differences.

The child's intellect develops at the pace at which his mind is stimulated. The earlier the stimulus is applied, the greater will be the mind's ability to acquire and store knowledge. Early mental stimulation can also create the need to acquire more knowledge in order to satisfy continuing intellectual demands. Even though a human being's brain at birth is only one-fourth the size it will be when he is grown, it is immediately responsive to stimuli. (As discussed later in the chapter, human brain capacity is virtually the same for all, though never fully utilized and commonly under-utilized.)

The child-rearing practices of the mother (or the person directly responsible for rearing the child) are the first factor in determining the levels of intelligence and achievement the child will attain. In both areas, the child is stimulated by the mother to achieve, intellectually and in the ways society rewards, proportionate to her interest in each.

The children who tend to develop the highest intelligence levels are the children of both dominant and nondominant mothers who have a greater-than-average interest in learning and consequently make strong demands for early intellectual achievements. The mental level of the mother, even if low, does not limit the child's intellectual accomplishments so long as she makes intellectual demands of him. Children tend to have average intelligence when their mothers make average demands on them for early intellectual accomplishments. Children of mothers who make few such demands and who have little interest in early childhood intellectual development tend to have the lowest intelligence.

Intellectual disparity among groups and countries is traceable to the active interest in education of the mothers. Mothers, through their child-rearing practices, determine the children's levels of mental stimulation. Where the dominance trait is skewed favorably among the mothers, the intellectual average of the children is likely to be higher than in a corresponding group or country with a less favorable dominance balance among the mothers. This holds true to an even greater degree in documenting disparity in achievement. Dominant and nondominant mothers providing early intellectual stimuli enhance a group or country's intellectual levels, but it is dominant mothers who determine a group's achievement levels.

The phrase "nature versus nurture" is euphonious but also latitudinal and ambiguous. "Heredity versus environment" places a simple concept (heredity) against an all-encompassing one (environment). "The word 'environment,' which is deliberately imprecise," writes Albert Jacquard, "covers such things as the nourishment absorbed . . . the radiation he was exposed to, the shocks he endured, the affection with which he was surrounded, the teaching, of all kinds, which he was given: in short, all the physical and moral influences which shaped the individual in the course of its development from the embryo." Perhaps the phrase *heredity versus child-rearing practices* is more descriptive when contemplating the origins of intelligence and achievement.

Technology presents an analogy. Computer hardware is dormant and unproductive by itself, as is computer software. Only when software is introduced to hardware will the computer function and produce. Could the human body and brain be compared to hardware and child-rearing practices and education to computer software?

dle dle dle glh glh glh

Charles Darwin presented the theory of evolution in *The Origin of Species by Means of Natural Selection*, published in November 1859. Although the entire first edition of 1,250 copies sold in one day, Darwin's work generally evoked ridicule and rejection. The initial storm of controversy climaxed during the June 30, 1860, British Association for the Advancement of Science meeting at Oxford with the celebrated oral duel between T. H. Huxley and Bishop Wilberforce.

Before publication of *The Origin of Species*, some Christian denominations already had an established creation date. They identified 4004 B.C. as the year in which the Garden of Eden and Adam and Eve, the first human inhabitants of the Earth according to the Bible, were created. In 1650 James Ussher (1581-1656), Archbishop of Armagh, calculated that date by studying the Old Testament. Beginning in 1701, 4004 B.C. was printed in the King James version of the Bible. Dr. John Lightfoot, Master of St. Catherine's College,

Cambridge, England, went a step further and identified the specific time of the earth's creation that year as 9:00 a.m., October 23rd.

As Darwin's work set the earth's habitation by humans well before 4004 B.C., the Creation as depicted in the first Book of the Old Testament was immediately subject to question. If evolution had validity, went the ensuing arguments, the Creation according to Genesis could not be true literally. Some Christian leaders felt threatened by Darwin's work and vociferously rejected his theory.

Many religious faiths and a sizable portion of the world's population still reject evolution. Some Christian leaders see either rejection of the Bible or of Darwin's theory as the sole alternative, without seriously considering the possibility of reconciling the two. Their rejection of evolution is much like the Roman Catholic Church's 1633 repudiation of Galileo's support for the heretical Copernican theory that the Earth revolves around the Sun. Today Galileo's discoveries and equations are universally accepted, and the Roman Catholic Church survives.

A few Christian leaders attempt to reconcile Christianity and evolution. Pierre Teilhard de Chardin, a French Jesuit priest, philosopher, and paleontologist, proposed that Christianity and evolution could coexist. Teilhard's background enabled him to blend science and religion. In China he helped in the discovery of the Peking Man's skull. He also worked with the dating of fossils in Asia. He was with the Wenner-Gren Foundation in New York City for the last two years of his life, and made two South African paleontology and archaeology expeditions. With his major works having been published posthumously, fame for Teilhard came after his death in 1955.

Teilhard believed the theory of evolution and the tenets of Christianity to be compatible and reconcilable. He developed a theory that mankind is evolving, mentally and socially, toward spiritual unity. He thought that just as man evolved physically, so too must man as a group evolve spiritually.

Because of the continuing religious controversy, basic knowledge about the human species accepted by scientists is unknown to most laymen and receives little or no attention from political or religious leaders. There appears to be confusion about mankind's evolutionary history, except among scientific scholars in fields such as biology and anthropology.

Some of that confusion manifests itself in intelligence and achievement studies. Evolution acknowledges that visible physiological human differences occur and are transmitted through genes from generation to generation. This knowledge leads many scholars and scientists to conclude that genes are also the major determinant in the distribution of intelligence and achievement among the earth's population.

Another element of confusion lies in the word "race." The concept of "race" or "racial origin" is a contemporary one. Racial determination, from its inception and as it exists today, occupies a minuscule time frame in the evolutionary process relative to the millennia humans have occupied the earth.

Possibly the concept of "race" began with Aristotle, then passed to Bernier in 1684, to Linnaeus in 1735, thence to Buffon in 1749. However, both Linnaeus and Buffon knew that all humans belonged to a single species. Buffon used the term "race" for convenience only.

In the essay "The Concept of Race in the Human Species in the Light of Genetics" from *The Concept of Race* (1964), Ashley Montagu succinctly states, "To sum up, the indictment against the anthropological conception of race is (1) that it is artificial; (2) that it does not agree with the facts; (3) that it leads to confusion and the perpetuation of error, and finally, that for all these reasons it is meaningless, or rather more accurately such meaning as it possesses is false. Being so weighed down with false meaning it were better that the term were dropped altogether than that any attempt should be made to give it a new meaning." Montagu notes that past scholars critical of the concept of "race" included Franz Boas, Blumenbach, Joseph Deniker, William Flower, Alfred Haddon, Herder, Lancelot Hogben, Julian Huxley, and T. H. Huxley.

Geography is the primary factor for identifying "racial origin" and "races," including: African Negroids, American Indians, Asian Mongoloids, Australoids, European Caucasoids, Melanesians, Micronesians, and Polynesians. But there is no evidence, for example, that American Indians existed as a "race" thirty thousand years ago. And no biological basis exists for determining "race." Therefore, racial determination has no value for forecasting future "races."

The names of new, continually appearing "sub-races" denote only ethnic groups or diverse cultures, as did past definitions of "race," rather than supposed different origins. The elimination of geographic barriers and the subsequent cohabitation and intermarriage among inhabitants of conquering and conquered nations increased the size and variety of the world's gene pool. Today, with geographic barriers virtually nonexistent, the gene flow among groups continues to expand worldwide.

The belief in and the commonplace use of the word "race" as applied to the human species afflicts many groups of humans. In the beginning, had people actually understood that humans represented a single, fully developed species, then "race" would not have been used to differentiate cultures. Without "race," the word hybrid to describe the offspring of mixed ethnic groups would not have been used, or the more derogatory expressions of cross-breed, half-breed, or mongrel, nor the term interracial marriage. The arrogant expressions "super race" and "master race" denote at best a fleeting cultural supremacy.

Without the term to influence our thought, it would be difficult to presume that "race" determines intellectual differences. If the origins of intellectual variances were considered solely cultural, perhaps different emphases would have been placed on developing and stimulating intellectual achievement.

The idea of evolution and the early theories that intelligence and achievement were inherited began with the publication of Charles Darwin's *Origin of Species*. These theories were furthered by Sir Francis Galton's *Hereditary Genius* (1869) and Darwin's *Descent of Man and Selection in Relation to Sex* (1871). Darwin's later work may have been unduly influenced by Galton; in *The Descent of Man* Galton is referred to ten times in the eleven chapters relating to man. Although *The Origin of Species* contains little about the possible heritability of intelligence, Darwin's initial work on evolution spawned studies in the field of inherited intelligence.

Even though archaeological findings and interpretations place mankind, *Homo sapiens sapiens*, on the earth for less than two hundred thousand years, our ancestors, *Homo erectus*, seem to have survived for 1.5 million years. *Homo habilis* existed before that for almost a million years.

The evolutionary process appears most obvious in humans in color and body configuration brought about by adaptation to environmental differences, such as climate, in diverse geographic locations. Skeletal remains found in Africa, Asia, and Europe show that man's physical evolution was fully modern thirty thousand years ago.

Unknown to supporters of evolution is at what rate the evolutionary process in the human species continues today. Size, especially height, is possibly the only discernible indicator of human change for thousands of years. The causes of height increases are either unknown or attributed to nutrition, but they are not ascribed to evolution.

While biological evolution is assumed to be occurring, the rate of change is imperceptible. Cultural rather than biological evolution has been the primary cause of change in human societies for at least the past thirty thousand years and especially the past ten thousand years. The differences in thoughts and attitudes among diverse groups of people, psychological mankind, result from cultural rather than biological transmission. *There is no evidence of the influence of biological evolution on human affairs during these periods.*

Biological evolution includes brain capacity to acquire, store, and release to other components of the body the information necessary for an organism to function in the environment and to continue the species through procreation. Darwin's theory of natural selection holds true equally for the inhabitants of Africa and for those who migrated from Africa to the Nordic countries. Individuals who adapted best to each environment survived, procreated, and passed on their genes.

Evolution of ancient man must be considered in the light of the extremely small numbers involved, small groups of individuals fighting for survival and propagating the species. Estimates put the number of mankind's ancestors, *Homo erectus,* a million years ago at only 125 thousand inhabitants worldwide. For perspective, consider these 1980 statistics: 123,000 population for Garden Grove, California, and Hampton, Virginia; 124,000 population for Peoria, Illinois; and 126,000 population for New Haven, Connecticut. This illustrates what an exceedingly small number of inhabitants were spread over the African continent, considered to be mankind's source, one million years ago. All human beings in the world today are descended from this small number; if an earlier date were used, the number would be still smaller. Every person has direct ancestral ties with every other human from the past as well as those living today.

Even with some movement among groups, membership changes within groups were probably small. Most members were likely to remain with the group in which they were born, breeding within the group. This also applied to each group's direct descendants on a scale unknown to civilized man. If the 125 thousand ancestors of man a million years ago comprised bands of fifteen, twenty-five, or thirty, the number of such groups would have been 8,333 or 5,000 or 4,166, very few relative to the geographic area and thus with limited chances for contact.

Such inbreeding, and interbreeding of small groups, could have continued until the appearance of Cro-Magnon Man when groups became considerably larger. Later, as agriculture allowed the development of more permanent settlements, still larger groups banding together created a proportionately larger gene pool.

From the estimated 125 thousand world population one million years ago to the time of the great new land mass discoveries in A.D. 1500, the world's population increased to about five hundred million, approximately one-tenth of today's population. Three hundred years later in 1800 the population reached the one billion mark. A mere 187 years later, the world's population had quintupled, and it is expected to pass the six billion mark by the year 2000.

Human evolution may have reached its zenith when humans reached the point of having the mental and physical capability to cope with the environment. Evolution by then had brought about an equal distribution of brain capacity among all humans.

Regardless of individuals' origins, all human brains today are close in size and weight, averaging 45.5 ounces and conforming to body weight. The brain's total size does not affect intelligence. People with larger heads are not more intelligent than those with smaller heads. Archaeological findings indicate that the cranial capacity of Cro-Magnon skulls was equal if not superior to that of today's humans.

Table 2 from RCA Corporation Advanced Technology Laboratories compares memory capacities.

Table 2. Memory Capacity

Memory device	Storage capacity (millions of characters)
Human brain	125,000,000,000
National Archives	12,500,000,000
IBM 3850 magnetic cartridge	250,000,000
Encyclopaedia Britannica	12,500,000
Optical disc memory	12,500,000
Magnetic (hard) disc	313
Floppy disc	2.5
Book	1.3

Based on the accuracy of this table and similar studies, one can conclude that the human brain has a magnificent storage capacity, equal to ten times the information stored in the United States National Archives and ten thousand times the knowledge contained in the Encyclopaedia Britannica.

Why then does inequality of intelligence exist among individuals and groups? Does not the distribution of genes, determining body configuration, height, color, et cetera, also determine brain size, brain capacity, and neurological functioning?

ᵔᶜ ᵔᶜ ᵔᶜ ₰ʰ ₰ʰ ₰ʰ

Genetic inheritance of intelligence and achievement was propounded by Sir Francis Galton in *Hereditary Genius: An Inquiry into Its Laws and Consequences,* the first publication on inheritance as the basis of intelligence and achievement in different groups. Galton's data incorporate and further Darwin's theory of evolution. Galton's book also contains an endorsement from his half-cousin, "I do not think I ever in all my life read anything more interesting and original.

Charles Darwin to Francis Galton on reading *Hereditary Genius*, 3rd December, 1869."

The book, as a first, is important. However, when considering *Hereditary Genius*, keep in mind the period in which Galton lived, since a society's values during a particular era influence individuals and their works.

England at the time had a rigid class system based on a patriarchal social outlook, and Galton was a highly placed male member of that system. Perhaps that was responsible for his focusing primarily on male ancestry, practically ignoring female lineage. Since that society placed less value on women, a mother's influence on her children's successes could easily be overlooked. The class system disguised any influence the mother had on her children.

Without a class system the success of a person from a poor family becomes more visible. Since his attainment of wealth, power, or fame cannot have depended upon an eminent father or grandfather, his mother's contribution to his accomplishments becomes highlighted. The mother's influence on a child's adult success is more readily apparent in a classless society.

After a class (or caste) system develops, the society maintains the system through marriages within class boundaries. Class size is a major factor in determining how long marriages between its dominant and nondominant members can successfully uphold the system. Another factor in determining the system's longevity is predicated on a country's expansionist policies or political upheavals. In addition, the realization of general affluence in a country accelerates the demise of a previously successful class system.

Class systems in unaffluent countries and in countries where outside entry into the system is difficult can be maintained for the longest period. History confirms this for aristocracies, plutocracies, oligarchies, monarchies, tyrannies, and other types of ruling parties or groups. Without exception, however, all class systems have a finite existence. Each fails, many times for the same reasons: a new interpretation of Galton's "regression" (discussed later in the chapter) and the country's overall level of affluence (discussed in Chapter XV, The Age of Affluence).

Class systems are designed to preserve individual family fortunes— money, goods, position, power, or the ownership of lands, minerals, or commerce. Each system has its roots in the dominance trait as exhibited by the successes of its men. Unless the system limits marriages of its members to others within the upper class, family fortunes can erode and disappear within two generations.

Class systems perpetuate family fortunes for years—although not totally within the confines of the male lineage in every generation—by marriages between its families. In a closed system, marriages combining given numbers of dominant and nondominant members of families within the class preserve family fortunes. The process reverses itself, nondominant to dominant and dominant to non-dominant unions, in each subsequent generation.

This means that a family fortune is not totally at risk of being lost by a nondominant son. He most likely will marry a dominant daughter of another family in the approved class, thereby providing wealth or its equivalent from both sides of the marriage. In the next generation, then, dominant sons of that union may increase the combined family wealth. This system perpetuates the transmission and growth of fortunes.

Marriages within the class system that existed in England during Galton's time preserved it to a point. Some families in the upper class were of the dominant wife, nondominant husband combination. The nondominant husband rarely achieved notable success, a detail usually overlooked in the family's history. Also ignored was the wife's role, she being a mere female: owing to the wife's dominance, the children were probably dominant and successful, especially the first born male.

In the same generation, time period, and class, the opposite circumstance will have occurred in other families in which there was a dominant husband and nondominant wife. The husband achieved outstanding success, duly noted in the family chronicles. The wife, again because she was a woman rather than because of her lower dominance level, usually was not mentioned. The children, nondom-inant because of their mother, probably were unsuccessful.

Examining a succession of marriages, one most often sees domi-nance paired with nondominance. Dominant men increased the wealth, land, and power or preserved them for future dominant men. In addition, there were some sequential generations of dominant males, for example, when a dominant man married a dominant woman and produced a son who was dominant because of his mother. In these families the chance for success was favorably skewed for two consecutive generations.

If the birth rate of dominant children equals or exceeds that of nondominant children, the class can continue indefinitely.

A deterioration of control by an upper class, in Galton's time as in any period, can be attributed to an imbalance in percentages of dominant and nondominant women. As a country becomes affluent, the number of births of dominant children falls because dominant women control their fertility. Although unacknowledged, this has been a consistent historical occurrence, especially evident in the upper class. Affluent dominant women frequently have fewer children than dominant women who have not yet attained affluence.

After a country realizes affluence, the number of dominant upper-class members available for marriage shrinks through the withholding of children by dominant, upper-class women. The system begins to deteriorate, and its control over the country diminishes.

Dominant individuals in the upper class, especially men, are the high achievers. When dominant women limit or stop having children during affluent times, in only one or two generations a majority of the class becomes nondominant, that is, with fewer members who gain power or fame or who achieve and produce wealth. Nondominant individuals can marry each other within the class according to custom, or they can break the class barrier by selecting a dominant marriage partner from a lower class.

When nondominant class members marry, the system can be maintained only temporarily. The children, because of the mother, are nondominant like their parents. If the first nondominant union does not dissipate the family wealth, the second nondominant marriage probably will. Thus, a family could lose everything in only one or two generations. If they choose instead to marry dominant members of a lower class, the family's fortune can be sustained longer. The dropping of class barriers, however, sets the stage for continued entry by the lower classes. As it loses its exclusivity, the class system becomes less important.

So long as marriages within the upper class balance dominant and nondominant partners, appearances indicate success to be a characteristic of upper-class families. This tends to hide a dominant mother's influence on the children. Family successes then can easily be attributed to genetic inheritance of the qualities needed to achieve individual success. The "proof" is visible in the achievements of dominant upper-class men.

The British class system during Sir Francis Galton's life formed his social frame of reference. It colored his thinking to such an extent that he drew incorrect conclusions from his data and ignored other information as irrelevant. As Raymond Fancher notes in *The Intelligence Men: Makers of the IQ Controversy*, "Families tend to share environmental circumstances as well as genes, and one can argue that eminence runs in some families because they provide their members with the material and psychological conditions particularly favorable to the development of their particular kinds of talent."

As educational and career opportunities became available to individuals from the lower classes and their members became highly successful, scholars could have begun the search again to determine why some people are high achievers and others are not. As some psychologists have noted, this did not happen in most cases; many studies of intelligence and achievement are only restatements or elaborations of Galton's original theory applied to more recent times.

In *Hereditary Genius* Galton sets forth the hypothesis that remains almost intact today as the basis for the theory of genetic inheritance of intelligence and achievement:

It has been shown in *Natural Inheritance* that the distribution of faculties in a population cannot possibly remain constant, if, *on the average*, the children resemble their parents. If they did so, the giants (in any mental or physical particular) would become more gigantic, and the dwarfs more dwarfish, in each successive generation. The counteracting tendency is what I called "regression." The *filial* centre is not the same as the *parental* centre, but it is nearer to mediocrity; it regresses towards the *racial* centre. In other words, the filial centre (or the fraternal centre, if we change the point of view) is always nearer, on the average, to the racial centre than the parental centre was. There must be an average "regression" in passing from the parental to the filial centre.

Galton further states, "The selection of the most serviceable *variations* cannot even produce any great degree of artificial and temporary improvement, because an equilibrium between deviation and regression will soon be reached, whereby the best of the offspring will cease to be better than their own sires and dams." and "I propose to show in this book that a man's natural abilities are derived by inheritance, under exactly the same limitations as are the form and physical features of the whole organic world." These and the following statements by Galton are incorrect relative to genetic inheritance.

Ability must be based on a triple footing, every leg of which has to be firmly planted. In order that a man should inherit ability in the concrete, he must inherit three qualities that are separate and independent of one another: he must inherit capacity, zeal, and vigour; for unless these three, or, at the very least, two of them are combined, he cannot hope to make a figure in the world. The probability against inheriting a combination of three qualities not correlated together, is necessarily in a triplicate proportion greater than it is against inheriting any one of them.

However, Galton notes exceptions and puzzles—exceptions on the maternal side, unsuccessful sons who had eminent sons, and in one particular group a small number of eminent fathers. In addition, he acknowledges some eminent wives thereby indirectly acknowledging mothers. Taken together, these provide clues from Galton's work for reasons of eminence other than heredity. Among Galton's exceptions and puzzles:

Finally the various results were brought together and compared, showing a remarkable general agreement, with a few interesting exceptions. One of these exceptions lay in the preponderating influence of the maternal side in the case of the divines; this was discussed and apparently accounted for.

Though the great Commanders have but few immediate descendants, yet the number of their eminent grandsons is as great as any other groups. I ascribe this to the superiority of their breed, which ensures eminence to an unusually large proportion of their kinsmen.

The next peculiarity in the table is, the small number of eminent fathers, in the group of Poets. This group is too small to make me attach much importance to the deviation; it may be mere accident.

Another approach to understanding intelligence and achievement focuses first on the mother or the person who rears the child. The mother, dominant or nondominant, and her interest in intellectual development provide a major answer to the stimulus of early learning in the child.

The pattern of "regression" set forth by Francis Galton occurs, but it is not linked to a "racial centre," as he suggests. "Regression" occurs simply as a consequence of negative assortative mating. Assortative mating describes marriages between individuals of approximately the same cultural background and educational level. Similarities in educational backgrounds usually mean comparable intellectual levels between husbands and wives.

Historically, as today, assortative mating applies to a preponderance of marriages. (Another term for assortative mating is homogamy —as when white people marry white people and tall people marry tall people.) Despite that, in the middle and higher classes, *many of these unions are products of negative assortative mating when considering dominance.* Negative assortative mating occurs when one marriage partner is dominant and the other nondominant. The added dimension of negative assortative mating in marriages between dominant and nondominant individuals has been overlooked, since it may be the only disparate element in otherwise assortative mating. Many marriages include one partner with more energy than the other, or one more sociable than the other, or one more friendly than the other. The trait of dominance, when considered at all, has been accorded no more weight than these and other similar ones in assessing negative assortative mating.

Consequently, we come to see that "regression" as Galton uses it in his various analyses applies to children of a marriage between a dominant husband and nondominant wife. It also applies to children of some marriages between nondominant partners. Contrary to Galton's belief, "regression" normally does not apply to children of two dominant parents or to children of a dominant wife and nondominant husband. In these cases "regression" is avoided; based on a dominant mother's educational interests and the demands she makes on the children to achieve, the intelligence or achievement, or both, of her children can be greater than the population's average and often greater than that of either parent.

Professor Eysenck's statement, "it is the children of the dullest and least successful who regress *upwards*," may be considering only half of the story. If he carefully reviews his data on the mothers of those children who he believes "regress upwards," he may need to revise his view. These mothers are undoubtedly less successful, but dull? No! Perhaps the Professor's statement is only an exercise in hyperbole.

Although every other recorded society suffered "regression" as described by Galton, this "regression" has been absent among Jewish people as a group for some four thousand years. The lineage and determination of Judaism has been and continues to be maternal, and a preponderance of Jewish mothers are dominant. As a group, Jews have not been afflicted by Galton's "regression" principally because of the dominance trait transmitted environmentally by the mother. Those who believe that Jews are a separate "race" must contend with a biological impossibility. Those who believe in Galton's "regression" of intelligence face over four thousand years of contradictory cultural evidence in trying to apply this theory to Jews. Biological determinists who believe in the concept of a Jewish "race" and in intellectual "regression" will encounter confounding and irreconcilable contradictions in attempting to mesh both beliefs.

The groups from which Galton selects eminent individuals in *Hereditary Genius* are Judges of England between 1660 and 1865, Statesmen, Commanders, Literary Men, Men of Science, Poets, Musicians, Painters, Divines, Senior Classics graduates of Cambridge, Oarsmen, and Wrestlers of the North Country. Galton further selects and analyzes 402 of his eminent individuals as to ancestry, siblings, direct descendants, and indirect descendants. These include 112 Judges, 46 Statesmen, 31 Commanders, 40 Literary Men, 47 Men of Science, 21 Poets, 16 Musicians, 19 Painters, 36 Divines, 10 Senior Classics Cantabrigians, 5 Oarsmen, and 19 Wrestlers.

The extent to which the patriarchal class system of his time influenced Galton surfaces in his analyses. In the study of the ancestry of each—fathers, mothers, grandfathers, grandmothers, great-grandfathers, great-grandmothers, uncles, aunts, great-uncles, and great-aunts—Galton chooses to mention 399 men (89 percent) and only 51 women (11 percent).

The pattern continues. For siblings, 260 brothers and 31 sisters are mentioned (again, 89 percent and 11 percent).

Direct descendants such as sons, daughters, grandsons, granddaughters, great-grandsons, and great-granddaughters include 286 men and 34 women (once more, 89 percent and 11 percent).

Indirect descendants comprise nephews, nieces, grandnephews, grandnieces, first cousins, and second cousins. (In one instance, a brother-in-law is included as an indirect descendant.) This count includes 255 men and 14 women (95 percent and 5 percent).

In the overall tabulation of ancestry, siblings, and descendants of 402 eminent people, Galton mentions 1,200 men and 130 women (90 percent and 10 percent). These percentages of men to women are so close that one begins to wonder whether Galton worked to a formula. At any rate it seems obvious that the patriarchal perspective of the time precluded an equitable look at women.

If the class system had not existed, perhaps *Hereditary Genius* would have included more data on the mothers of eminent individuals. Galton missed the implications and importance of the uncles he listed who were brothers of the mothers of his eminent people. The trait of dominance is implied by the mention of uncles, even though their sisters, the mothers, were overlooked. This holds true also for Galton's listings of maternal great-uncles; likewise the dominance trait deriving from mothers is implied throughout Galton's descriptions of the nephews' lineage.

It may be easier to relate ancestors and descendants of contemporary eminent men to dominance levels in the maternal line. Research on the Fords, Rockefellers, or Kennedys should show:

Henry Ford's mother Mary was far more dominant than his father William. Henry was dominant; Henry's wife Clara J. Bryant was not. Their son Edsel Bryant Ford was nondominant, and his wife Eleanor Lowthian Clay was dominant. Edsel and Eleanor's sons Henry II, Benson, and William were dominant, as was their daughter Josephine. Henry Ford II's first wife Anne McDonnell and their son Edsel II were both considerably less dominant than Henry II; his second wife Cristina was dominant, and so on.

Eliza Davison Rockefeller, the mother of John Davison Rockefeller, was dominant; the father, William Avery Rockefeller, was not. John Davison Rockefeller was dominant; his wife Laura Celestia Spelman was not. Thus, their son John Davison Jr. was not dominant. John Jr.'s wife Abby Greene Aldrich was dominant. Their daughter Abby and sons John Davison 3rd, Nelson Aldrich, Laurance Spelman, Winthrop, and David were dominant.

Joseph P. Kennedy and his wife, Rose Fitzgerald Kennedy, were both dominant as were their healthy children. Research should identify which of the children had dominant or nondominant spouses and which offspring would be expected to be dominant or nondominant.

Studies of male executives in the top echelons of America's largest corporations, undoubtedly intelligent, dominant, and energetic, would yield conclusions similar to those reached concerning Galton's eminent people. Research would also reveal data on dominance not considered by Galton. With few exceptions, the top executives' wives would be nondominant, their marriages long lasting, and their children nondominant (not achieving outstanding success). The minute number of highly successful offspring of first marriages by these executives would be in direct proportion to their few marriages to dominant women. Even a cursory look at the executive histories of General Motors, Exxon, and other major corporations would confirm these findings, along with the successes of many of the executives' grandsons from their sons' marriages to dominant women (little different from the grandsons' successes cited in Galton's Commanders).

The dominance trait is also found in the leaders of criminal organizations. The Mafia is perhaps the world's most widely known and discussed criminal group. Mafia chieftains represent one highly dominant group in America. Research will show that these leaders are sons of dominant mothers who normally marry nondominant men. Further inquiry would reveal that in most cases motherly demands made on Mafia leaders differ little from those made on executives who reach the pinnacle of corporate success, on prominent politicians, and on other successful, achievement-oriented adults. Just as other successful dominant men usually choose nondominant wives, so do Mafia leaders, and these wives rear nondominant children. Consequently, contrary to some popular fiction, sons do not succeed their fathers as heads of the large Mafia families.

Some may suggest that Galton's eminent people and their families were different people of another time to whom the rules of dominance do not apply. This thought prompted research on the mothers of Galton's eminent men. The researcher found little information about the mothers of several of the men and, in some instances, the fathers as well. Among these were Henry Brougham, Francis North, John Bedford, Thomas More, Andrea Doria, Hannibal, Lord Nelson, P. Cornelius Scipio, Jacques Benigne Bossuet, Claude Adrian Helvetius, Giovanni Baptista Porta, Dante, Ben Jonson, Sophocles, Virgil, Lope de Vega, Jan van Eyck, Sir Anthony van Dyck, Tiziano Vecelli (Titian), Ebenezer Erskine, Bernard Gilpin, John Guyse, John Hooper, John Knox, Alexander Nowell, John Welch, and the Reverend Dr. William Selwyn.

Research on Galton's George Canning, William Lamb, Sir Robert Walpole, Armand-Jean du Plessis Richelieu, Charlemagne, John Churchill (Duke of Marlborough), Arthur Wellesley (Duke of Wellington), Washington Irving, Thomas Babington Macaulay, Lucius Annaeus Seneca, Alexander von Humboldt, John Keats, Mendelssohn, George Herbert, Oliver Cromwell, Sir Philip Sidney, Alexander Pope, Johann Wolfgang von Goethe, Martin Luther, and even on Francis Galton himself revealed much data showing immense influence deriving from the child-rearing practices of their dominant mothers.

If Sir Francis Galton had specifically searched for history's most dominant mothers, he would have found a treasure-trove among the mothers of his eminent men.

∿ ∿ ∿ ∿ ∿ ∿

Hereditary Genius, being the first work of its kind, has exerted a strong continuing influence on scholars and scientists. This scrutiny of Sir Francis Galton's work may help highlight errors that are still being perpetuated. There are hundreds of eminent people (as defined by Galton) living today with high dominance levels that were transmitted environmentally to them by their mothers' child-rearing practices. It seems evident that Galton's eminent individuals do not differ in this respect from the eminent people of the present.

Charles Darwin's theory of the evolution of species, including the human species, was the foundation for new knowledge to help reconstruct man's ancient past. Sir Francis Galton set in place another building block, as to achievement. He believed that the qualities making up ability were transferred through inheritance. Galton thought that to become eminent an individual must inherit capacity, zeal, and vigor. (These terms are very similar to intelligence, dominance, and energy.) Galton incorrectly interpreted his data, placing undue weight on the importance of heritability while neglecting environmental factors, primarily child-rearing practices. He thereby steered the search for understanding of the source of intelligence and achievement onto a tangential course.

More recently the psychologist Arthur R. Jensen, in the field of intelligence testing, seems to furnish support for the position that heritability rather than environment is the primary source of intelligence. His writings have contributed to the current belief of some psychologists and much of the public that intelligence is 80 percent inherited and 20 percent environmental. For reasons set forth throughout this book including the following information, I believe that Jensen's conclusion that intelligence is primarily genetically inherited is wrong.

In the 1960s Sir Cyril Burt, the then-eminent British psychologist, propounded the idea that intellectual heritability was 80 percent or more. In "How Much Can We Boost IQ and Scholastic Achievement?" (an article published in 1969), Jensen deduced that IQ heritability ranged from 70 to 90 percent and that in the groups studied it was around 80 percent. He based his conclusion on several studies, but weighted Burt's studies more heavily than the others.

Leon Kamin, an author and a psychologist at Princeton, became interested in the nature versus nurture debate. In 1972 Kamin began questioning and bringing to light discrepancies and flaws in many studies purporting to advance the heritability of intelligence concept. He concluded that Burt's studies were not only wrong but also fraudulent. Without Burt's studies, the evidence for high intellectual heritability seemed weak.

After being contacted by Kamin, Jensen reviewed Burt's studies and in the mid-1970s published a report on Burt's discrepancies. Burt's work was totally discredited by the late 1970s, and by the end of the decade the psychological community agreed that the studies had been deliberately fraudulent. By the early 1980s Jensen concluded that IQ heritability was probably 70 percent. He also cautioned that after reviewing more studies heritability might be found to be near 50 percent.

In *Bias in Mental Testing* (1980), "Validity and Correlates of Mental Tests, Occupational Level, Performance, and Income," Jensen writes of a study by Waller (1971) using the IQ scores of fathers and sons obtained from their high-school records. According to Jensen, in instances where the son has a higher IQ than the father, the son attains more occupational success. The reverse occurs when the son has the lower IQ; he falls below the father's occupational success.

Some psychologists question whether all the occupational levels used in Waller's study are truly different. However, where the occupational levels are not in question, I believe most of the variances can be traced to the dominance trait transmitted by mother to son. When a son's IQ is higher and he attains a higher occupational level than the father, I expect the mother to be more dominant than the father and to have transmitted that dominance to her son; he then becomes more successful than his father. When the son's IQ is lower and his attainments fall below the level of the father's, the mother is probably less dominant than the father. This pattern is evident today in many American families in the highest seven income categories. It could be true of high income groups worldwide.

In *Straight Talk About Mental Tests* (1981), "Social Class and Race Differences in Intelligence, IQ in White and Black Populations, Age of Subjects," Jensen notes, "The average black IQ deficit does not change beyond age 5 for the vast majority of the black population. . . . The fact that the 15-point black deficit remains stable after age 5 means that its causes, whatever they might be, must be sought in factors whose influences are already fully established before school age."

Jensen could be correct but for reasons unrelated to heredity. Hereditarians and environmentalists agree that by age six intelligence has become reasonably stable. Environmental influences, particularly the efficacy of the mother's encouragement and demands during the first five years (the time frame used by Jensen), have already shaped to a great extent a child's future interest in intellectual achievement. Therefore, future generations need not be affected by the mental differences of current generations.

If black leaders and others desire to increase the intelligence and achievement levels of future generations, that can be accomplished. It can be done for any country's inhabitants. The degree of commitment and will of the group or country would determine its success.

Many people who consider themselves strongly religious decry Darwin's theory of evolution, but find no conflict in subscribing to Galton's and Jensen's beliefs. Many of the same people feel no moral conflict in separating the human species into "races." Possibly they also accept the idea that personality traits affecting human behavior are genetically transmitted, so that the good and bad are unalterable. By accepting that this is the way things are, they may feel no need to concern themselves with attempts toward the betterment of mankind.

A bizarre modern offshoot of *The Descent of Man* and *Hereditary Genius* was the creation of the Repository for Germinal Choice, a sperm bank founded with apparently good intentions in 1980 by the eyeglass magnate Robert Graham. At least three Nobel Laureates donated sperm to the program; one was William Bradford Shockley, a 1956 co-winner in physics.

In 1980 Syl Jones interviewed Dr. Shockley for *Playboy*. According to Dr. Shockley: "The major cause for American Negroes' intellectual and social deficits is hereditary and racially genetic in origin and thus not remediable to a major degree by improvements in environment." When asked how his children turned out, Dr. Shockley responds:

In terms of my own capacities, my children represent a very significant regression. My first wife—their mother—had not as high an academic-achievement standing as I had. Two of my three children have graduated from college—my daughter from Radcliffe and my younger son from Stanford. He graduated not with the highest order of academic distinction but in the second order as a physics major, and has obtained a Ph.D. in physics. In some ways, I think the choice of physics may be unfortunate for him, because he has a name that he will probably be unlikely to live up to. The elder son is a college dropout.

When asked about his children's IQs, Dr. Shockley says he does not know. When asked about his parents' IQs, Dr. Shockley answers, "Terman measured my mother and, as I recall, it was above 150." One can conclude that Dr. Shockley was reared by a dominant mother, married a nondominant woman, and had nondominant children.

Oddly enough, the majority of the offspring of mothers participating in the Repository for Germinal Choice sperm-bank program will probably be high achievers and considerably above average in intelligence. Presumably, most women participating in the program are dominant, whether married or single, want great futures for their children and will take advantage of every avenue, real or imagined, to achieve that result. If dominant, a recipient of sperm from the bank could be expected to stimulate and demand intellectual achievement in her child, who then should become a high-achieving adult.

Leon Kamin states in *The Intelligence Controversy*, "The most influential and widely read reviews of the research literature on IQ have been written by ardent hereditarians." Consequently, many intelligent people still believe that intelligence is 80 percent inherited and 20 percent environmental. These numbers are often used to support the status quo. Perhaps the need some people have to feel superior makes them susceptible to theories indicating, as they see it, that they have inherited some exclusive property.

Kamin is an outspoken advocate of environmental factors as the primary source of IQ differences. In *The Intelligence Controversy*, Kamin stands almost alone in the academic field of intelligence with his statements, "In fact the possibility cannot be excluded that IQ heritability is actually zero." and "What counts is the mother, not the genes." I believe he is right.

Chapter X

Discrimination

Dominance levels, as previously outlined, regulate the achievements of individuals. Class structures increase opportunities for some people to capitalize on their intellectual capabilities and limit possibilities for others by confining them to a specific social class. The more rigid the class system, the less likely the lower classes are to breach the barriers and enter the upper class. Intellectual development becomes the prerogative of the upper class and is erroneously considered its birthright. An understanding of how dominance is related to intellectual achievement and to differences in cultural, ethnic, and social groups can explain how and why societies at different times discriminate for or against specific groups.

The most frequent definition of discrimination is, "treatment or consideration of, or making a distinction in favor of or against, a person or thing based on the group, class, or category to which that person or thing belongs rather than on individual merit." Discrimination is exercised more often *against* than *in favor of* something. More people are aware of discrimination that is *against* rather than *in favor of* them.

When discrimination is employed *in favor of* an individual, group, class, or category, the reasons are often identifiable since they appear logical and seem to be based on a quid pro quo. Something of value is gained by those who discriminate *in favor of* and by the beneficiaries.

Politics provides a public showcase for *in favor of* discrimination, as when one segment of commerce receives preference over another. Federal and state governments bestow special tax treatment *in favor of* specific commercial or income groups. The favor usually means offsetting costs to other commercial or income segments, yet legislative *in favor of* discrimination is presented in a positive manner, its beneficiaries identified while those harmed are ignored. Consequently, this discrimination is rarely viewed as overly negative or openly resented by the public.

Discrimination can occur *in favor of* individuals, for example, as in the passing out of well-paying jobs through nepotism or personal connections. Often, the person harmed by not being hired is unaware of the reasons someone else was hired; therefore, little negativism or resentment develops.

When discrimination is applied *against* a group, class, or category of people, the acts are usually conspicuous and resented by those discriminated against. The dominance trait is a factor in such discrimination; at different times throughout history both dominant and nondominant people have faced discrimination.

ෆ ෆ ෆ ෆ ෆ ෆ

The longest known cycle of *against* discrimination is against Jews. Religious differences are blamed, but religion is only something obvious at which people can point. Perhaps high dominance levels among Jews are the basic cause of *against* discrimination.

James Thomas Flexner in *The Young Hamilton: A Biography* mentions Alexander Hamilton's "great respect for the Jews," and in a footnote states:

Among his papers is a fugitive scrap, evidently once part of an essay, which reads, ". . . progress of the Jews and their [illegible] from the earliest history to the present time has been and is entirely out of the ordinary course of human affairs. Is it not then a fair conclusion that the cause also is an extraordinary one—in other words, that it is the effect of some great providential plan? The man who will draw this conclusion will look for the solution in the Bible. He who will not draw it ought to give in another fair solution."

Without drawing a conclusion as to a providential plan, may not one suggest that a solution lies in the dominance trait?

One facet of the Jewish faith that has been a primary contributor to high dominance levels among Jews could be said to have influenced the success along with the discrimination and persecution suffered by Jews. Halachah holds that children of a Jewish mother are Jewish regardless of the father's religious faith; lineage is traced through the mother. *The Jewish tradition of determining religious descent through the female line has maintained high dominance levels to an amazing degree among Jews.*

If the determination of Jewish descent had been patrilineal, Jews probably would not be recognized as a major, distinct cultural entity today. Their achievements would have faded over time as did those of the Greeks, Romans, Ottomans, Spaniards, British, and many others. They might have followed the path of such nomadic groups as the Scythians, Sarmatians, and Hsiung-nu, and disappeared as a separate culture. At best they would simply be members of a small religious group similar to numberless other small sects from earlier times like the Parsees.

On the whole, dominant Jewish men prefer to marry nondominant Jewish women and nondominant Jewish men prefer to marry dominant Jewish women. There is little difference in this respect than in gentile marriages. *Only the large beginning base of dominant Jewish women is dissimilar.* The higher ratios of dominant Jewish mothers produce more dominant than nondominant Jews. Consequently, nondominant Jewish daughters of successful dominant fathers and nondominant mothers are the most sought-after wedding prizes.

The preponderance of Jewish interfaith marriages are between Jewish men and gentile women. Dominant Jewish men in first-time marriages outside their faith, especially in affluent times, usually select nondominant wives. The children of these marriages will be nondominant like their mothers. Unless the mother converts to Judaism, the children are not Jewish according to Halachah. Although some nondominant offspring of these marriages convert to Judaism, many do not and are simply assimilated into society. If descent of these nondominant children of fathers born into Judaism were patrilineal, the Jewish people today would be little different from any other population segment of equal size.

According to Steven Bayme, 1988 director of communal affairs for the American Jewish Committee, "American Judaism is essentially pluralistic in nature. Jews here have a choice of Conservative, Reform, Reconstructionist and Orthodox."

Some Reform rabbis disregard Halachah pertaining to matrilineal descent and recognize the children of Jewish fathers as Jews. This occurs when Jewish men marry gentile women and the wife does not convert to Judaism; the children are considered Jewish.

Through this practice Reform synagogues may be bringing greater problems to the future of Judaism than those which surfaced in the proposed amendment of Israel's Law of Return, considered late in 1988. By increasing the number of nondominant Jews, the Reform will contribute to the diffusion of the trait of dominance in a portion of the American Jewish population to a range similar to that of Protestantism and other religious groups. Diffusing the dominance trait in this way will help to culturally assimilate Jews into American society by reducing their success rate. However, in times when national or international problems confront the Israelis or Jews elsewhere, this lessening of generational dominance levels could leave dominant Jews vulnerable. Their religion would still exist, but the support group of other dominant Jews would be smaller.

When a Jewish woman marries outside her faith, her children are still designated Jewish. If a dominant Jewish woman marries a nondominant Gentile, their children will probably be dominant like the mother. Then the dominance trait and Judaism are legacies to the next generation from the Jewish mother.

Being Jewish never protected its women from historical occurrences of rape and the plundering and sacking of cities. Although genetically different, children of these rapes were still Jewish and were reared by a Jewish mother. Whether the rapist was a Mongol tribesman, a Vandal invader during the sack of Rome in 455, or a Visigoth plundering Spain in 612 made no difference; the issue of these encounters were Jewish and most likely developed high dominance levels from their mothers.

Jews as a group have maintained their superiority of intellect and achievement for over four thousand years, even while other civilizations, one by one, lost both. This is primarily attributable to the dominance trait. Possibly for this simple reason, Jewish contributions to civilization for over 160 generations have continuously been greater than those of any other historical group.

The exile or dispersion known as the Diaspora refers to the Jewish communities existing outside Judah; the first significant Diaspora began with the Babylonian Exile in 586 B.C. and became a permanent state. It may have been the Jews' salvation. Religious exiles are likely to marry within their cultural group, since they naturally cling together and are commonly considered outsiders. The Diaspora and its effect on the dominance trait through endogamy preserved the dominant Jewish culture.

Archaeological findings indicate the past existence of dozens of civilizations. Civilizations and cultures are founded, attain a certain level of achievement, decline, and disappear or are absorbed by new civilizations. In the four thousand years since Abraham of the Old Testament, many great cultures have risen and fallen. Even within the relatively short New Testament period of two thousand years, accounts chronicle various cultural failures and assimilations. Had Jews remained a nation and the world's Jewish population been contained within a single limited region, it probably would have failed. The Diaspora prevented the Jewish culture's decay and helped create the single exception to history's long list of failed cultures.

The trait of high dominance and its resulting successes surely must have been a major cause of envy, resentment, and fear of Jews—especially in those competing for success or in the process of failure. Often Jews seem intimidating to those equally as dominant and successful; even successful dominant people are insecure and feel menaced by competition. Regardless of ethnic background, dominant groups everywhere evoke envy and fear. "Fear," writes Karl Menninger, "is often the only external manifestation of hate." And Cyril Connolly states, "There is no hate without fear. Hate is crystallized fear, . . . We hate what we fear and so where hate is, fear is lurking. . . . Hate is the consequence of fear; we fear something before we hate it . . ."

Robert Burns' quote, "Oh wad some power the giftie gie us to see oursels as others see us!" applies to Jews (and non-Jews) in historic and modern contexts. No one truly sees himself as others see him. It is doubtful that many dominant people (Jews or non-Jews) see themselves as aloof, overly proud, too aggressive, excessively demanding or, most importantly, threatening to others. Dominant Jews of both sexes probably see themselves as productive, hard-working, and achieving. Many correctly believe they are making contributions in their fields of endeavor, especially those who have greatly benefited society in areas such as medicine and the arts. At the same time, though they may be aware of envy, they may not understand its cause; they mistakenly believe that opportunity is the same for all, as they do not understand the differences in ambition in dominant and nondominant people.

Adolf Hitler could not rationally have believed that Jews were inferior. He, along with many Germans, saw the achievements and mental superiority of Jews as a group. Hitler first feared, then hated the Jews, even though they represented less than one percent of Germany's population. His hate was translated into an effort to eradicate an entire segment of society—genocide on a larger scale than ever attempted by modern man. Results of the Holocaust are well documented. The six million murdered Jews represented over one-third of the world's then-current Jewish population.

If fear and hatred of Jews had not filled Adolf Hitler's mind, the outcome of World War II might have been different. Before Hitler's rise to power, many German Jews espoused their country's nationalism. A sizable number considered themselves as much German as Jewish, an integral part of Germany and her fortunes. Jews from other European countries also lived in Germany and considered it home. It is doubtful that Hans Bethe, Max Born, Albert Einstein,

James Franck, Leo Szilard, and Edward Teller would all have fled Germany had Hitler welcomed and rewarded their participation in Germany's expansion. (According to Richard Rhodes, Bethe said: "I was not Jewish. My mother was Jewish, and until Hitler came that made no difference whatsoever.") These brilliant Jews made contributions, direct and indirect, to making the first atomic bomb. Many others of the six million Jews who wanted to stay in Germany and its conquered countries would have answered an appeal to duty and service; instead they were eventually murdered.

Modern European anti-Semitism did not originate with Hitler. In August 1888, near the time of Adolf's conception, four thousand gathered at the Western Railway terminal in Vienna, Austria, to cheer Georg von Schonerer. Schonerer led the pan-German Party, a small but zealous anti-Semitic group, and represented the parliamentary district that included Hitler's parents. Another demagogue and Jew-baiter, Dr. Karl Lueger, came to the political forefront in Austria in that same period of hard times when bankruptcies multiplied. Austrian anti-Semitism was well entrenched before Hitler's birth.

Envy, fear, and hatred have been directed against many dominant people through the ages. The magnitude of the problem usually surfaces when a dominant group is or becomes a distinct minority within an overwhelmingly large nondominant segment in a given country or geographic area. This appears to be the case with Israel, a country with many dominant citizens who are a minority among large numbers of Arabs in neighboring countries.

After World War II the United Nations General Assembly voted to partition British-ruled Palestine into an Arab state and a Jewish state. The modern state of Israel was founded on May 14, 1948, with 600 thousand citizens. Since then Israel has become enormously visible given its small size. The fear and resultant hatred of Israel by adjacent countries has grown tremendously. Neighboring populations appear primarily nondominant if one judges by their national achievements in modern times but, as with all nations, they are headed by dominant leaders.

No absolute historical pattern of Jewish persecution has been established. But persecutions of dominant individuals, including Jews, occur again and again during times of transition. During the decline and rebirth of an empire or great nation, the nondominant majority often persecutes the dominant minority because when the numbers of less prosperous citizens increase, they become envious of those who are more successful.

The Spanish Inquisition, aimed primarily at Jews and Muslims, began during a transitional period in Spain before it became a world power near the end of the fifteenth century. Non-Catholics were pressured to convert to Roman Catholicism. Jews who converted but still practiced Judaism were called Marranos (Pigs). After the marriage of Ferdinand and Isabella uniting Aragon and Castile in 1469, the government denounced the Marranos as a threat to Christianity.

A bull secured from Pope Sixtus IV in 1478 authorized Catholic kings to name inquisitors. The Pope later decided that the inquisitors were too harsh, and he attempted to limit the Inquisition's powers. Pope Sixtus IV failed; his authority was not as strong as that of the Spanish kings.

In the first year of Spain's reign as a world power, the edict of March 31, 1492, ordered Jews to convert to Roman Catholicism. Jews who refused to abandon their faith were forced to flee to more tolerant countries.

During the transition year of 1763 in the thirteen British colonies no Jewish persecutions occurred. Approximately 150 thousand unconverted Jews lived in Spain in 1492 (1 in 60), whereas in America in 1763 Jews numbered only about two thousand (1 in 800).

The Weimar Republic was established in 1919 shortly after World War I. The ravages of unprecedented inflation in the immediate postwar years set the stage for the Republic's demise and Adolf Hitler's ascent to power. Hitler was appointed Chancellor of Germany in 1933. That year he established an absolute dictatorship. Parallels exist between Spain in 1492 and Germany in 1933. Both periods were detrimental to Jews; both coincided with the fall of a prior regime.

During the Romanov reign in czarist Russia in 1881, pogroms spread through the country. Jews remember that year as "the year the pogroms began." They began in the Ukraine, spread to the Ukrainian cities of Kiev and Odessa, and then throughout Russia and

Poland, affecting hundreds of thousands of Jews. Those were troubled times, times of transition for Russia, well past the Romanovs' high noon of achievement. In only thirty-six years after the pogroms began, Romanov Russia expired and Bolshevik rule began.

Changing population percentages in the United States do not bode well for America's Jews. In 1940 the United States population numbered 132.1 million of which an estimated 4.9 million or 3.7 percent (1 in 27) were Jewish. The population in 1950 was 151.7 million with an estimated five million Jews or 3.3 percent (1 in 30). By 1960 the population increased to 179.3 million with 5.3 million or 2.9 percent (1 in 34) estimated to be Jewish. The 1984 population was calculated at 237.6 million with approximately 5.8 million Jews, 2.4 percent (1 in 41). The Jewish portion of the 1960-1984 population increase of fifty-eight million approximated five hundred thousand, less than 1 percent of the total (1 in 116).

If Jews wished to raise their proportions in society, they could take steps such as the following, but undoubtedly will not, as they are extreme measures: (1) immediately institute a campaign to raise the rate at which Jewish women give birth, thus keeping the percentages of dominance and nondominance at their current levels in the Jewish population; (2) embark on a worldwide adoption program whereby dominant Jewish women adopt and raise non-Jewish infants of whatever ethnic ancestry as Jews, but with a larger proportion of female than of male adoptees so as to increase the dominance trait over the generations; (3) vigorously proselytize.

In the second scenario, the ratio of male to female adoptions is preeminently important. Male infants reared by dominant Jewish mothers will affect the following generation only. A higher ratio of female adoptions, however, will greatly influence future generations. These female infants would become dominant Jewish mothers and by the sheer numbers of their future offspring would dramatically raise the dominant portion of the Jewish population.

Although evangelism would be new, Jewish acceptance of large numbers of converts is not. Before Christianity, thousands of pagans joined the Jewish community. An interesting historical sidelight involves the large-scale conversion of the Parthians. These aggressive fighters and horsemen of northern Persia conquered much of the old

Persian empire. Thousands became Jewish with both leaders and common people embracing the faith. Parthia was the only nation the Romans attacked but were unable to defeat; for three hundred years they overcame the Roman legions sent to conquer them.

As, however, it is highly unlikely that any of the above courses of action will be adopted, Jews may find themselves threatened in the near future as never before in this country. That a pogrom or other stringent persecution could occur in the United States may appear inconceivable. At present Jews and most other Americans no doubt would react to such a prospect with disbelief.

The potential for an increase of envy of Jewish citizens has been created by a lowering of our adult dominance levels since 1964, and a decrease in the proportion of Jews in the population along with an increase in their affluence. In 1969 Jewish family incomes were 72 percent greater than corresponding incomes in the remainder of the United States, the largest disparity in the country's history. (These changes are further discussed in Chapter XV, The Age of Affluence; Chapter XVI, The Age of Intellect; and Chapter XVII, The Age of Decadence.)

Though not overly influenced themselves by the country's dropping intellect since 1964, Jews stand to be inversely affected. Even if the intelligence level of American Jews stays in the same range, any percentage decline in the general population's level will become, in effect, a percentage increase in Jewish intelligence compared to the average. The same would be true with the dominance trait. If it remains static in Jews but diminishes in the general population, as is happening, then although they themselves are unchanged Jews will be considerably more dominant relative to the general population. Therefore, Jews may be destined shortly to become even more successful, as apparently they became during similar periods in other societies in the past and so subject to resentment.

If Jews can come to understand the role of dominance levels, they may better understand their past, and might avoid reliving portions of the past. If this could happen, mankind then can benefit even more in the future from Jewish contributions to civilization.

שׁ שׁ שׁ שׁ שׁ שׁ

In the United States, discrimination *against* white men as a group, whether dominant or nondominant, does not exist on any significant scale. There are two primary reasons: the country has a patriarchal society that generally sets a higher value on men than on women, and the majority of the population is white. Consequently, any *against* discrimination is directed against specific individuals rather than the group as a whole.

Nondominant white women experience some job discrimination in the United States. This discrimination lies primarily in the struggle for jobs held by nondominant white men, although in some jobs a nondominant white woman may be first choice over a nondominant white man. Such discrimination particularly affects single women and single mothers competing with men for lower-paying jobs.

Discrimination without apparent logic *against* a group plagues dominant white women. Sigmund Freud's quote, "Anatomy is destiny," continues to type all women as physiologically and psychologically the same. Freud's quote also types men, contributing to the perception that men and women are different. Physiologically this is true. Psychologically, however, it is generally false. According to numerous psychological personality surveys, highly dominant men and women, if their dominance levels are equal, have equivalent psychological needs to achieve.

Fairly representative of the confusion among various schools of thought on psychological differences between men and women are the statements by the editors of *The New Encyclopaedia Britannica, Volume 19* (1979) in the article "Status of Women, Theories and Beliefs Regarding Male-Female Differences:"

In conclusion, no statement can with any certainty be made about the origins of feminine or masculine personality traits beyond saying that psychosexual orientation appears to be the outcome of complex interactions among genetic, hormonal, and environmental factors whose relative importance in the whole process of character formation is impossible to ascertain. This view is now almost universally accepted, by biologically oriented scholars no less than by psychologists and sociologists.

This view demonstrates the willingness of many to accept an undefined unknown as the cause of differences. It avoids the necessity of focusing on the power of the prevailing culture, including child-rearing practices of mothers, to influence individual psychological traits. It allows the perpetuation of discrimination by implying that men and women are psychologically different instead of focusing on individual psychological differences.

The right to vote did not convey equal rights to women any more than did granting women citizenship in ancient Athens. The different outlooks and goals of women with high dominance and women with lower dominance successfully inhibit consensus in the political arena by which they could obtain rights truly equal with those of men. This lack of solidarity among women coupled with a greater amount of political agreement among men forestalls equal rights for women. Men continue to maintain social and political control.

At the inception of the United States, there were more dominant individuals of both sexes than perceived opportunities. Men grasped the opportunities. Women were relegated to what society considered the lesser although important task of child rearing or to socially acceptable occupations such as nursing or teaching. Dominant women provided the country with dominant children; dominant men continued to take advantage of new opportunities as they became available. This discriminatory cycle continued for generations until the nation became affluent.

When sufficient affluence is attained in a country, circumstances occur that point up the unfairness of discrimination against dominant women. They now become a contending force in two areas. First, and with the greatest portent for the future of any free society, is their withholding or limiting of children. Perhaps this is the dominant woman's way of sharing in society's affluence without child-rearing responsibilities. Whatever the specific reason, as affluence increases, dominant women deliver fewer or (in many instances) no children. At a time of national affluence, a high percentage of this group of their own volition practice birth control in various ways including abortion.

Affluent women are probably among the first and most likely to be informed about and to use artificial birth-control methods regularly. They are more able than the poor to afford contraceptives and to obtain abortions. Working, affluent couples clearly recognize that these practices increase their joint income and improve their standard of living. Dominant women are less likely to be affected by religious mandates concerning birth control than their less dominant counterparts. Consequently, in affluent countries, the first to have fewer or no children are likely to be the most dominant, affluent, and intelligent women. The less affluent and less educated are most apt to continue their standard childbearing practices or to be denied the full opportunity to use artificial birth control should they desire it.

Contrary to common belief, artificial birth control and abortion did not originate in the last few generations. They were prevalent in ancient times and probably reached a zenith in every great civilization when affluence was realized. It is possible that once a country attained affluence, its dominant women always had fewer children than their nondominant counterparts. Although there are no statistics that refer to the childbearing practices of dominant women in other eras, declining birth rates occurred time and again throughout history.

The culturally caused withholding of children was recognized as a factor contributing to the decline of ancient Greece. The Greek historian and politician Polybius, ca. 200 B.C.-ca. 118 B.C., publicly denounced Greece's declining birth rate, equating its drop to suicide for the country.

The introduction of chemical means of birth control in the early 1960s and the growing affluence of the United States accelerated the decline in the birth rate particularly among dominant women. The advent of legalized abortion in 1973 hastened the decrease even more. Abortion alone accounts for 1.5 to 1.7 million fewer births annually, approximately 25 percent of all pregnancies. The ratio of abortions between dominant and nondominant women is unknown.

A second force exerted by dominant women in the United States involves their recent penetration of the work force at executive levels. After several years of affluence in a large society, opportunities to gain power, fame, and wealth become greater than the number of dominant men available to grasp them. Vacancies in leadership positions because of a lack of dominant men allow dominant women to fill the void. "Nature," according to Spinoza, "abhors a vacuum."

Discrimination *against* dominant women has ameliorated but only from blatant to subtle. Dominant women threaten men, dominant and nondominant, since many compete for the same jobs. Generally speaking, however, dominant men feel most threatened by dominant women. Dominant men's phobias of domination (brought about by dominant mothers) affect their attitudes toward dominant women. Except for some Jewish men and those few men who are willing to recognize merit (coupled with the wish to serve their personal ambitions by utilizing such talents, which denies them the luxury of discrimination), the dominant woman can expect to face an uphill battle to reap rewards commensurate with her achievements.

The numbers of dominant men and women are approximately equal during their most productive years (ages thirty-six through sixty). Since the birth rate approaches an equal distribution of boy and girl babies, the same across-the-board estimate can be made for dominant men and women reared by dominant mothers. Consequently there should be equal numbers of white men and white women in the highest-paying positions in all fields, for example, in the medical and dental professions. The same equal success ratios should hold true for black men and black women, and so on for other ethnic groups. Count how many men and women from any ethnic group attain high-achieving positions. Although the disproportionate numbers of men over women in such positions may be attributed to a disinclination and lack of desire by specific dominant women for high position, generally they reflect the operative degree of discrimination by gender in the business and professional world.

Until recently the medical and dental professions presented a glaring example of discrimination *against* dominant women in the United States. In 1970 the percentage of women physicians and dentists was 8.1 percent versus 91.9 percent for men. In 1980 the percentages rose to 11.8 percent for women versus 88.2 percent for men. The trend continues upward as dominant women fill the void created by the decrease of dominant men choosing these fields. By 1982, 31 percent of first-year medical students were women. Although a small surplus of physicians and dentists exists, these professions remain extremely profitable and continue to attract dominant individuals. (The percentage of women lawyers quadrupled from 2 percent in 1954 to 8 percent in 1980 and, in 1984, 39.3 percent of all law students were women.)

In the Soviet Union, the ratio for physicians and dentists in 1970 was 74 percent women versus 26 percent men. In 1979 the percentages were 70 percent women and 30 percent men. Although the prestige and pay in medicine is small compared to the United States, a physician or dentist in the U.S.S.R. is well regarded. In addition, the losses of men during World War II and the purges of Joseph Stalin created a huge vacuum in that country. Women took advantage of these circumstances in far greater proportion than their percentage in the population. If no drastic changes occur in Soviet politics, the ratio of women physicians will trend down until it duplicates the existing male/female population percentages.

One cannot make direct comparisons between communist and capitalistic societies as to discrimination *against* dominant women. However, let us try a hypothetical example. In the United States in 1983, an estimated one out of each 364 persons was a physician or dentist. Of these 645 thousand physicians and dentists, 86 percent were men and 14 percent were women. If all these physicians and dentists were gathered simultaneously in one location, and a catastrophe such as an earthquake destroyed them, at the end of the next twenty-five years (one generation), what percentage of the American-born physicians and dentists would be male and what percentage female?

Naturally, in the immediate aftermath, physicians of all nationalities would gravitate to the United States to fill the vacuum. Then medical schools would restaff and expand, and new American-born medical and dental students would reflect male/female proportions equal to those of the country's general population. With such a catastrophe, the male-controlled society could not afford the luxury of discriminating against dominant women in medicine.

Over time discrimination *against* dominant, achieving women may weaken even more as the percentages of dominant people of both sexes drop. Job successes lessen dominant women's desire for or time to give to children, further diminishing the number of children born to dominant women. The withholding of children by dominant women will cause a continuing change in future dominance ratios in the general population. This is borne out somewhat by "The Corporate Woman Officer," a 1986 Heidrick and Struggles study of women corporate officers in America's largest industrial and service companies. Their average annual cash compensation (base and bonus) was $116,810.00, and 53.7 percent had no children.

Dominant women also encounter discrimination in their search for religious leadership. Women in Protestant denominations have been more successful than Roman Catholic women in achieving leadership positions. Dominant, religious, Roman Catholic women with strong needs to achieve are presumed to be among those agitating for greater participation in the Church's hierarchy, including the priesthood. With opportunities to move up the organizational ladder, women may be in a position to more effectively promote Church reforms favoring women's needs, reforms that would affect dominant women, the leaders, to a greater degree than nondominant women.

Perhaps the most subtle *against* discrimination shows up in some state divorce laws in the United States. Although affecting few as a percentage of overall divorces, these laws are ironically significant because they are created primarily by dominant men. *Against* discrimination involves divorces between dominant husbands and nondominant wives, particularly in the top six income categories.

In this configuration, the husband achieves financial success. The wife, by her choice and with her husband's concurrence, chooses not to work outside the home. She is the respected homemaker, rearing the children and maintaining the home. This union exemplifies the perfect marriage; it represents America's ideal family. However, the truth may be otherwise.

It may be that the greater the husband's success, the greater the pressure exerted against him by his wife. She may want him to conform to her expectations of what a marriage should be, for example, in the amount of time she believes he should spend at home. The more the husband achieves, the more insecure the marriage becomes. The wife may grow resentful and envious of the husband's success.

The husband then has at least two problems: his work, necessary to fulfill his psychological need to achieve, and his wife's unhappiness. She seems to have few achievement needs outside the home and is unable to obtain satisfaction, either in her life or through his success.

After many years of marriage, they may divorce. In many instances they reach an amicable settlement with the wife being well provided for financially. However, in some cases the wife becomes vindictive and uses the services of a divorce lawyer trained to capitalize on such resentments. In the August 28, 1985, issue of *The Wall Street Journal*, "Divorce Becomes a Big Business As Cases Grow in Size, Complexity," Nilda R. Weglarz notes, "At least 11,000 attorneys across the country now concentrate on divorce proceedings, according to the American Bar Association. In 1980, there were only 700."

Divorce laws designed to protect women and children sometimes provide this nondominant wife with windfall profits. Double irony surfaces in the statements, "She has devoted her whole life to her family. She has developed no marketable skills and her age drastically impairs her future earnings potential." This wife had little outside work experience because she chose not to work. Had she been a male she would have been expected to work, and had she been a male her lower dominance level would have resulted in less pay than that of her more dominant husband. Divorce costs come from the earnings of her husband. Many state laws bring discrimination to bear here *against* the successful dominant husband in the upper six income categories.

Few dominant wives in first-time marriages ever garner wealth in this fashion, other than those who marry nondominant sons with inheritances from wealthy families. After a divorce, they must continue working or secure jobs to support themselves.

The dominant wife of a successful dominant husband is often the second wife and usually much younger than the husband. She may capitalize on the divorce laws, although this happens infrequently, since the successful husband usually protects himself by a prenuptial agreement after the experiences of the first marriage and divorce.

Divorce laws were originally enacted to protect dependent wives and children in all income categories with no consideration of dominance traits. Wives were female and were categorized as all alike. Most state laws on alimony and community property treat all husbands and all wives the same.

Divorce between a dominant wife and nondominant husband after many years of marriage usually entails a much smaller settlement because the husband's income and net worth probably are less than more successful dominant men. Even when the dominant wife achieves success, the nondominant husband is likely to make considerably smaller demands than a nondominant wife. Settlements involving community property are sometimes a different matter. Divorce laws then work *against* the dominant wife, many times placing assets she accumulated over a lifetime in jeopardy.

There are many marriages between dominant women and nondominant men. The wife usually works and sometimes the husband remains at home. Although the dominant wife rarely earns an income equal to that of a dominant husband, she faces similar problems. As stated above, if the marriage ends in divorce, discrimination is *against* the dominant wife. The wife's net worth is treated like that of a successful dominant husband. Although the net worth involved is probably less, the nondominant husband may take advantage of and be rewarded by divorce laws originally designed to protect wives and children. As time passes and more dominant women obtain financially rewarding careers, successful dominant wives with nondominant husbands will increasingly face demands from their spouses very similar to those sometimes made by nondominant wives on successful dominant husbands.

In the lowest two income categories, most divorces occur between nondominant couples. Protection for the wife through alimony and property settlement is ineffective, since there is little money or debt-free property. If there are children, the mother and children face financial hardship. Nondominant wives in these income categories must, if not working, obtain employment to provide food and shelter, notwithstanding age or lack of experience.

◅ ◅ ◅ ▻ ▻ ▻

Broad-scale discrimination exists *against* several large population segments in the United States—blacks and Hispanics to mention two. They face discrimination whether dominant or nondominant, male or female. Discrimination against blacks is based primarily on color, against Hispanics on color and language.

The black population of the United States in 1983 approximated twenty-eight million. In 1980 the census recorded 26.68 million black citizens. In 1970 the figure was 22.58 million. In 1960, 1950, 1940, and 1930 the figures were 18.87, 15.0, 12.86, and 11.89 million, respectively. Since 1930 the country's black population has grown considerably faster than the white population.

Blacks are the only ethnic group that did not immigrate to the New World voluntarily. (A relatively small number of freedmen immigrated from the Caribbean islands.) They were brought here against their will and sold as slaves. Judging by achievement levels, most of the black population in the United States as well as in Africa, today as in the past, is believed to be nondominant.

A black child's upbringing as concerns the dominance trait is the same as that of any child of any color: if the mother is dominant (and a large number of black mothers are dominant), the expectation is that her children, especially the first born, will be dominant; if the mother is nondominant, her children will be nondominant. The color of the mother or child has no relevance to the dominance trait; the factor that is germane is the dominance level of the person rearing the child.

Often black mothers are heads of families and raise their children alone. Many of these women were abandoned by their husbands. Because they love their children they assume the responsibility for them which their husbands relinquished, committing themselves to doing the best they can for them. The usual conclusion by onlookers is that these mothers are matriarchal and dominant, and that the black community as a whole is matriarchal. It may or may not be the case that such mothers are dominant. The confusion arises because many personality traits simulate dominance in both men and women, for example, the traits of criticalness and unfriendliness, as described in Chapter I, Dominance and Nondominance. A beset mother fighting alone for her children may exhibit such traits out of desperation rather than dominance. Black mothers, in common with all mothers, are either dominant or nondominant, and they live in a patriarchal society despite the family responsibilities they shoulder.

The mistaken belief in genetic inheritance as the major source of intelligence and achievement is pervasive. Many Americans who have embraced this belief condemn blacks to a future no brighter than their present. In effect, blacks as a group are expected to maintain exactly the same levels of intelligence as are present in the black population today; few possibilities for change are envisioned. Consequently many misguided or prejudiced individuals see little reason to try to alter the odds.

Discrimination *against* blacks as a group can be described using the same subgroups as for whites: dominant male, dominant female, nondominant male, nondominant female.

Affirmative action has not produced the intended results. True, it has assisted many nondominant black men and women. Yet the program has failed to elevate dominant black women to equal status with dominant black men. Dominant, energetic, intelligent black men have achieved outstanding success without the aid of affirmative action.

The dominant black man has needs to excel, to achieve, and to lead to the same degree as any other dominant man. Every description of dominant men of any group fits dominant black men equally well. Since the United States population is predominantly white, to achieve success a dominant black man must operate within the white majority. In the competition for executive promotions, it is presumed that dominant white men do not view a dominant black man as any more of a threat than a dominant white man; possibly the black man is viewed as a lesser threat, since he must overcome the extra factors of color and minority status. The dominant black man may face less discrimination than the dominant white woman but only because his group is smaller.

The strongest discrimination *against* dominant black men usually comes from nondominant white men. This group is believed to constitute considerably more than a mere majority of white men. Thus, dominant black men regularly contend with discrimination. The dominant black man's success becomes a "put-down" to the unsuccessful white man. The dominant black man faces blatant discrimination from many white men in the lowest three income categories and subtle discrimination from some in the upper seven categories. Ironically, nondominant black men also frequently resent the early successes of dominant black men and, like unsuccessful white men, perceive those successes as "put-downs."

Dominant black women, existing in the same ratios as dominant black men, face the same sort of discrimination *against* their group as do dominant white women. Added to the stigma of being female is that of color. They stand almost alone in any fight to achieve, to lead, to accomplish, or to reap the rewards society gives to dominant white men, dominant black men, or dominant white women in that order. As described earlier, if discrimination did not exist, dominant black women would have success ratios similar to those of dominant black men.

Perhaps the greatest discrimination *against* any group in the United States today is toward dominant black women. For insight into the double handicap of color and sex, consider the following hypothetical occurrence.

A white man's employment is terminated. Whatever his dominance level, what would be the most traumatic blow possible to his ego with the resultant anger and resentment? Being unemployed is bad enough, but having to tell his wife that he was fired by a black woman would probably be the most wounding to his ego. The blow would be slightly less harsh if he were fired by a white woman, less still if by a black man, the most bearable if by a white man.

Discrimination *against* nondominant black men and women as a group (attributable to color and minority status) is particularly noticeable in entry level employment. There are no differences in merit between hardworking nondominant blacks or whites of either sex in the lowest two income categories. Near the bottom of the economic ladder, it is hard for nondominant blacks to secure first-time jobs with set entry level pay scales when there is no government intervention and the applicant majority is white. Usually blacks only obtain these jobs if whites do not want them. The next higher pay levels for first-time employment become increasingly harder for black men and women to attain unless the country's economy is expanding.

In time poor black (and poor white) men and women may realize that minimum wage laws are often detrimental to them. According to a labor market specialist at the Brookings Institution, raising the minimum wage increases the employment difficulties of unskilled workers. Union members probably benefit most from the minimum wage laws; as the rates increase, unions usually raise their wages proportionately. Although many of the concept's proponents believe they are helping to increase the incomes of the poor, others know that is not the case.

Eliminating minimum wage laws should benefit hardworking, poor, nondominant blacks. They could compete directly in the job market. Even though they might receive less beginning pay, getting the job would be easier. If they cannot get the job they have no potential for future advancement. Once on a job where work quality can be measured, they are apt to be rewarded for good performance. This thought must be tempered by consideration of the eroding work ethic brought about by national affluence. The clear change in national attitude away from "a day's work for a day's pay" is borne out somewhat by a massive crackdown on illegal immigrants during 1987. Many hardworking Mexican illegals were doing the jobs Americans simply would no longer do. Even though they began work at or below minimum wages, they were earning one and a half to two times the minimum wage at the time they were arrested and deported.

Eliminating minimum wage laws is unlikely given the temper of the times. A good argument exists for raising the minimum wage. *The Wall Street Journal* tallied compensation for the nation's top executives over the ten years ending in 1987. The *Journal* found that salaries and bonuses for chief executives alone grew by 12.2 percent annually to an average of $595 thousand. Hourly wages increased by only 6.1 percent annually, inflation rose by 6.5 percent, and profits improved by a tiny 0.75 percent. Stockholders raised no hue and cry for rollbacks of chief executives' salaries. Therefore stockholders, realistically, have no grounds to begrudge sharing such largess with hourly wage earners at the bottom level.

Minimum wage laws would become fair if full employment were guaranteed at that rate. If city, state, or federal jobs were the only minimum wage jobs and if full employment were guaranteed, then unemployment and unemployment compensation could be eliminated. However, corporations would probably oppose this, even though they bear the bulk of unemployment compensation costs; they would probably consider such a policy socialistic or worse.

Discrimination that benefits the nondominant white majority is more often meant to be *in favor of* the whites than *against* nondominant blacks. Nevertheless, blacks of both sexes bear the brunt of this discrimination. Even though they are not being directly discriminated *against*, the results are the same.

During an expanding economy, nondominant black men and women are pulled up because they take the lower-paying jobs that nondominant whites of both sexes abandon for higher-paying jobs. When the economy turns down, unless there is government intervention, *in favor of* discrimination ensures the nondominant white majority first choice of available jobs.

Hispanic is not a satisfactory word by which to describe the combination of immigrants from Central America, Cuba, Mexico, Puerto Rico, and South America, but no other word presents itself, Latin or Latino being at least equally poor. Discrimination *against* individuals of these ethnic groups varies greatly in different geographic areas of the United States. For example, in 1989 one would see little discrimination *against* former Cubans and their descendants living in Miami, Florida.

In the Hispanic population of the United States, discrimination in most places is similar to that faced by blacks. When subgrouping Hispanics in the same way as blacks and whites (that is, dominant male, dominant female, nondominant male, nondominant female), virtually no differences exist in the last three groups of Hispanics as compared to blacks. The dominant Hispanic woman encounters job discrimination almost to the same degree as the dominant black woman. *In favor of* and *against* discrimination is approximately the same for nondominant Hispanic men and women as for nondominant black men and women.

The dominant Hispanic man faces less *against* discrimination than his black counterpart. The advantage accrues from several factors. Many Hispanic cultures accept and reward dominant men, and successes of dominant Hispanic men in nearby countries are known to their white counterparts in the United States. There are also financial, political, and economic ties among dominant men from these countries and their counterparts in the United States. These associations and familiarities temper discrimination *against* dominant Hispanic men.

⚜ ⚜ ⚜ ♫ ♫ ♫

Discrimination has always existed and can be expected to continue. Although most think in terms of eliminating it, it is more realistic to work to counter it. An important step involves designing jobs to satisfy the needs of people with different dominance levels. Gainful employment with dignity for those with lesser degrees of dominance just may be an obtainable goal.

Chapter XI

Migrations and Immigrations

Long before recorded history, migrations and immigrations took place among hominid populations. Archaeological evidence indicates that within concurrent time periods ancient humans lived at different sites separated by great distances. The scant knowledge available about them comes primarily from prehistoric remains of bone fragments and flint tools. These provide little insight into their daily routines or their reasons for living in particular areas. Current ideas are reconstructions based on minimal amounts of information.

The lack of solid data on the motives of ancient man's migratory patterns creates a great deal of speculation. One theory presumes that man has a single source, that Africa is the cradle of the human species, and that from there migrations populated the world. It is supposed that ancient migrations were little different from those of recent times, only vastly slower. Although having little archaeological support, another supposition favors the idea that man developed from various sources, springing forth almost simultaneously in several diverse areas.

The first theory, with a great amount of archaeological support, is the leading belief today—that the human species originated in East Africa. Scientists theorize that migrations from Africa began in the vicinity of one million years ago and that hominids first settled throughout Africa and Asia.

Ancient humans were nomadic, drifting from one location to another. The journey from the Olduvai Gorge in Tanzania to Egypt's Nile Valley represents only a small segment of archaeological time whether the journey involved one thousand or ten thousand generations. The move from the Nile Valley to the Tigris and Euphrates rivers in present day Iraq entailed an even shorter period of archaeological time.

The migrations probably proceeded from East Africa along generally northward routes. The earliest migrations took thousands of generations to gain momentum. Food shortages or overcrowding are unlikely to have been solely responsible for migratory movements. One million years ago, Africa's food supply apparently was large compared to the small number of hominid inhabitants.

The evolutionary process of natural selection would have caused physiological adaptations during the movement north. Psychologically the dominance trait in ancient humans may have been one factor stimulating the northward movement. Thus dominance levels could have been a psychological force behind the continual migrations, with evolution a modifier adapting humans to cope with their new environments. Over hundreds of thousands of years, ancient man developed the physical characteristics necessary to live in varied climates.

Not everyone participated in the migrations. Many remained in the vicinity of their ancestral home. During each migratory phase, some stayed or settled along the way while others continued onward. The process by which some set forth to new places while others stay behind and preserve the status quo continues to this day.

By allying dominance and achievement, one can recognize dominance in the later patterns of migration. Many ancient humans who remained in the tropical areas of Africa probably had lower dominance levels than those who moved on, preferred maintaining the status quo, and left few artifacts reflecting achievement. The more dominant individuals were among the migrants who moved on to other areas. Millennia later the greater accomplishments by descendants of the more dominant were recorded for history, as in ancient Egypt and later in other geographic locations northward.

The migratory movement and the evolutionary process were inordinately slow. The gene pool was small because of the few hominids, the number of young produced by each generation, and the many generations involved. Since the groups were small so that inbreeding and close interbreeding would have occurred, the evolutionary process probably proceeded at an approximately equal pace in each band regardless of its geographic location.

The physiological trait of color is easily traced. Ancient humans and their descendants who remained in the direct sunlight of equatorial Africa retained their dark skin. The descendants of those who moved further north adapted to the lesser amounts of sunlight by gradually lightened skin color, which corresponded in degree according to the distance moved from the tropics. Latitude determined skin color. Other recognizable evolutionary changes include exterior facial features and hair.

We readily accept that nature adjusts animal color in accordance with environmental need. For example, the arctic rabbit is white in winter and brown in summer; this is a proven annual occurrence that people willingly acknowledge. Yet many find it strange to think that ancient black men became brown, then tan, then white after they settled in different latitudes. To some it is simply unbelievable; to many it is emotionally unacceptable. As Arthur Schopenhauer states in *Supplements to the World as Will and Idea*, "the white color of the skin is not natural to man, . . . by nature he has a black or brown skin, . . . consequently a white man has never originally sprung from the womb of nature, . . . there is no such thing as a white race, . . . every white man is a faded or bleached one."

Skeletal construction has been the same in all humans for at least thirty thousand years. Today human bone configurations, including the skull, reflect little or no changes among populations. They are the same for Africans and for those living in northern areas such as Sweden.

Toynbee notes the "challenge of the environment" as the genesis of civilization. The prehistoric migrations of early hominids encompassed hundreds of thousands of years. Well before the first agricultural settlements around ten thousand years ago, humans had adapted superbly to cope with the widely varying environments in populations scattered around the world. With agriculture's development, a new way of life began; humans increasingly abandoned their nomadic ways to live in permanent settlements. After settlements were successfully established, the more dominant inhabitants were probably among those who conquered other communities or established new ones. Many of the less dominant inhabitants remained near their birthplace. However, from time to time, some must have moved simply out of necessity, to survive.

The dominance trait influenced mankind's conquest of the physical world. Presumably later groups who chose to continue the nomadic life contained mainly dominant individuals, those wanting freedom from the constraints imposed by permanent settlements. In still later periods, dominance is evident in the nomads of the sea, whether traders or plunderers.

Archaeologists surmise that the first immigrants to the North American continent were Asian. At different periods from ten to possibly thirty thousand years ago, several groups crossed the Bering Strait from what is now the Soviet Union into what is presently Alaska. The strait was then exposed land and passable because of receding seas.

Scientists consider it unlikely that today's Alaskan Eskimos are direct descendants of the first immigrants. Most likely the Eskimos descended from more recent settlers, a theory substantiated by the blood type B prevalent in Eskimos and almost nonexistent in American Indians, descendants of the original Asian incomers.

Before these migrations, the entire North and South American continents contained no humans. The trail of immigration tracked from what is now Alaska into Canada and throughout the contiguous forty-eight states of the United States. Later generations continued the migration into Mexico, the southernmost portion of North America. Continuing south, migrants settled Central and South America.

At each stage of immigration, the most dominant people established and controlled territories. The most dominant individuals also established rules and rituals for the group. Later, each tribe's more dominant segments, which may have comprised whole families and entire social groups, were among those most likely to continue migrating southward because of being the most adventuresome.

Doubtless it was the more contented individuals, avoiding risks, who stayed behind and maintained established conditions. The percentages of dominant people remaining in the established territories were probably relatively static; if only a small base of dominant mothers stayed, dominance would then be transmitted to fewer children.

We can deduce dominance levels from archaeological findings that indicate what a group achieved. Great civilizations succeed in large part because of high dominance levels in their populations, since dominant individuals are most involved in the development and growth of their cultures. Accomplishment or lack of accomplishment closely corresponds to the percentage of higher or lower dominance in a population.

The original Asian immigrants undoubtedly included dominant and nondominant individuals. By 1521 when Hernando Cortez conquered Mexico, most of the Asian descendants, based on what they had achieved in the New World by then, appear to have been nondominant. Outstanding achievement, a hallmark of high dominance, is recognizable in specific cultures but not in the overall native population.

The southern movement by descendants of the more dominant tribes culminated in three major cultural areas in North, Central, and South America. High dominance levels appear evident when their achievements are compared to the lesser accomplishments of other descendants of the original immigrants. These dominant cultures, at their zeniths, included the Aztecs in what is now Mexico City and central and southern Mexico; the Mayas in what are now the Mexican states of Campeche, Yucatan, and Quintana Roo and the countries of Belize, Honduras, El Salvador, and Guatemala; and the Incas from the northern border of what is now Ecuador through Peru to the Rio Maule in central Chile.

Based on their cultural accomplishments at the time of Cortez, the Aztecs, concentrated in the Valley of Mexico, had the largest number of dominant individuals of any society in North America. In the past hundred years, individuals with high dominance (one spur initiating migration) appear to have consistently moved from south to north in Mexico. This geographic shift became noticeable during the Mexican Revolution of 1910-1920 as demonstrated by the strong participation of northern Mexican revolutionaries.

Today, a high proportion of dominant Mexicans still seems to be found in the northern states as evidenced by their successful food production in the state of Sinaloa and industrial production in the state of Nuevo Leon, particularly in Monterrey. Indications of high dominance also appear in the growing participation of the northern states in the conservative opposition political party. Apparently the opposite is occurring in Mexico City where one out of four of the country's citizens lives. That area's overall population percentages now seem increasingly skewed toward nondominance, a significant change from the dominance levels existing at the time of Hernando Cortez.

The disparity in cultural achievements between the descendants of the original Asian immigrants who stayed in Canada, the United States, and northern Mexico and those who continued the move south (eventually becoming the Aztecs, Mayas, and Incas) is too great to attribute to climate. Canada and the northern portions of the United States have cold and temperate climates, similar to Europe; the southern states are warm; northern Mexico is hot; the Valley of Mexico, Mexico City, is cool; and there are climatic differences throughout South America. It seems likely that the differences in cultural achievements relate more to dominance levels in the populations than to the climate in which the cultures were located.

Had Europeans not intervened, groups of dominant natives might have continued to splinter, migrate, and consolidate. In time elaborate social systems surpassing those of the Aztecs, Mayas, and Incas probably would have developed.

rle rle rle sh sh sh

Immigrations to the present United States (excluding the small number of earlier European settlements on the lower east coast) began on the upper east coast and were primarily British. Judging by their achievements, many of the immigrants were dominant. They brought their families, including some dominant wives and hence dominant children. In many instances, the extended families of dominant men also migrated, and included dominant sisters whose children usually were dominant. Dominant mothers ensured a continuation of high dominance levels for generations.

Early immigrants had many reasons for coming to the New World: freedom from religious persecution, increased economic opportunity, free or inexpensive land, and the desire for personal freedom. Will and Ariel Durant in *The Lessons of History* succinctly make the point that, "only the man who is below the average in economic ability desires equality; those who are conscious of superior ability desire freedom . . ."

The movement of entire families was one key to the future successes of the New World immigrants. If the men had come alone, as originally occurred in much of Latin America, the results of the first British immigration might have been dramatically different. Families were instrumental in making colonization of the United States a phenomenal success. Later, indentured servants came, of whom some of both sexes had high dominance levels. Others who came from English prisons were not convicts as we know them; often, their crime was being born poor.

The differences—and today's end results—between the settling of the United States and the conquering of Mexico and Peru are tremendous. The Conquistadors conquered and plundered. Men came alone. Years passed before European families arrived to settle and subsequently migrate throughout Mexico and Central and South America.

Although the conquests of Mexico and Central and South America were brutal, perhaps today's descendants of the original inhabitants fared better than those in the United States and Canada. It is of small consequence if vast numbers of the current inhabitants of Mexico and Central and South America are nondominant. Their populations increased. The same is not true of the Indians of Canada and the United States.

Diseases brought by the European invaders decimated the populations of Mexico and Central and South America since they lacked immunity to European viruses, and the Conquistadors plundered, pillaged, and killed large numbers of the inhabitants. Still, the Europeans interbred with and often married the natives. The resulting offspring, with immunity from many death-dealing European viruses, were allowed to prosper within the boundaries set by their conquerors.

Populations survived and increased from the time of Cortez and Pizarro to the present. Their descendants threw off the European yoke and gained their freedom. In Mexico, although there are between eight and ten million Indians, 90 percent of the population is *mestizo*, having both Spanish and Amerindian blood.

In the United States the original inhabitants and their descendants fared poorly. Since most of the English settlers and later immigrants brought their families or soon sent for them, there was little interbreeding or intermarriage with the natives. Few social ties developed. The immigrant families competed with the Indians for territory.

The northernmost inhabitants of the New World offer little evidence of high dominance if one judges by the achievement levels of their particular cultural groups at the times of conquest and colonization, and compares them to the accomplishments of the Mayan, Aztec, and Incan civilizations. This was true for the Canadian Indians and southward in lesser degrees throughout the United States.

During the struggles with the European settlers, the Indians were nearly eradicated from the face of the earth and lost virtually all their land. In 1890 about twenty million Indians lived in the United States. The 1980 census recorded 1.37 million Indians. Of those, 332 thousand lived on 260 reservations, isolated from the mainstream of the country's culture, growth, and prosperity.

The United States has had more immigrants than any country. Principally Anglo-Saxons settled the original thirteen colonies, mainly from the British Isles. Additionally, nine out of ten of the five million European immigrants from 1820 through 1860 came from Great Britain, France, Ireland, and Germany. Until about 1850, the population (excluding slaves) remained relatively homogeneous: white, Anglo-Saxon, and Protestant.

The population increases during the 1830s and 1840s were particularly significant, since they consisted largely of immigrants. About 250 thousand Europeans came to the United States in the first three decades of the nineteenth century, but ten times that number arrived from 1830 through 1850. From 1851 through 1920, a flood of thirty-one million newcomers arrived. By the late 1880s most immigrants came from central and southeastern Europe: Italy, the Balkans, Poland, and Russia.

Large waves of immigrants began arriving in 1851, well before the Statue of Liberty's placement in 1886. "The New Colossus" written by Emma Lazarus in 1883 and affixed to the statue in 1903 ends with the invitation:

> Give me your tired, your poor,
> Your huddled masses yearning to breathe free,
> The wretched refuse of your teeming shore,
> Send these, the homeless, tempest-tossed, to me:
> I lift my lamp beside the golden door.

Many immigrants pouring into the country before 1886 and for several subsequent years fulfilled the terms of Lazarus' invitation and brought something more, much more. A large percentage of the immigrant families brought high dominance levels with them. In addition, dominant relatives often followed. For the United States, this transfusion of dominant individuals resulted in phenomenal growth and success never before experienced by any country in modern history.

An internal migration also occurred. By 1763, after much of the Atlantic Coast had been settled, the first of several stages in the movement from the East Coast westward began.

Pioneers moved across the Appalachian Mountains until about 1815. After the War of 1812, a western and southern movement settled the areas around the Great Lakes, the Gulf of Mexico, and the Mississippi Valley. During the 1840s, 1850s, and 1860s, the Great Plains, the Rocky Mountain region, California, Oregon, and Utah were settled.

The leaders and promoters who paved the way during the western migrations included such men as Daniel Boone, James Bridger,

Christopher (Kit) Carson, David Crockett, William Fargo, Meriwether Lewis, Zebulon Montgomery Pike, and Brigham Young.

These leaders shared two common denominators, masculinity and dominance. Daniel Boone and Jim Bridger appeared reclusive in addition to being dominant; they found happiness in solitude. Brigham Young and the Mormons found religious freedom. Others gained personal freedom. The opportunities for leadership provided a challenge for all and profits for many.

The settlers of the western United States who migrated from other parts of the nation differed little from the foreign immigrants (and, in many instances, included newly arrived immigrants) in that all sought freedom, adventure, and opportunity. Most wanted land and material goods; they accepted the risks of moving west in view of the potential rewards. Risk-taking is a behavioral characteristic of the dominance trait, exhibited from the time the first Asians crossed the Bering Strait and spread southward over the continent, through the final settlement of the United States by the movement of dominant Americans and Europeans from the East to the West Coasts.

The migrations from the East and Midwest to the West Coast began in earnest when Mexico ceded California and the southwestern portion of the country to the United States after the war of 1846. They accelerated with the discovery of gold in California. After the first surge of adventurers bent on finding gold, families followed.

Because the western United States was settled last, varying degrees of difference in outlook exist today from the East to the Midwest to the West Coast. The viewpoints considered characteristic of the Western states in particular are illustrated in the terms *individualistic, entrepreneurial, rugged individualist,* and *pioneer spirit.* Perhaps they reflect a difference in the percentages of dominant and nondominant populations, with dominance ratios increasing as one moves farther west.

New York and Boston are well known for achievements that reflect high dominance—in the stock markets, banking and investment firms, national and international corporate headquarters, major law firms, and prestigious schools. Individual dominance percentages are extremely high in these enclaves, but these and similar centers of achievement account for only a small portion of the population. Conversely, the magnitude of public social services and the numbers on welfare rolls today indicate extremely high percentages of nondominance in the overall populations of northeastern metropolitan areas.

Undoubtedly the nation will reach a dominance mean, since there are no new frontiers to challenge the United States population.

◌◌◌◌◌◌

Two large, recent migrations to the United States came from Cuba beginning in 1959 and from Indochina (Vietnam, Cambodia, Laos, and Thailand) during and after the Vietnam War, which ended in 1975. Both resulted from political upheavals. Their sheer numbers and the compressed periods involved accelerated immigration patterns. The European immigrations spanned decades; those from Cuba and Indochina occurred much more quickly. They were akin to earlier political migrations from Europe transpiring in small bursts after political upheaval. Waves of Armenian immigrants, for example, came after political strife in 1893 and 1896, and again in 1915; Russian immigrations increased beginning with the Russian Revolution of 1917; about forty thousand Hungarians arrived after the abortive anticommunist rebellion of 1956.

These political revolts and resultant immigrations had five things in common: (1) the immigrants fled their homeland to save their lives with little hope of returning; (2) many came from the political right (other than refugees from fascist regimes in the 1930s and 1940s)—they were more the *haves* than the *have-nots*; (3) as a percentage of the overall population, more of the immigrants were more highly dominant than those on the winning side who remained; (4) although many were stripped of their material possessions, they had advanced skills in their chosen fields and these skills and knowledge left the country with them; and, (5) the most successful men managed to leave with their immediate families and many of their siblings and the siblings' families. These shared characteristics helped ensure their successes in the democratic, capitalistic environment of the United States.

The ongoing migrations from Central America, Haiti, Ireland, Mexico, and Puerto Rico are entirely different. A majority of undocumented workers come for jobs because of overpopulation in their countries. They fill a vacuum in low paying jobs, which many members of an affluent society deem undesirable. They do not share the five common characteristics of dominant persons escaping political upheavals; they are the *have-nots*. One can presume that most, though not all, are nondominant.

These immigrations are similar to those from Ireland during the Irish famine of the 1840s and the migrations of blacks from the rural South to the industrialized North during 1900-1930 and 1940-1970. Those movements also reflected a need for jobs.

Before the Irish famine, Irish immigrants to colonial America were predominantly Protestants from Northern Ireland. They considered themselves Scotch-Irish, and many were dominant. The immigrants escaping the Irish famine were Roman Catholics primarily from rural areas. They were poor although less so than many remaining in Ireland. They were less dominant than the Irish immigrants of colonial times but more dominant than most of their countrymen who stayed behind.

The scope of migrations from the Caribbean and Central American countries, Ireland, and Mexico will continue in direct proportion to their lack of jobs at home, high birth rates, and the willingness of the United States government to allow them entry.

To return to the immigrations of the refugee *haves* to the United States from Indochina, Cuba, and Nicaragua; they had another thing in common. They fled the turmoil which ensued when entrenched rightist governments became so corrupt and repressive that they were overthrown. In many cases they themselves had been active or passive participants in the corruption or at least beneficiaries of it. In this way they helped precipitate the political upheavals which brought the "left" to power in their countries and caused them to have to seek asylum elsewhere.

The immigrations from Cambodia, Laos, Thailand, and Vietnam were set in motion by the authoritarian ruler of Vietnam, Ngo Dinh Diem, and culminated when his government was overthrown by Nguyen That Thanh, known as Ho Chi Minh—He Who Enlightens. Those from Cuba were caused by Fulgencio Batista, who was overthrown by Fidel Castro, and those from Nicaragua were set in motion by Anastasio Somoza Garcia and continued by his sons Luis Somoza Debayle and Anastasio Somoza Debayle, who was overthrown by the Sandinistas.

The swift withdrawal of many dominant people from their native lands practically ensures that these lands will decline in a new "leftist" environment. Economic failures brought about by new political regimes have occurred in Cambodia, Laos, Thailand, Vietnam, and Cuba, and are materializing in Nicaragua. All happened over a short period. They are particularly noticeable when compared to the successes of the refugee immigrants in their new environments, especially the United States, where they have generally become model citizens and distinct assets.

By granting them asylum, the United States creates a means of escape for these refugee *haves*. During the years before the political chaos comes to a head, many take the steps necessary to abandon their country. Knowing they have a safe haven, some smugly continue to participate in the governmental corruption or at least uncourageously stand by without intervening. Had there not been a place available to them to which they could retreat with their wealth intact, they—those who were not involved in the corruption and repression and even some who were—might have tried to stop or limit the excesses and thus prevent the government from being destabilized. If they have no escape hatch, more of the *haves* might help their countries if only in their own self-interest.

A transition is occurring in Mexico. There are few affluent Mexicans without financial deposits in the United States and other free-world countries. Capital is moved supposedly to protect against inflation, but that could be achieved to some extent by investing in Mexico's land and tangibles. Actually, protection from inflation is only one consideration. Investments in the United States and other free-world countries in real estate, money markets, and equity markets pave the way for a permanent departure if it proves necessary. It seems safe to infer that these wealthy Mexicans are preparing for political asylum if a chaotic change in the Mexican government occurs. Many of the most successful people in Central and South America seem to be taking the same precautionary measures.

If there were no possibilities of political asylum in other countries, wealthy, successful, dominant Mexicans might attempt to reduce corruption in the government and law enforcement agencies of their country, since their lives could depend on it. They might try, for instance, to limit the growing police involvement in private affairs;

they might implement changes to increase the general prosperity of the country.

Mexico is important to the United States. We share one of the longest borders in the world. Mexico's stability is vital to us. One reason for its stability is that Mexico apparently has a higher percentage of dominant citizens than do Central and South American countries. Currently the country does not appear to need a dictator of the "right" or "left."

rle rle rle sh sh sh

Another migration involving dominance occurred between 1820 and 1865 when black American freedmen moved to Liberia. They founded the country in 1822; it became a republic on July 26, 1847. Many Liberian names have roots in the United States; the capital, Monrovia, is located on the banks of the Saint Paul River. Liberia is the only black African state that never came under colonial rule.

The black founders probably came from the most dominant, risk-taking, entrepreneurial segment of the American black population of the time. These Americo-Liberians and their descendants must have been dominant in contrast to the overwhelming majority of the native Liberians, since although they were a minority segment of the population at the country's founding and are a 5 percent minority today, they maintained control of the country for 158 years, until 1980. In that year the government was overthrown by members of the Liberian Krahn tribe led by Master Sergeant Samuel Doe.

rle rle rle sh sh sh

Over the past hundred years, mass immigrations have reached the limits set by the confines of the earth's land masses. With no new lands available for discovery and settlement, future migrations can occur only if: (1) one country conquers another, gaining land for immigrants from the victor's homeland; (2) one country voluntarily opens its borders to immigrants from another country; or, (3) compatible countries allow themselves to be peacefully subsumed under one governing body. The translation of the territories of

Hawaii and Alaska into states within the United States are examples of the third alternative.

In 1987 the world population was estimated at 4.975 billion; over eighty million people are added annually. Every three years the increase equals the entire world population at the time of Christ.

Will and Ariel Durant in *The Lessons of History* present a dichotomy concerning population control:

Until that equilibrium of production and reproduction comes it will be a counsel of humanity to disseminate the knowledge and means of contraception. Ideally parentage should be a privilege of health, not a by-product of sexual agitation.

On the other hand,

The third biological lesson of history is that life must breed. Nature has no use for organisms, variations, or groups that cannot reproduce abundantly. She has a passion for quantity as prerequisite to the selection of quality; she likes large litters, and relishes the struggle that picks the surviving few; doubtless she looks on approvingly at the upstream race of a thousand sperms to fertilize one ovum. She is more interested in the species than in the individual, and makes little difference between civilization and barbarism. She does not care that a high birth rate has usually accompanied a culturally low civilization, and a low birth rate a civilization culturally high; and she (here meaning Nature as the process of birth, variation, competition, selection, and survival) sees to it that a nation with a low birth rate shall be periodically chastened by some more virile and fertile group.

Populations continue to grow and countries continue to endure catastrophes such as war and drought, which produce death and famine. Yet these catastrophes have only minimally slowed the world's population growth. Dr. I. J. Good, the Oxford scientist, states, "Should the population continue to expand at the current rate it will only be 3,500 years before we shall have converted into people all the matter that can be reached during that period."

All species live within and are governed by the same boundaries of territory and food supply. Mankind is the only species that has temporarily broken out of these ecological boundaries. The overpopulation permitted by sovereign states without regard to individual well-being and quality of life will stimulate dramatic cultural evolution in humans to cope with stress, tension, hunger, and starvation.

All land areas are currently controlled without major questions of ownership by individual sovereign states. The possibility of peaceful mass immigration to new territories on the planet is now part of mankind's past. Unless space exploration provides new habitation, almost all humans will be born, live, and die within set boundaries.

Chapter XII

Dictatorships, Socialism, and Democracies

Democracy + Private Ownership = Capitalism.
Democracy + Public Ownership = Socialism.
Dictatorship + Private Ownership = Fascism.
Dictatorship + Public Ownership = Communism.

Leonard Roy Frank

To a great extent, governments are based on the people governed. Individuals and their overall personality makeup (the country's collective attitude) dictate the form of government that eventually prevails in each society. Over an extended period, the majority of a country's people can rarely be changed to fit a political regime that runs contrary to their collective attitude. Consequently, a political system that functions well for one society is less successful when adopted by other societies.

McClelland's *Achieving Society* provides in-depth calculations, studies, and comparisons of achievement differences in modern cultures and countries. McClelland's criteria for measuring *n-achievement* (needs for achievement) differences of modern nations include production and use of electricity per capita, economic growth, entrepreneurial activity, income per capita, passenger kilometers flown per month per thousand inhabitants, birth rates, and children's stories. A common thread in the comparisons is a consistently greater ratio of individuals with high *n-achievement* in successful countries and a consistently lower ratio for countries with lower levels of national achievement.

The dominance levels of the population, in numbers and as a percentage of the whole, are the achievement wellsprings from which a country's political structure evolves, whether that structure is aristocratic, democratic, dictatorial, socialistic, or takes some other form. The political environment can be classified as the end product of a nation's individuals. Thus, internal political shifts are partially attributable to changes in the population's collective needs for achievement, its dominance ratios.

Of course, factors other than dominance ratios contribute to a country's political environment. Their influences, while important, do not have the same continuing effect as do human resources. Natural resources, for example, are eventually depleted. Human resources, however, are lasting, their effect seen with clarity in times of great achievement and less evident during periods of decline.

One recurring aspect of political environments is governmental repression; no civilization has ever totally freed itself of repression. The severity of oppression can be expressed in degrees; owning slaves and tampering with voting rights represent wide variances in the exercise of suppression.

Repression appears to be a particularly complex issue for countries in which ethnic or religious minorities coexist with a majority population of different ethnicity or religious belief. It may be that a difference in dominance levels rather than ethnic or religious differences is the major contributor to oppression.

"It is bad to be oppressed by a minority, but it is worse to be oppressed by a majority. . . . from the absolute will of an entire people there is no appeal, no redemption, no refuge but treason." Lord Acton's 1877 statement fits one of the more obvious, virulent forms of political repression, that directed against dominant minorities in countries having a huge nondominant majority. Historical examples abound. The Protestant Huguenots of France were persecuted in the sixteenth through eighteenth centuries. Pogroms against the Jews in Russia exploded during the 1880s. Armenians were massacred by their Turkish conquerors between 1893 and 1896. In 1915 several hundred thousand Armenians died when the Turks drove them into the Syrian desert to starve.

The 1966 repression of the Ibos, a tribe in Nigeria with a high percentage of dominant men and women, was somewhat disguised as they were persecuted by their fellow black countrymen, a nondominant majority from other Nigerian tribes. In 1967 the Ibos attempted to isolate themselves by forming the country of Biafra in eastern Nigeria. They failed and, over the next three years, tens of thousands were eliminated by murder and starvation.

Though less common, repression also occurs in countries in which both the suppressed minority and the population majority have high dominance ratios. Nazi persecution and genocide of Jews between 1933 and 1945 provides one example.

Another form of repression occurs when a dominant minority abuses the human rights of the nondominant majority. Are the nondominant majorities suppressed in Soviet bloc countries? Is this happening in Northern Ireland, South Africa, and some Central and South American countries?

rle rle rle sh sh sh

Charles Darwin's great discoveries transmitted in *The Origin of Species*, although not directly relating to man, make him the unmatched discoverer and delineator of physical man. Sigmund Freud discovered psychological man. His first major work, *The Interpretation of Dreams*, was published in 1900—thirty-one years after Galton's *Hereditary Genius* and twenty-nine years after Darwin's *Descent of Man*.

Darwin's understanding of man's physical evolution appears greater than his grasp of psychological man and the dominance trait. In *The Descent of Man and Selection in Relation to Sex*, Darwin states:

Thus the reckless, degraded, and often vicious members of society, tend to increase at a quicker rate than the provident and generally virtuous members. Or as Mr. Greg puts the case: "The careless, squalid, unaspiring Irishman multiplies like rabbits: the frugal, foreseeing, self-respecting, ambitious Scot, stern in his morality, spiritual in his faith, sagacious and disciplined in his intelligence, passes his best years in struggle and in celibacy, marries late, and leaves few behind him. Given a land originally peopled by a thousand Saxons and a thousand Celts—and in a dozen generations five-sixths of the population would be Celts, but five-sixths of the property, of the power, of the intellect, would belong to the one-sixth of Saxons that remained. In the eternal 'struggle for existence,' it would be the inferior and *less* favoured race that had prevailed—and prevailed by virtue not of its good qualities but of its faults."

Darwin presents a view that, though harsh, was held by many dominant individuals then. Even today, that reflects the attitude of some dominant individuals toward their less dominant countrymen. It seems most prevalent among dominant citizens controlling countries in which much of the population is nondominant.

Dominant and nondominant individuals have little understanding of or regard for what the other believes relevant; their priorities are different. The small dominant population and the larger nondominant population have differing views on whether the majority is actually suppressed. Regardless of the followers' dominance levels, leaders are invariably highly dominant.

Contrary to popular opinion, the developed need to be obedient seems greater, on the whole, in the highly dominant than in the less dominant segment of society. Of course, not all dominant individuals respect society's rules just as not all nondominant people break its laws. High intelligence appears to boost respect for obedience in the nondominant citizenry just as high levels of affluence and power seem to encourage disobedience by dominant citizens.

Popular wisdom holds that the United States can export democracy to any country and make it work. Some even believe that it is a country's leaders who prevent the formation of democracy, a position W.W. Rostow takes in *Politics and the Stages of Growth*, "Democracy was always conceived as a combination of liberty and the assumption of responsibility. . . . The rule has not changed in the past twenty-five hundred years; and the peoples of the contemporary developing world appear capable of living by it—if given half a chance by their leaders." But Will and Ariel Durant in *The Lessons of History* state, "Nature smiles at the union of freedom and equality in our utopias. For freedom and equality are sworn and everlasting enemies, and when one prevails the other dies." Leaders cannot change the ratios of dominance levels in a country's population. Democracies, such as that of Athens under Pericles from 463 B.C. to 431 B.C. or that existing in the United States today, can function successfully only with a high percentage of dominant people.

In a country with high ratios of individual dominance, people with diverse needs to be in control are constantly at odds on policy formation. As a matter of course, these individuals form groups with others holding similar opinions; representatives of these separate groups meeting to govern or control a population have different priorities. Since each group has needs to control, a single leader finds it difficult to attain cohesion among them; thus compromises are made and democracy flourishes.

The scarcity of national achievements by Russia until recently indicates that the bulk of the population has been nondominant. Although communist dictatorships have shortcomings that democracies consider morally wrong, communism is a viable political structure for governing large numbers of citizens with low dominance levels. Between 1945 and 1949, even excluding those who escaped by emigration, the populations of countries that came under Soviet control as spoils of war still had a recognizable number of dominant people and were not well suited to communism. But countries coming under Soviet domination or influence beginning in 1949 such as China, Cuba, Nicaragua, and Vietnam possessed markedly nondominant population percentages, a factor in their embrace of communism.

Compared to earlier political systems in Russia, the communist government has improved the economic situation of most citizens. The battering cycles of famine and death before and during the early years of communism up to 1938 are only memories. Today there is sufficient food, shelter, and warm clothing. Since 1960 food consumption has doubled. The work week has been shortened from six to five days.

Tremendous strides have been made in developing the country's resources. In 1983 the U.S.S.R., the world's largest crude oil producer, pumped twice as much oil as Saudi Arabia. Natural gas reserves are estimated at 40 percent of the world total. The country channels its human resources by targeting many for specific purposes. It has 1.5 million researchers with scientific degrees, 25 percent of such specialists in the world.

In less than three generations a small group of dominant Soviets succeeded in lifting the country to its present world position. Although the cost in Russian lives was great, only one country, Germany, has invaded its borders since 1920. Before that Russia had a long history of intervention or invasion by foreign powers. As late as 1918-1920, fourteen foreign governments intervened in Soviet affairs, primarily to overthrow the Bolshevik regime. In spite of its harried past, the Soviet Union has become one of two world superpowers. The country attained superpower status despite its World War II losses of an estimated fifteen to twenty million servicemen and civilians.

Among Soviet-controlled countries, the dominance ratios appear more favorable in those countries that became communist as a result of the political division negotiated at Yalta in February 1945, for example, the German Democratic Republic (East Germany). East Germany's estimated population in 1983 was 16.7 million and the Soviet Union's was estimated at 272.5 million. On the basis of percentage of population, East Germany consistently wins more Olympic medals than does the U.S.S.R. If all Soviet bloc countries are included, East Germany's feat becomes even more outstanding. If one considers Olympic success as one measure of national achievement, that East Germany has such a high proportion of wins in relation to its population is not surprising, for its population though small has a high percentage of dominant people. The need to achieve is evident in other areas. East Germany's productivity levels are higher than any Soviet bloc country or the U.S.S.R.

Dominance can also be seen in the 3.5 million people who fled East Germany between 1945 and 1961. (Of these, an estimated five hundred thousand returned.) At the time, the loss of three million persons severely damaged the East German economy. Most who left are likely to have been dominant, those who most wanted freedom and were willing to take dangerous risks for it. They emigrated to Western countries that offered greater potential for achievement and liberty.

In 1945 Korea was divided into North and South Korea. North Korea was placed under Soviet supervision and South Korea under American jurisdiction. At the time of division, Korea's industrial might was in the North and the South was primarily agricultural. The partition stimulated a mass move of dominant people from the North to the South. Industry and commerce shifted from North Korea to South Korea, a result of the concentration of dominant individuals, those originally from the South and those who fled the North. This is the source of South Korea's industrial and commercial success.

Whatever the political system of a country may be, it seems to be that if the populace is nondominant it will not have great accomplishments. A comparison of communist Poland and democratic Ireland helps make the point. The population ratios of both countries, based on past and current world achievements, are skewed toward nondominance. Ireland enjoys more freedom with democracy than does Poland under the U.S.S.R. But Ireland is no economic success story, and emigrations increase annually—some expatriates arrive in other countries legally, some illegally.

Comparing communism in the Soviet Union to democracy in the United States is not a valid means of assessing the Soviet system of government, since democracy has never existed in Russia. A more realistic comparison would be the U.S.S.R. versus Russia under the Tsars or Poland under the U.S.S.R. versus Poland under the rule of the Magnates. Those feudal systems were also dictatorships and allowed even fewer human rights than communism does today.

Before 1917 the Tsars owned huge estates, administered by managers and maintained by serfs. Serfs went with the land when it was given by the Tsars in return for favors. Cycles of hunger and starvation prevailed. Some conclude that the Soviet Union's communal farm system is superior to that of the Tsars. Even though a failure when measured against the successes of free enterprise farms, the State and to some extent the farm commune workers benefit from the system. Workers are gainfully employed, not wards of the state or recipients of welfare. They make social contributions to their level of competence, support themselves, and provide food for most, though not all, of the remaining populace.

Since Soviet communism prohibits direct ownership of private property, few incentives exist in farming to reward or interest dominant people with high needs to achieve. Cities act as magnets drawing the more dominant from rural areas. The Soviet Union has increasingly changed from rural to urban since 1918. Urban populations have more than tripled. Moscow has a population of 8.2 million. Twenty-two other cities have populations exceeding one million, and 272 have more than one hundred thousand.

If the Soviet economy grows and provides more industrial jobs for the general population, communal farming stands to become less productive. When that occurs farming enterprises will become more capitalistic as a means of increasing productivity. Present American derision of Soviet farming will shift to consternation. It is bad enough to lose a large purchaser of United States grain, but worse still for a good customer to become a major competitor.

The government implements the philosophy of gainful employment for all, as in farming, throughout the Soviet bloc in most areas including manufacturing, commerce, and government bureaucracy. Jobs are created for everyone regardless of dominance level. On the surface, the system is based on the premise of equality. This is false. No real equality exists because, as in all nations, dominant, achieving individuals secure most of the highest and more rewarding positions.

Although its upper class comprises a tiny percentage of the population, a class system exists in the U.S.S.R. Only about 10 percent of the adult population belongs to the Communist party. Initially the class system rewarded only dominant male party members who were successful. It now includes the extended families of these dominant, successful men—many of which include nondominant children. In the U.S.S.R. as in the United States, dominant men tend to marry nondominant women who rear nondominant children. Rewarding the nondominant children of dominant, successful party members through a hereditary class pattern as the U.S.S.R. now does is in direct opposition to party tenets.

Power, fame, and wealth are the three greatest measurements of success. Soviet communism sanctions power and fame, but its doctrine limits the creation of individual wealth. This restriction is circumvented somewhat by perquisites of automobiles, chauffeurs, second homes, good medical facilities, culinary delicacies, and imported products sold in restricted stores.

Of the three motivators, wealth is most easily discernible. Money is not only seen, it is particularly envied and resented by a largely nondominant population. The communist class system created in 1917 was not resented by the bulk of the people because it was not centered on wealth. Today resentment of the perquisites enjoyed by Soviet officials festers but, by not allowing individual fortunes, communism defuses some built-in envy and anger in the nondominant majority. The dominant segments of society, motivated by a desire for money but denied the opportunity to acquire wealth, react by not contributing as much as they otherwise might to the country's economy.

In the sphere of dominance, communism is, in effect, a parallel world to capitalism, with opposite problems. Consequently, the Soviet Union has not reached a true understanding of capitalism and the overall dominance levels and achievement needs in capitalistic populations, nor have capitalists understood the lower achievement needs and dominance levels of the Soviet bloc peoples. Even though democracies and dictatorships occupy opposite political poles, the difference in the composition of their dominant and nondominant populations is one reason both systems work.

One of communism's serious problems is its refusal to accommodate all dominant men with needs to lead and achieve. The achievement needs of dominant, non-party members as well as some party members are under-utilized in the Soviet economy. Some become involved in entrepreneurial efforts such as managing sectors of an illegal underground economy in the manufacture, distribution, and sale of goods for personal profit. They are lost to politically acceptable activities that would benefit the overall economy. Discrimination against many of the U.S.S.R.'s more than two million Jews also robs the nation of economic benefits. By not using the success potential of dominant men to the fullest, communism limits its economic success.

The full employment principle of Soviet-style communism accommodates nondominant men and women fairly successfully. It also succeeds in accommodating dominant women. One indication: there are more women engineers in the Soviet Union than in the rest of the world.

Perhaps the greatest future internal threat to communism (which should eventually become an asset) is a potential increase in births of dominant people, those with needs to achieve. Although their percentage of the overall population may be small, without the limiting of the birth rate that affluence brings, actual numbers could become large. With its narrow hierarchical structure, communism is almost certain to continue facing defections, strife, and the possibility of insurrections unless it adjusts so as to accommodate any increased numbers of men and women with needs to achieve. Walls are only a temporary way to retain the dissatisfied; to their advantage, financial incentives and political changes are evolving as longer-term policies.

Democracies, on the other hand, face a problem in accommodating nondominant people as their numbers increase. To the present time they have been quite successful in accommodating achievement-oriented men and recently, to a lesser degree, dominant women.

Communism is not a viable political system for countries with a high proportion of dominant citizens. Communism has never been an *internal* threat to Australia, Canada, Great Britain, Israel, Japan, the United States, West Germany, or the white population of South Africa. Regardless of financial recessions, depressions, economic hardships, or even defeat in major wars, as in the cases of Germany and Japan, they have not been susceptible to communism because the overall dominance level in each is relatively high.

Socialism is a political straddle between a democracy and a dictatorship. Current socialistic governments attempt to accommodate dominant minorities and nondominant majorities.

Socialism and Soviet-style communism share some characteristics, since both governments intervene in almost all functions of society. They differ dramatically in employment. Socialism provides subsidies to the nondominant majority without enforcing specific job requirements. Conditions such as requiring a specific number of work hours per week or meeting production quotas are rarely imposed. Communism, on the other hand, requires the nondominant majority to hold jobs and work a specified number of hours each week; the government also attempts to force production goals. Under socialism most people enjoy greater personal freedom, since the choice of whether to work and in what area rests to some extent with them. Under some communistic regimes, they would be forced to work in a field chosen by the government.

Two factors of a population's dominance levels continually affect socialistic countries. The first involves the simultaneous accommodation of a nondominant majority and a dominant minority; the second, the country's birth rate. In socialistic countries where the number of nondominant individuals is not an overpowering part of the whole and the birth rate is below the world average, socialism can prevail longest. Some dominance level changes from one generation to another occur in the population but, with a low birth rate, any resulting political changes right or left stay within a narrow range. Consequently, such countries have managed for many years to avoid political extremes and are unlikely to acquire a dictatorship of either the right or the left.

France and Sweden provide examples of countries with socialistic governments, low birth rates, and fairly constant dominance ratios in the population. (Sweden technically is a monarchy, but a constitutional one with western-style parliamentary government.) Although at times apparently vacillating between governments more accommodating to the nondominant segment and those more sympathetic to the dominant minority, the countries remain stable. Unlike some socialistic countries, they have little need to fear internal threats that would allow a dictatorship to develop.

The birth rate acts as a major political force in any country. When nondominant individuals constitute the bulk of the population and the birth rate is above the world average, governments of all types seem to be in constant danger. An above-average birth rate presages a huge numerical increase in the nondominant adult population segment and places the country in an untenable economic position. At some point, the government must decide whether to continue accommodating the expanding nondominant majority of the population or to curtail governmental expenditures by decreasing social services.

Two situations, separately or in combination, often account for the emergence of dictators from either the "right" or "left." In one case, a declining percentage of dominant people limits the activities of dominant political groups, decreases opposition to a dictatorship, and makes it possible for a single leader to seize control. In the second situation, when fewer dominant persons are available to provide legislation and law enforcement, civil disobedience and criminal activity increase. If lawlessness prevails, the country at some point needs a dictator to provide leadership for a society out of control and no longer capable of being governed by peaceful means.

A move from socialism to communism would be by an indirect route, one that leads to a communist dictatorship via a rightist dictatorship. In a socialistic country with a continually growing population, it eventually will become impossible to obtain enough funds to continue accommodating the nondominant segment. A sequence of events is as follows. As tax revenues constrict, the government implements an austerity program designed to reduce subsidies and entitlements. The government then favors the dominant minority and represses the nondominant majority, causing general unrest. A rightist dictatorship emerges, which initially brings order to the country.

At a later stage, a dominant, charismatic person appears to lead the repressed nondominant majority. This new leader of the "left" overthrows the rightist government. Some socialistic countries that fit the early stages of this pattern are El Salvador and Honduras and perhaps Mexico.

Dominant individuals, a minority in socialistic countries, are the most vulnerable to taxation and bureaucracy. Tax revenues subsidize the poorer classes in their quest for economic equality. Those with money, from the middle class to the rich, find ways to evade paying unreasonable taxes. Without ever greater taxes, inflation occurs and the value of the country's currency erodes. Eventually the upper limits of taxation are reached. Then, if a growing birth rate adds to the imbalance between dominant and nondominant citizens, social spending increases, the value of the country's currency decreases, and inflation becomes a certainty.

The financial burdens of a government trying to accommodate a burgeoning birth rate increase. Dominant individuals who cannot acquire wealth because of excessive tax or inflation levels are unlikely to work to capacity, lowering productivity. Those already wealthy frequently transfer their capital to countries where investments can reap greater rewards or where at the least they can avoid confiscation. As capital investments fall, major repairs to existing machinery necessary for profitable ventures are curtailed, productivity of private enterprise shrinks, and the economy may grind to a halt.

Since 1949 China, Cuba, Vietnam, and Nicaragua each made a political change directly from the far right to the far left without the buffer of socialism. The United States, having backed the rightist government in its struggle to retain control, refused to support the new leftist government even though any actual differences between the two regimes were small. The Soviet Union filled the vacuum. These countries then "fell" to communism. A similar situation was materializing in the Philippines under Ferdinand Marcos. That country is, at least temporarily, operating without a dictator.

Based on China's current achievements and a peasant population ratio of 80 percent, an overpowering majority of the country's people appear to be nondominant. Still, Chinese immigrants to the United States fit the pattern of immigrants of other nationalities who achieve success in this country. Among the most dominant people in China, these immigrants are not representative of the country's overall dominant and nondominant percentages. The success rate of the new Taiwanese, for example, since their migration from mainland China beginning in 1949, would approximately match the successes of ousted Chinese and Indochinese now in the United States.

After a communist dictator ousts a rightist dictator (a strongman), many of the nation's *haves* abandon their country for a haven in another country. Owing to a new sense of equality and euphoria among the citizens, dictatorial aspects of the new communist regime are overlooked, as is a realistic assessment of the country's chances for increased economic achievement under the new government.

Whether in industry, agriculture, or finance, the most dominant individuals are the leaders, organizers, and profit-makers. Their ousting or flight shrinks an already small dominant population segment even more. Additionally, many of the dominant individuals remaining become active in the new government, and that limits their participation in the commercial, profit-making activities needed to increase a country's prosperity. Communist regimes that develop after political upheaval frequently become financial drains on the Soviet Union. Cuba's estimated financial subsidies from the U.S.S.R. in 1985 were more than $4 billion, approximately 40 percent of Cuba's total annual budget.

The ratios of dominant to nondominant people set the political environment, but the nationalistic bent of a country determines whether it accepts or rejects foreign investments. Whatever its political doctrine, each country has national pride, nationalism being particularly strong in some. This can express itself in fear of foreign business competition and foreign exploitation. Distrust of other political systems combined with limitation or prohibition of foreign investment and ownership effectively inhibits an inflow of capital.

In democracies foreign investments are generally welcomed and in some countries, including the United States, solicited. Achievement-oriented individuals in democracies usually recognize the need for capital to take advantage of economic opportunities. Though foreign investments entail foreign ownership, the citizens believe they can control the risks associated with the foreign presence and these investments are not seen as an affront to national pride.

Certain countries with populations skewed favorably toward dominance, like Japan, still inhibit foreign competition. In time increasing needs for capital to finance growth will silence opposition to foreign involvement in their economies.

In countries where dominance is skewed unfavorably, resistance to foreign competition is frequently the fiercest and the longest lasting. In Mexico many businesses are now confined to a maximum of 49 percent foreign ownership. Attitudes can change; the Mexican government is reconsidering its policy of limiting foreign investments to a minority percentage of a company's ownership. Rescinding this law could produce meaningful changes in the government's foreign investment policy, temporarily benefiting the economy through an infusion of foreign capital.

Welcoming foreign capital is a radical departure from communist doctrine. Yet unexpectedly China's leaders are now expressing interest in foreign investment and ownership—this in a country which has banned all foreign investments since 1949.

rle rle rle sh sh sh

Beginning with the first immigrants at Jamestown in 1607, the United States population was fundamentally dominant. It continued to be success-oriented because of the birth rate of dominant mothers and the continued influx of dominant immigrants. From the nation's inception, one idea brought colonists to the United States and permeated the principles set forth in the Declaration of Independence and the Bill of Rights; the ideal of individual freedom became the country's watchword. The founding fathers believed that government should be limited to specific, stated tasks. Rights not explicitly designated as the responsibility of the government belonged to the people. Only in this way did the Declaration's framers believe individuals could be protected from governmental oppression.

The country's political system accommodated a citizenry of mostly dominant individuals with great needs for freedom. The legislative, judicial, and executive branches worked well in conjunction with the needs of dominant individuals to acquire power, fame, or wealth, and the country benefited from their accomplishments. At the same time, checks and balances curtailed the possibility that too much power might be amassed by any individual or group. The checks and balances protected citizens from the negative effects of high individual dominance levels, most specifically those aimed at acquiring extensive amounts of power that could be used to subjugate the population. The founders understood the perils of unchecked individual power and of overly strong governmental powers; they knew that, if left completely to their own devices, some people might attempt to gain power in greater and greater amounts.

Freedom was the watchword, and individual freedom was its result. Since most of the population was dominant, had great needs to achieve, and had the freedom to attempt to attain large goals, American democracy and its brand of capitalism became a wonder to other countries as each accomplishment fostered still another. Many countries marveled at this concept of democracy and its resultant successes without realizing their major cause, that the United States had a heavy concentration of highly dominant people enabled by their system of government to search for freedom, opportunities, and success.

The country's first major test of democracy came eighty-five years after the Declaration of Independence with the Civil War in 1861.

The War Between the States was not a revolution; it was not fought between dominant and nondominant groups or between *haves* and *have-nots*. Judging by the accomplishments of the North and the South, we can deduce that the white majority of each was dominant. No matter which side won, high dominance with its achievement orientation would prevail and ensure that the victorious government would continue to function with a dominant population majority. After the war, achievement opportunities were still available to soldiers of the losing side. Many escaped the scenes of defeat and found freedom in the western United States. A number emigrated to Brazil and attained success there.

Freedom, independence, and liberty continue to be the rallying cry of dominant Americans. The less dominant call out for equality and security.

The nation faces the task of accommodating increasing numbers of nondominant citizens while retaining a democratic form of government. A review of the histories of earlier democracies may reveal that one of the greatest internal threats to a democracy is an increase of nondominant people born in or immigrating to the country. In the United States, it is highly probable that further large nondominant population increases will come through changes in the citizenship laws governing aliens. (A comparison of the recent successes of small numbers of dominant Asian newcomers to the great numbers of new immigrants from other areas highlights the dominance of most Asian immigrants and the nondominance of many of the others.) Affluence is another important factor accelerating a decline in dominant domestic births as affluent dominant women limit the number of children they have.

At the country's founding, individuals shouldered personal and social responsibilities; they expected the government, in accordance with constitutional limitations, to abstain from these areas. As the nondominant portion of the population grows, demands that the government assume greater and greater social welfare responsibilities increase. To continue functioning successfully, American democracy must absorb the increase of nondominant citizens into society in an economically productive way while preserving their dignity and rights as individuals.

The architects of United States democracy were dominant as were the designers of Soviet communism. The difference was not in the founders, since all leaders are dominant. They both succeeded, albeit in very different ways, because their philosophies of government fit the difference in percentages of dominant and nondominant people in each country at the time of political inception—1776 for the United States and 1917 for the Soviet Union. A dictatorship would have failed in 1776 in the United States, and democracy would have failed in Russia in 1917.

riz riz riz sh sh sh

Two broad schools of thought exist as to how the history of mankind has progressed since recorded time. One states that the influence of rare individuals and events is the major factor affecting historical change. The other affirms that mankind's history moves in recurring cycles, the rare individuals and events being products of those cycles.

Both views are important. Viewing the histories of empires as recurring cycles need not diminish the influence of great individuals and rare events. It is hard to disentangle at a given time in an empire's cyclical development the mutual effects of the social climate, that is, the collective attitude of the population, and the occurrence of a seminal event or appearance of a great individual. Which calls forth which?

Alexander the Great's conquests, for example, can be considered from both perspectives: as a product both of unusual events and great leadership and of a fortuitous social milieu. An unusual event, the assassination of his father (Philip of Macedon) at an early age, provided a young Alexander with a successful, aggressive standing army and the tactical advantage of the phalanx. Another unusual event, or lucky happenstance, was Alexander's use of the phalanx. Napoleon Bonaparte notes, "He gave only a few battles, and his triumphs were due to the order of the phalanx rather than his generalship." But when Alexander faced powerful opponents and tactical disadvantages he remained undefeated, a testimony to his enormous abilities as a leader.

Even with this rare individual and these unusual events, Alexander's successes still could be a consequence of the repetitive cycles of empire. Macedon was an upstart nation regarded by its contemporaries as barbaric. The collective attitudes of the Greeks and Persians reflected the different cyclical stages they were then in; both were established, affluent, and declining, in contrast to their war-like beginnings. Could an earlier, younger, and more aggressive Greece or Persia have been overrun by a Philip or an Alexander? Perhaps that part of the world was decadent, deteriorating, and ripe for Alexander's conquest.

Insightful leadership that delayed but did not reverse a country's decline happened in France with Richelieu's Edict of Grace on June 28, 1629. For years French Huguenots had been cruelly persecuted and murdered; in 1628 much of France called for the extinction of all Huguenots. Richelieu's Edict granted amnesty to Huguenots who had participated in the rebellion, guaranteed freedom of Protestant worship, and opened military and civil service positions to all without question of creed.

According to Durant, "With a wisdom tragically lacking in Louis XIV, the great Cardinal recognized . . . the immense economic value of the Huguenots to France. They abandoned revolt, gave themselves peacefully to commerce and industry, and prospered as never before." Although financially beneficial to France, Richelieu's action ran counter to French public opinion.

Cardinal Richelieu's intervention ended three decades later, and France's downward cycle continued. Some four hundred thousand Huguenots (of an estimated 1.5 million in France in 1660) in the decade before and after the Revocation escaped across guarded borders at the risk of their lives, much like people fleeing communism. Tales of heroism survived for a century. During 1669 Huguenot emigrants captured by the French were arrested and their belongings confiscated. Anyone in France aiding a Huguenot's escape faced condemnation to the galleys for life.

Several countries, including the British colonies in America, in cyclical stages differing from that of France, became the beneficiaries of Huguenot achievements. Protestant countries opened their borders to the fugitives. Four thousand Huguenots found a home in Geneva, boosting that city's population 25 percent, to twenty thousand. By

1697 over a fifth of Berlin's population was Protestant French owing to the efforts of the Elector of Brandenburg. In Holland a thousand homes were constructed to shelter the Huguenots. The Dutch government provided loans for Huguenots to establish businesses and guaranteed them all the rights of citizenship; Jews and even Catholics in Holland raised funds for Huguenot relief. Charles II and James II, though Roman Catholics, recognized the value of the Protestant Huguenots, gave material aid, and provided for their assimilation into England's economic and political life.

Besides providing new industry and trade in the United Provinces, the Huguenots volunteered in the English and Dutch armies and fought France. Their skills in crafts, commerce, and finance benefited countries that were in their upward cycles to the detriment of France in its downward cycle. Huguenot immigrants to England paved the way for English influence over French thought by Bacon, Newton, and Locke. Protestant Europe profited from France's religious bigotry.

It would take very unusual events or very great leadership to break the force of a nation's collective attitude or, more directly stated, the force of the country's composition of dominant and nondominant citizens. Cycles appear hard to reverse or even deflect. It is now easy to recognize how much France lost with the loss of the Huguenots and how much other countries gained. Would Richelieu's efforts to accommodate the Huguenots and to retain their vitality for France have prevailed had he been a greater leader? Or was the force of the cycle too strong for any leader to reverse?

An estimated two million Jews, approximately one of every 136 citizens, live in the Soviet Union. Most are assumed to be dominant and potentially high achievers. During this swing of the Soviet cycle, might not the Soviet Union reap large economic, intellectual, and scientific gains by restoring their religious freedom and allowing them to pursue their achievement needs? For this to happen, however, the Soviets must grant the same freedoms to all Soviet citizens. In this phase of the country's ten-generation cycle (as described in Chapter XIII, The Law of Ten Generations) these freedoms appear to be starting under Soviet restructuring and openness. But expectations for democracy and freedom may be hope divorced from reality: the attendant ratios of dominance and nondominance seem to provide weak underpinnings for democracy; and democracy, such as that in Classical Greece, Republican Rome, or the United States, has never existed in Russia's history.

History clearly indicates how large groups of striving individuals, like the Soviet Jews, have changed the course of nations. However, the events or leaders must be very unusual indeed to surmount a country's ongoing cycle upward or downward.

Lester C. Thurow's Foreword to *The Great Depression of 1990* by Dr. Ravi Batra notes, "If one could find cyclical regularities, the analyst could go beyond descriptions of the past and make predictions about the future. History would come alive as a predictive science."

Possibly Isaac Asimov is prophetic when in *Foundation and Earth* he bases his story on the work of a scientist of the future who:

devised psychohistory by modeling it upon the kinetic theory of gases. Each atom or molecule in a gas moves randomly so that we can't know the position or velocity of any one of them. Nevertheless, using statistics, we can work out the rules governing their overall behavior with great precision. In the same way, Seldon intended to work out the overall behavior of human societies even though the solutions would not apply to the behavior of individual human beings.

The following chapters demonstrate that past and present cyclical regularities do exist, and provide a possible explanation of cycles and their timing. Perhaps individuals can use this information to better understand themselves, their country, and its place in the world today.

BOOK TWO

PART III
Cycles of History

Chapter XIII

The Law of
Ten Generations

Philosophers and historians have long recognized that civilizations begin, develop, flourish, decline, and fail. They have speculated on the existence and influence of cycles, searching for reasons to explain why certain series of events are interchangeable among large successful cultures.

An understanding of the past provides a basis for predicting the future; with the ability to predict the future comes the possibility of altering or controlling it. But predicting the future has never been particularly rewarding. Prophets warn of potential danger to a civilization's well-being, and encourage change, but their prescriptions go unheeded. After all, changes beneficial to a society rarely suit the citizens' short-term self-interests. Consequently, many predictors meet the fate of Cassandra, the prophetess daughter of Priam and Hecuba of Greek mythology. She was cursed by Apollo so that her prophecies, though true, were never believed.

The concept of studying the past to develop an understanding of behavioral patterns that influence the future has been discussed pro and con. According to Louis Ferdinand Céline, "Those who talk about the future are scoundrels. It is the present that matters." And "History," said Henry Ford, "is more or less bunk." On the other hand Aldo Leopold, the environmentalist, notes, "It is reasonable to suppose that our social processes have a higher volitional content than those of the rabbit, but it is also reasonable to suppose that we, as a species, contain population behavior patterns of which nothing is known because circumstance has never evoked them. We may have others the meaning of which we have misread."

Could the rise and fall of great civilizations contain enough common factors to reveal a sequence of circumstances invariable under like conditions? Can patterns in the changing population behaviors of empires be discovered so as to correlate the causes and sequences of events? If so, could they be viewed as natural law?

Philosophers and historians have tried since ancient times to determine how and why the past repeats itself. Each built upon his predecessors' works to increase human understanding. Through the ages, their studies have identified common threads.

The Greek philosopher Plato (427-347 B.C.) was an early contributor to the idea of history's repetitiveness. He foresaw the rise and decline of future great states. Plato reduced political evolution to the sequential occurrence of these four regimes: monarchy, aristocracy, democracy, and dictatorship. Plato predicted that Athenian democracy would fail and be followed by a dictatorship; nine years after his death, as he foretold, Athenian democracy failed and was succeeded by a Macedonian dictatorship. Plato's *Republic* contained perhaps the earliest description of Western child-rearing practices designed to avoid what he identified as the last stage of political evolution, dictatorship.

The Greek politician Polybius, believed to have lived between 200 and 118 B.C., is recognized as a great historian. He predicted, then witnessed, the collapse of Greece. Although his dire predictions of the country's downfall were well known, his prophecies and proposed remedies were disregarded.

After Greece's fall, Polybius secured the best possible settlement with Rome on behalf of his countrymen. In time statues honoring him were erected in Lycosura, Mantineia, Pallantium, and Tegea. The inscription on the statue at Lycosura read, "Greece would never have come to grief, had she obeyed Polybius in all things, and having come to grief, she found succour through him alone."

Best known for his account of Rome's ascension to world power in the third and second centuries B.C., Polybius offers good advice for modern politicians: "All historians have insisted that the soundest education and training for political activity is the study of history, and that the surest and indeed the only way to learn how to bear bravely the vicissitudes of fortune is to recall the disasters of others."

Niccolo Machiavelli (1469-1527), an Italian statesman, patriot, political philosopher, and writer, became a great writer because he was first a great thinker. His forceful writing, understanding of contemporary politics, and tremendous insight into human nature produced literary masterpieces that were simple, honest, and easily understood. Possibly for these very reasons, the man and his works have been judged cynical or immoral. Few historians' works have been so misconstrued or vilified.

Machiavelli was the first to write about historical cycles based on the idea that human nature does not change, and he pioneered a political science founded on the study of man. His thoughts on human nature (human behavior-psychology) preceded Sigmund Freud's by some four hundred years. Even today, the belief that human nature remains constant is widely disputed and mankind's technological advances are sometimes confused with improvement in his basic nature.

Edward Gibbon (1737-1794), considered the greatest English historian of the eighteenth century, continued to expand the cyclical theory. His epic work, *The Decline and Fall of the Roman Empire* (1776-1788), traces a continuous story from the second century to Constantinople's fall in 1453. Gibbon's meticulous detail provides insight into the similarity of the circumstances that attended the declines of later empires.

Brooks Adams' (1848-1927) most important work, *The Law of Civilization and Decay* (1895), culminated his quest to determine whether a science of history was possible. Adams believed in, and searched history for, common clues to develop a law of the rise and decline of civilizations.

Adams' basic theory that all civilizations follow cycles was disturbing because it presumed that United States democracy would eventually deteriorate. His mixture of philosophy and theory was well received by the public, including Theodore Roosevelt, but denounced by many academicians. Roosevelt reviewed Adams' book in *The Forum* in 1897; he grasped Adams' theory and arguments, and understood the philosophy and its application to the American people and to the country's development.

Arnold Toynbee (1889-1975) began his major work, A *Study of History*, in 1927; he published twelve volumes between 1934 and 1961. Toynbee developed a philosophy of history itself. He analyzed the cyclical development and decline of civilizations, contending that historical study should examine common factors governing their growth and decay rather than individual nations or states.

Toynbee believed that a civilization's beginning stage was caused by a creative minority, somehow mystically inspired, who provided leadership to a passive majority. He envisioned that finally a stage of disintegration would be reached: a breakdown of social solidarity into internal social classes, and the majority's being contained by force as in the latter days of the Roman Empire.

Will and Ariel Durant, modern American historians, coauthored the last four volumes of an eleven-volume series, *The Story of Civilization* (1935-1975), amplifying the subject of historical cycles. Their 102-page *The Lessons of History* (1968) is probably the most concise summation ever written of Western history.

Historians continue to study and build on earlier knowledge, and the past continues to repeat itself. Recent publications on the cyclical nature of history include *The Cycles of American History* by Arthur M. Schlesinger, Jr., published in 1986, and Paul Kennedy's *Rise and Fall of the Great Powers*, published in 1987.

rle rle rle sh sh sh

"The Fate of Empires," an essay by Sir John Glubb published in 1976, is among the best of the analyses of cycles wherein great nations rise and decline. Born in Preston, England, on April 16,

1897, Sir John found his place in history as a professional soldier rather than as a historian. (Glubb stated in his autobiography, "I have been often vilified as the man who led an army wantonly to attack the innocent newborn state of Israel. I can only state in my defense that military commanders do not start wars. To do so is the prerogative of governments.") He died in Sussex on March 17, 1986.

"The Fate of Empires" contains astute observations by a non-scholar. Glubb accepted invitations to speak at universities in the United States but was never extended that courtesy in his native country. Possibly to British scholars he lacked the proper academic credentials. Even if proven right, outsiders are rarely accepted by the academic community.

Glubb presents three basic themes. First, he identifies six specific stages through which a great nation passes during its rise and fall. Second, these stages correspond with those of other empires no matter when each country held world prominence. Third, each nation's rise and fall covers some 250 years, noted as ten generations. Its fall can be either gradual or swift. Although the nation might continue to exist after ten generations, it is no longer a great power.

Glubb lists the six stages of empire as the Age of Pioneers (Outburst), the Age of Conquests, the Age of Commerce, the Age of Affluence, the Age of Intellect, and the Age of Decadence. The sequence resembles the physical course of life: birth, childhood, adolescence, adulthood, old age, and death.

The following excerpts are from "The Fate of Empires":

An interesting deduction from the figures seems to be that the duration of empires does not depend on the speed of travel or the nature of weapons. The Assyrians marched on foot and fought with spears and bow and arrows. The British used artillery, railways and ocean-going ships. Yet the two empires lasted for approximately the same periods.

Immense changes in the technology of transport or in methods of warfare do not seem to affect the life-expectation of an empire.

One of the very few units of measurement which have not seriously changed since the Assyrians is the human 'generation', a period of about twenty-five years. Thus a period of 250 years would represent about ten generations of people. . . .

Again and again in history we find a small nation, treated as insignificant by its contemporaries, suddenly emerging from its homeland and over-running large areas of the world. . . .

The Prophet Mohammed preached in Arabia from A.D. 613 to 632, when he died. In 633, the Arabs burst out of their desert peninsula, and simultaneously attacked the two super-powers. Within twenty years, the Persian Empire had ceased to exist. Seventy years after the death of the Prophet, the Arabs had established an empire extending from the Atlantic to the plains of Northern India and the frontiers of China.

The Arabs ruled the greater part of Spain for 780 years, from 712 A.D. to 1492. . . . During these eight centuries, there had been no Spanish nation, the petty kings of Aragon and Castile alone holding on in the mountains.

The agreement between Ferdinand and Isabella and Christopher Columbus was signed immediately after the fall of Granada, the last Arab kingdom in Spain, in 1492. Within fifty years, Cortez had conquered Mexico, and Spain was the world's greatest empire.

. . . The new conquerors are normally poor, hardy and enterprising and above all aggressive. The decaying empires which they overthrow are wealthy but defensive-minded. . . .

The first stage of the life of a great nation, therefore, after its outburst, is a period of amazing initiative, and almost incredible enterprise, courage and hardihood. These qualities, often in a very short time, produce a new and formidable nation. These early victories, however, are won chiefly by reckless bravery and daring initiative.

The Age of Conquests, of course, overlaps the Age of Commerce. . . . but gradually the desire to make money seems to gain hold of the public. . . .

The first half of the Age of Commerce appears to be peculiarly splendid. The ancient virtues of courage, patriotism and devotion to duty are still in evidence. The nation is proud, united and full of self-confidence. . . .

. . . Duty is the word constantly drummed into the heads of young people.

The Age of Commerce is also marked by great enterprise in the exploration for new forms of wealth. Daring initiative is shown in the search for profitable enterprises in far corners of the earth, perpetuating to some degree the adventurous courage of the Age of Conquests.

The first direction in which wealth injures the nation is a moral one. Money replaces honour and adventure as the objective of the best young men. Moreover, men do not normally seek to make money for their country or their community, but for themselves. Gradually, and almost imperceptibly, the Age of Affluence silences the voice of duty. The object of the young and the ambitious is no longer fame, honour or service, but cash.

. . . No longer do schools aim at producing brave patriots ready to serve their country. . . . The Arab moralist, Ghazali (1058-1111), complains . . . of the lowering of objectives in the declining Arab world of his time. Students, he says, no longer attend college to acquire learning and virtue, but to obtain those qualifications which will enable them to grow rich. . . .

That which we may call the High Noon of the nation covers the period of transition from the Age of Conquests to the Age of Affluence: the age of Augustus in Rome, that of Harun al-Rashid in Baghdad, of Sulaiman the Magnificent in the Ottoman Empire, or of Queen Victoria in Britain. . . .

All these periods reveal the same characteristics. The immense wealth accumulated in the nation dazzles the onlookers. Enough of the ancient virtues of courage, energy and patriotism survive to enable the state successfully to defend its frontiers. But, beneath the surface, greed for money is gradually replacing duty and public service. Indeed the change might be summarised as being from service to selfishness.

Another outward change which invariably marks the transition from the Age of Conquests to the Age of Affluence is the spread of defensiveness. The nation, immensely rich, is no longer interested in glory or duty, but is only anxious to retain its wealth and its luxury. It is a period of defensiveness, from the Great Wall of China, to Hadrian's Wall on the Scottish Border, to the Maginot Line in France in 1939.

. . . Ample funds are available also for the pursuit of knowledge.

In the eleventh century, the former Arab Empire, then in complete political decline, was ruled by the Seljuk sultan, Malik Shah. The Arabs, no longer soldiers, were still the intellectual leaders of the world. During the reign of Malik Shah, the building of universities and colleges became a passion. Whereas a small number of universities in the great cities had sufficed the years of Arab glory, now a university sprang up in every town.

The Age of Intellect is accompanied by surprising advances in natural science. In the ninth century, . . . the Arabs measured the circumference of the earth with remarkable accuracy. Seven centuries were to pass before Western Europe discovered that the world was not flat. Less than fifty years after the amazing scientific discoveries under Mamun, the Arab Empire collapsed. . . .

. . . When the Mongols conquered Persia in the thirteenth century, they were themselves entirely uneducated and were obliged to depend wholly on native Persian officials to administer the country and to collect the revenue. They retained as wazeer, or Prime Minister, one Rashid al-Din, a historian of international repute. Yet the Prime Minister, when speaking to the

Mongol Il Khan, was obliged to remain throughout the interview on his knees. . . .

One of the oft-repeated phenomena of great empires is the influx of foreigners to the capital city. Roman historians often complain of the number of Asians and Africans in Rome. Baghdad, in its prime in the ninth century, was international in its population—Persians, Turks, Arabs, Armenians, Egyptians, Africans and Greeks mingled in its streets.

. . . While the empire is enjoying its High Noon of prosperity, all these people are proud and glad to be imperial citizens. But when decline sets in, it is extraordinary how the memory of ancient wars, perhaps centuries before, is suddenly revived, and local or provincial movements appear demanding secession or independence. . . .

Frivolity is the frequent companion of pessimism. . . . The Roman mob, we have seen, demanded free meals and public games. Gladiatorial shows, chariot races and athletic events were their passion. In the Byzantine Empire the rivalries of the Greens and the Blues in the hippodrome attained the importance of a major crisis.

The heroes of declining nations are always the same—the athlete, the singer or the actor. . . .

The works of the contemporary historians of Baghdad in the early tenth century are still available. They deeply deplored the degeneracy of the times in which they lived, emphasising particularly the indifference to religion, the increasing materialism and the laxity of sexual morals. They lamented also the corruption of the officials of the government and the fact that politicians always seemed to amass large fortunes while they were in office.

The historians commented bitterly on the extraordinary influence acquired by popular singers over young people, resulting in a decline in sexual morality. The 'pop' singers of Baghdad accompanied their erotic songs on the lute, an instrument resembling the modern guitar. In the second half of the tenth century, as a result, much obscene sexual language came increasingly into use, such as would not have been tolerated in an earlier age. . . .

An increase in the influence of women in public life has often been associated with national decline. The later Romans complained that, although Rome ruled the world, women ruled Rome. In the tenth century, a similar tendency was observable in the Arab Empire, the women demanding admission to the professions hitherto monopolised by men. 'What,' wrote the contemporary historian, Ibn Bessam, 'have the professions of clerk, tax-collector or preacher to do with women? These occupations have always been limited to men alone.' Many women practised law, while others obtained posts as university professors. . . .

Soon after this period, government and public order collapsed, and foreign invaders overran the country. The resulting increase in confusion and violence made it unsafe for women to move unescorted in the streets, with the result that this feminist movement collapsed.

The people of the great nations of the past seem normally to have imagined that their pre-eminence would last for ever. Rome appeared to its citizens to be destined to be for all time the mistress of the world. The Abbasid Khalifs of Baghdad declared that God had appointed them to rule mankind until the day of judgement. . . .

The belief that their nation would rule the world forever, naturally encouraged the citizens of the leading nation of any period to attribute their pre-eminence to hereditary virtues. They carried in their blood, they believed, qualities which constituted them a race of supermen, an illusion which inclined them to the employment of cheap foreign labour (or slaves) to perform menial tasks and to engage foreign mercenaries to fight their battles or to sail their ships.

History, however, seems to suggest that the age of decline of a great nation is often a period which shows a tendency to philanthropy and to sympathy for other races. . . .

State assistance to the young and the poor was equally generous [in the Arab Empire of Baghdad]. University students received government grants to cover their expenses while they were receiving higher education. The State likewise offered free medical treatment to the poor. The first free public hospital was opened in Baghdad in the reign of Harun al-Rashid (786-809), and under his son, Mamun, free public hospitals sprang up all over the Arab world from Spain to what is now Pakistan.

The impression that it will always be automatically rich causes the declining empire to spend lavishly on its own benevolence, until such time as the economy collapses, the universities are closed and the hospitals fall into ruin.

In due course, selfishness permeated the community, the coherence of which was weakened until disintegration was threatened. Then, as we have seen, came the period of pessimism with the accompanying spirit of frivolity and sensual indulgence, by-products of despair. It was inevitable at such times that men should look back yearningly to the days of 'religion', when the spirit of self-sacrifice was still strong enough to make men ready to give and to serve, rather than to snatch.

In this manner, at the height of vice and frivolity the seeds of religious revival are quietly sown. . . .

It is of interest to note that decadence is the disintegration of a system, not of its individual members. The habits of the members of the community have been corrupted by the enjoyment of too much money and too much power for too long a period. The result has been, in the framework of their national life, to make them selfish and idle. A community of selfish and idle people declines, internal quarrels develop in the division of its dwindling wealth, and pessimism follows, which some of them endeavour to drown in sensuality or frivolity. . . .

Decadence is a moral and spiritual disease, resulting from too long a period of wealth and power, producing cynicism, decline of religion, pessimism and frivolity. . . .

It has been shown that, normally, the rise and fall of great nations are due to internal reasons alone. Ten generations of human beings suffice to transform the hardy and enterprising pioneer into the captious citizen of the welfare state. . . .

Perhaps, . . . the successive rise and fall of great nations is inevitable and, indeed, a system divinely ordained. But [to know] even this would be an immense gain. For we should know where we stand in relation to our human brothers and sisters. . . . If we could accept these great movements as beyond our control, there would be no excuse for our hating one another because of them.

Glubb examines eleven great nations and identifies their tenure as empires. Table 3 comes from "The Fate of Empires."

By identifying the Roman Republic and the Roman Empire as separate epochs, Glubb thus acknowledges each as an independent ten-generation cycle, but he seems to miss the implications of this division. As Glubb views a completed 250-year cycle as final, nonrecurring, he overlooks the possibility that there can be more than one ten-generation cycle in each empire or great nation.

Table 3. Eleven Great Nations

The Nation	Dates of Rise and Fall	Duration in Years
Assyria	859-612 B.C.	247
Persia (Cyrus and his descendants)	538-330 B.C.	208
Greece (Alexander and his successors)	331-100 B.C.	231
Roman Republic	260-27 B.C.	233
Roman Empire	27 B.C.-A.D. 180	207
Arab Empire	A.D. 634-880	246
Mameluke Empire	1250-1517	267
Ottoman Empire	1320-1570	250
Spain	1500-1750	250
Romanov Russia	1682-1916	234
Britain	1700-1950	250

⚜ ⚜ ⚜ ⚘ ⚘ ⚘

We can apply Glubb's ten-generation cycle throughout history. We can assume that nomads who subjugated affluent, established civilizations were dominant because of their aggressive conquests. As time passed, the conquerors became affluent and sedentary. Dominance levels in the population waned. Their cities were overrun by a more dominant, vigorous, less affluent group—often other nomads. So the cycle repeated itself.

Nomads became horsemen around 3500 B.C. Some of the earliest were mentioned by the Greeks and Chinese as Scythians (identified by some historians as the first horsemen), Sarmatians, Yueh-chih, and Hsiung-nu.

The Scythians supposedly moved from the Volga basin to the southern Russian steppes around 700 B.C. and conquered the occupying Cimmerians. They abandoned their nomadic ways, settled in cities, and became affluent. Herodotus identified four major Scythian tribes: the Auchatae, the Catiari, the Paralatae, and the Traspians. Ten generations later, between 500 and 400 B.C., their power and empire peaked.

In 346 B.C. another group of nomadic horsemen, the neighboring Sarmatians, crossed the Don River and overran Scythian territory. High dominance in Sarmatian women can be concluded because they fought alongside the men. As Herodotus notes of them, "No girl shall wed till she has killed a man in battle."

Glubb's six stages of growth and decline fit many civilizations, among them Etruria. The Roman historian Livy, writing around the time of Christ, recalls that, "Etruria filled the whole length of Italy with the noise of her name." The Etruscan civilization emerged around 750 B.C. with abrupt evidences of a new people in central Italy who built cities rather than the primitive villages of earlier times.

The empire peaked around 500 B.C., ten generations after its entrance on the world stage. The Etruscans directly controlled or exerted a major influence over northern Italy from south of Venice on the Adriatic Sea to the Tyrrhenian Sea. Their territory included much of the Po Valley and the center of the peninsula from the Apennines westward.

The Etruscans lost power gradually. After becoming affluent, Etruria's commercial ventures at home and abroad began to fail. Accelerating class conflicts added social problems to a major business decline. Weakened, Etruria began to succumb to the more vigorous citizens of Rome. Veii, "the wealthiest city in Etruria" according to Livy, fell to the Romans in 396 B.C. Etruria allied itself with Rome to survive against other intruders, but that did not suffice. The Etruscans disappeared as a civilization.

Etruscan soothsayers foretold that the empire's prominence would last ten *saecula* (Etruscan centuries). If a *saeculum* consisted of one hundred years, the prophecy was in error. These empire builders are not alone in misjudging the longevity of their civilization. Adolf

Hitler promised a thousand-year Reich for Nazi Germany. Great Britain's adoption of Rudyard Kipling's "Take up the White Man's burden" (although a misinterpretation of Kipling's meaning) is a burden it no longer assumes. On the wane is the United States' dedication to John Louis O'Sullivan's "Our manifest destiny." The Soviet Union's course based on Karl Marx and Friedrich Engels' *Communist Manifesto* and its "Abolition of private property" is also doomed to failure.

China is often viewed by Westerners as having been one long, stable civilization until the change to communism. Its dynasties were independent epochs, however, each with its own cycle. Four of the last five dynasties approximate Glubb's ten-generation span: the T'ang, 289 years; the Sung, 319 years; the Ming, 276 years; and the Ch'ing (Manchu), 267 years.

Parallels have been drawn between the emergence of Napoleon and of Hitler. In the popular short-term view, the beginning of Hitler's dictatorship signaled a new Germany that ended with World War II, and Napoleon and France constituted a parallel. However, using a ten-generation perspective, Hitler and Napoleon signaled the early stages of new, recurring ten-generation cycles. Their attempts at world domination represented the Age of Conquests in cycles unfolding in Germany and France.

During the reign (1643-1715) of Louis XIV, the Sun King, France led the world as an intellectual and cultural center. France's Age of Decadence began during this period, accelerated, then ended with the Revolution of 1789. The stage was set for Napoleon, who began his rule of France in 1799 as a member of the Consulate, as part of a new cycle.

Germany was little different, following in France's footsteps some 135 years later when Hitler came to power. From the late 1800s until 1916, Germany was the world's leading intellectual and cultural center. Several outstanding American universities were modeled after German educational institutions of that period. Few would disagree that Germany also became the most decadent nation in the Western world from that time into the 1920s.

Germany is now well into its current ten-generation cycle. Its Age of Conquests under Hitler failed, but it is succeeding in its Age of

Commerce. Still to come are its Ages of Affluence, Intellect, and Decadence.

Japan is no stranger to ten-generation cycles and their seemingly inevitable sequences. The Muromachi (or Ashikaga) shogunate began with the acclaimed Kemmu restoration (Age of Outburst) in 1333. The new shogunate was in every sense a military dictatorship to reform a country out of control. Near the end of the cycle, from 1583 to 1598, the countrywide Taikō land survey was conducted. The ensuing exorbitant taxes reduced the farmers to rural serfdom, exploited prisoners of the land. Decadence, corruption, and civil disorders followed in the final phase of the cycle. After ten generations (267 years) the failure of aggressions against Korea in 1592 and in 1597 contributed to the cycle's end in 1600.

Japan's next and most recently completed cycle followed the same course. In 1600 Tokugawa Ieyasu established his military rule nationally by winning the Battle of Sekigahara, which involved all daimyo in the country. Thus began the ten-generation (267 years) Tokugawa shogunate. The Age of Outburst started with the establishment of Ieyasu's Edo *bakufu* with its sweeping social restructuring. (The *bakufu*, literally, "tent headquarters" was an adaptation of a system Shogun Yoritomo created some four centuries earlier to govern his warrior vassals.) In the latter half of the seventeenth century, commercial activities expanded. Industry was promoted and cities were developed. Later, as in ten-generation cycles throughout history, Japanese artistic expression flowered; masterpieces were created in the fine arts and crafts. Still later, the same progression occurred in scholarship during the Age of Intellect. Coincidental with the weakening of the *bakuhan* system, dramatic new movements took place in advanced learning. Additionally, the study of European modern sciences spread, from medicine to military technology.

As with all ten-generation cycles, the latter days of the epoch proved remarkably similar to the close of Japan's previous cycle. Besides the usual economic stagnation, government corruption, villainy, and venality which signaled the end, there was also a great famine. Rural uprisings and city riots reached unprecedented peaks. Along with domestic problems, foreign pressures increased. Near the end of the cycle, from 1841 to 1843, the chief senior councillor, Mizuno Tadakuni, instituted massive government reforms to cope with chaotic conditions. The reforms failed. One generation later in 1867 it was all over. Even though the cast of characters, the good and the bad players, had changed from the previous epoch, the span and general course had not. Another ten-generation cycle had come and gone.

Eighteen sixty-eight initiated Japan's current ten-generation cycle. Its Age of Outburst started that year with the Meiji rule and restoration, whose authority reestablished law and order. The new rule ended the rural insurrections, city havoc and rioting, and corruption by government officials. The Age of Conquests began in 1894 with the Sino-Japanese War, giving Japan control of Formosa, the Pescadores Islands, and the Liaotung Peninsula with its Port Arthur naval base. It ended in 1945 with the country's surrender in World War II. Japan is reaping the rewards of its Age of Commerce and is approaching its Age of Affluence. In 1988, in this present cycle, the Japanese are undoubtedly nearer to their future Ages of Intellect and Decadence than to their Meiji beginning 120 years ago.

ᴎᴇ ᴎᴇ ᴎᴇ ᴚ ᴚ ᴚ

Glubb portrays the beginning (outburst) to the end (decadence) of a great nation's cycle as encompassing ten generations, 250 years. A human generation includes those born and living at approximately the same time. The time span of a generation is the period from the birth of a mother to an average of her age at the birth of each child. Thus, a generation easily varies from thirteen to forty-five years, the approximate limits of child-bearing age. An average generation for ancient man might have been as short as seventeen years if the first birth occurred at age thirteen and the last at age twenty-one.

A twenty-five-year span is used in this book to denote a generation and to distinguish each birth generation of individuals growing up at the same time. For centuries, twenty-five years has been deemed the length of a generation.

The accomplishing age of individuals can also be termed a generation. An accomplishing generation is the twenty-five-year span during which the group members are age thirty-six through sixty. This age group consistently makes the greatest contributions to a country's growth, improvement, well-being, and change. There are exceptions of course; contributions of consequence are made by individuals under thirty-six and over sixty. Nonetheless, the most changes, good or bad, in any given twenty-five-year period come from the thirty-six through sixty age group.

With that in mind, two different generations are always in focus: the birth generation of those through age twenty-five and the accomplishing generation, those age thirty-six through sixty.

In terms of maximum earning potential, scientific discoveries, and other individual achievements, the twenty-five-year period from age thirty-six through sixty becomes more meaningful and fitting than any other twenty-five year grouping. This can be somewhat confusing as members of the same accomplishing generation belong to different birth generations.

ᘐᘐᘐᘐᘐᘐ

History can be observed from an entirely different perspective by accounting dominance levels (especially of the accomplishing generations) the principal cause of the cyclical course of empires. Empires expand and prosper when overall dominance levels are high. Conversely, lower overall dominance levels combined with affluence are a major contributing factor to their decline. The dominance trait can be considered not only in studying the birth, rise, and decline of past cultures but also when analyzing present large societies. The overall dominance levels of a country can be measured by the amount of achievement and leadership that its people demonstrate.

By studying the ebb and flow of dominance in great modern nations from the standpoint of their six cyclical stages, we can determine the rise and fall of civilizations more closely than if forecasting without considering the dominance trait. We can use specific types of events to determine the beginning and ending dates of each stage. Such information proves useful in comparing cycles of coexistent great nations. World events affect all, but each nation responds differently depending on the stage of progress it occupies.

The Age of Outburst begins when a major occurrence or chain of events produces a discernible, continuing change in the economic or political direction of a country. A dramatic redirection of the country's aims and interests signals the end of this Age.

The start of the Age of Conquests may be marked by the year in which the country first gains control over a foreign power and reaps the spoils thereof. The country holds to a doctrine of intervention or conquest throughout this Age, whether at war or temporarily at peace. The Age of Conquests ends when the country voluntarily ceases to use force of arms to gain spoils or control, or when a war ends in defeat rather than victory.

The Age of Commerce may be determined by looking at the pattern of export-import ratios. It begins when the country's sales of domestic goods consistently exceed its purchases of foreign goods, and ends when purchases of foreign goods consistently exceed sales to foreign markets.

The Age of Affluence begins when a country becomes significantly wealthier than other great nations. The Age ends when the country's wealth is greatly diminished or exhausted.

The advent of the Age of Intellect may be marked by an enormous increase in the opening of new institutions of higher learning. Another indicator is the world prominence given to the intellectual achievements of the accomplishing generations. The end comes with the closing of large numbers of colleges and universities in conjunction with the aging or death of the accomplishing generation of that particular era. Without their achievements, an ongoing decrease in the country's overall intellect becomes apparent.

The Age of Decadence commences with sudden macroscopic changes in morals and values that are clearly evident to all. As the Age continues, less visible changes progressively weaken the social fabric. At its end, force and repression may be used to stem major civil disorders, or the country may be overrun by foreign invaders.

Such indicators are useful in observing the course of a great nation. The following chapters will consider the ten-generation cycle in the United States, first, its Ages of Outburst, Conquests, and Commerce, all of which are deemed to have ended. Discussions of the Ages of Affluence, Intellect, and Decadence, still in progress, follow in separate chapters.

For simplicity's sake, single years are used to mark beginning and ending dates of the various Ages, the years having been selected in accordance with an event that generally indicates each Age, but other choices of date and event might prove equally valid. In any case, the period each Age encompasses is far more significant than its exact beginning or ending date; it is not specific years but general trends that matter. The recognition of such trends, combined with consideration of the dominance trait, helps promote understanding of the society in which one lives.

Chapter XIV

The Ages of Outburst (Pioneers), Conquests, and Commerce

To analyze the Age of Outburst in the United States, a starting date is needed. 1776? That year of the signing of the Declaration of Independence represents the nation's political birth. But the fight for independence had already begun at Lexington and Concord in 1775. The First Continental Congress convened at Philadelphia in 1774, and demonstrations against British controls included the Boston Tea Party in 1773, protesting one form of taxation. Colonials were wounded and killed by British troops at the Boston Massacre in 1770. The social and cultural makeup of the United States was firmly established before any of these dates. So what is the earliest date for American society as it currently exists?

The year 1763 is a logical beginning date for the United States as a country. Two events that year precipitated a change in perspective concerning the thirteen colonies by the British Crown and the colonists.

One was the Treaty of Paris ending the French and Indian War, an extension of the European Seven Years' War in which the colonists fought on behalf of Great Britain. The war was the last stand taken by the colonists for the British.

The second was the British Proclamation of 1763 drawing an absolute, map-marked boundary beyond which any further westward movement by British subjects was prohibited. The colonies had been individually created and colonized through royal grants and each was subject to royal rule. In most cases, they had been treated as separate entities by British political and private agencies. By setting forth one boundary for all, the Proclamation of 1763 recognized and treated the thirteen colonies as a single unit. Thus 1763 is considered here to be the date of origin of the country as we know it today.

Table 4 sets forth the birth generations for the United States since 1763.

With 1763 as the de facto beginning of the United States, 1988 became the first year of its tenth birth generation. Table 5 summarizes the sixth through the tenth birth generations and the eighth through the tenth accomplishing generations, completing a ten-generation period (250 years) for the United States.

Table 6, which identifies United States Presidents by accomplishing generations, indicates, often dramatically, differences in national priorities and the quality of presidential leadership from one accomplishing generation to the next. Significant differences also appear between the administrations that begin and end each presidential accomplishing generation, such as between Theodore Roosevelt and Herbert Hoover, and in time John Kennedy and George Bush. Perhaps the differences result more from cyclical timing than quality of leadership.

The Age of Outburst (Pioneers) started in 1763 and continued for 127 years. The sheer size of the sparsely populated New World made America's Age of Outburst exceedingly long compared to those of previous empires. Many Americans view this period, covering the first five birth generations, as the country's most heroic. The era of the tribulations of America's settlers remains one of the nation's most heralded. The outburst of initiative and pioneering effort fired

Table 4. Birth Generations - 1988

(1738-1762 - Last British Colonial)

Born	Generation
1763-1787	First
1788-1812	Second
1813-1837	Third
1838-1862	Fourth
1863-1887	Fifth
1888-1912	Sixth
1913-1937	Seventh
1938-1962	Eighth
1963-1987	Ninth
1988-2012	Tenth

Table 5. Ages of Birth and Accomplishing Generations - 1988

Birth Generation	Current Ages	Years of Birth
Tenth	First birth year	1988 through 2012
Ninth	1 through 24	1963 through 1987
Eighth	25 through 49	1938 through 1962
Seventh	50 through 74	1913 through 1937
Sixth	75 through 99	1888 through 1912

Accomplishing Generation	Current Ages	Years of Birth
Tenth	13 through 37	1952 through 1976
Ninth	38 through 62	1927 through 1951
Eighth	63 through 87	1902 through 1926

Table 6. Presidents of the Unites States, Accomplishing Generations

Accomplishing Generation	Born	Presidents
First	1727-1751	George Washington, John Adams, Thomas Jefferson, James Madison
Second	1752-1776	James Monroe, John Quincy Adams, Andrew Jackson, Martin Van Buren (born 1782), William Harrison
Third	1777-1801	John Tyler, James Polk, Zachary Taylor, Millard Fillmore, Franklin Pierce (born 1804), James Buchanan
Fourth	1802-1826	Abraham Lincoln, Andrew Johnson, Ulysses Grant, Rutherford Hayes
Fifth	1827-1851	James Garfield, Chester Arthur, Grover Cleveland, Benjamin Harrison, Grover Cleveland (2nd term), William McKinley
Sixth	1852-1876	Theodore Roosevelt, William Taft, Woodrow Wilson, Warren Harding, Calvin Coolidge, Herbert Hoover
Seventh	1877-1901	Franklin Roosevelt, Harry Truman, Dwight Eisenhower
Eighth	1902-1926	John Kennedy, Lyndon Johnson, Richard Nixon, Gerald Ford, James Carter, Ronald Reagan, George Bush
Ninth	1927-1951	
Tenth	1952-1976	

the world's imagination. Thousands of books have extolled the pioneers' magnificent personal accomplishments. Films have immortalized the sung and unsung heroes of the westward movement. Pioneer and western themes dominated television for years. The Age is still revered. Many states, cities, and towns have erected monuments and hold celebrations honoring local founders and heroes from that time.

In 1890 the Superintendent of the Census declared that there was no longer any frontier separating the settled and unsettled parts of the United States. Now the country could concentrate on consolidating its continent-wide holdings. With this, the Age of Outburst (Pioneers) ended.

⚜ ⚜ ⚜ ♫ ♫ ♫

To enter the Age of Conquests, a nation acquires something of substance such as territory, spoils, or control through intervention or conquest. Though the American Revolution gained political freedom for the colonists, they wrested no land or power from Great Britain; they already possessed the land. From the Revolution until the mid-1800s, except for the Indian wars, negotiation and money were used in pursuit of land.

In 1803 the United States purchased the western half of the Mississippi River basin from France. The Louisiana Purchase of 828 thousand square miles was not a conquest but a peaceful acquisition that doubled the country's size.

The War of 1812 culminated with Britain's agreement to refrain from future intervention in United States access to the oceans. It entailed no acquisition of territory or control over any of Great Britain's domains.

Florida was not among the spoils of war. Territorial disputes over the area had continued for years among Spain, France, and England. England traded Havana to Spain for Florida in 1763. Floridian loyalty during the American Revolution mainly favored England. After the Revolution England returned Florida to Spain. The United States was in constant conflict with the Spanish presence alongside American settlers. During the War of 1812, while Spain still owned Florida, General Andrew Jackson captured Pensacola, a British base where the English employed Indians and runaway slaves to harass American settlers in Florida. Spain ceded the disputed territory to the United States by a treaty signed in 1819 and ratified in 1821.

The purchase of Alaska from Russia in 1867 also constituted a peaceful acquisition. Although consummated during the country's Age of Conquests, no force was used; indeed, most citizens believed the United States foolish to spend good gold for bad land. The public ridiculed its prime negotiator, Secretary of State William Seward, referring to the purchase as "Seward's Folly."

The intermittent wars with the American natives yielded conquests and territorial acquisitions. They were directed, on the whole, against individual tribes whose land ownership seemed questionable to the settlers; these wars were not against a nation as such. No common language existed among the Indian tribes, limiting any united effort on their part against the usurping of their lands.

In 1832 the Black Hawk War in Illinois and Wisconsin pushed the Sauk and Fox Indians west across the Mississippi. An eight-year war begun in 1835 (Second Seminole War) with the Florida Seminoles resulted in their being sent to Oklahoma. An 1864 battle at Sand Creek in southeastern Colorado Territory left nine American soldiers dead; more than four hundred Indian men, women, and children were killed while awaiting surrender terms. General George A. Custer and 264 soldiers of the 7th Cavalry died at the Battle of the Little Big Horn in 1876 during the Sioux Indian War. The Apache Indian leader Geronimo surrendered in 1886. In 1890 at the Battle of Wounded Knee, South Dakota, about thirty American soldiers and more than two hundred Indian men, women, and children died. That was the last major conflict between United States troops and native Indians.

The Age of Conquests began in 1846 with the Mexican War. This was the first conflict in which the United States acquired territory and spoils. Although the United States paid Mexico $15 million and assumed $3 million in American claims at the signing of the Treaty of Guadalupe Hidalgo on February 2, 1848, the conquest netted almost half of what had been Mexican territory. Mexico ceded claims to what are now Arizona, California, Nevada, Utah, and parts of Colorado, New Mexico, and Wyoming. (In 1845, before the war began, the nation resolved the question of Texas, then a Republic, by annexation.)

Other foreign interventions occurred after the war with Mexico. On July 8, 1853, Commodore Matthew C. Perry, determined to alter Japan's policy of isolation, entered the fortified harbor of Uraga, Japan, with four ships. The Japanese reluctantly received Perry, thus stalling for time to build the country's defenses. In February 1854 Perry reappeared with nine ships in what is now Tokyo Bay. That threat ended on March 31 with a treaty between the two countries opening Japan to United States trading. Japan was a weakened and decadent nation near the end of its ten-generation cycle; the 267-year Tokugawa Regime ended thirteen years after Perry's second visit.

On March 20, 1896, in a situation destined to replay itself, Marines landed in Nicaragua to protect United States property during a revolution.

At Havana, Cuba, on February 15, 1898, the American battleship Maine was blown up with 260 fatalities. The United States blockaded Cuba on April 22, and Spain declared war two days later. The United States destroyed the Spanish fleet in the Philippines on May 1 and captured Guam on June 20. Puerto Rico was taken between July 25 and August 12. On December 10, 1898, Spain agreed to cede the Philippines, Puerto Rico, and Guam to the United States and to approve Cuban independence; the United States agreed to pay $20 million to Spain for the Philippines.

In 1900 the United States helped suppress the Boxer Rebellion in China. (The then-decadent Manchu dynasty, which began in 1644, ended its ten-generation cycle eleven years later.) In 1914 an American blockade of Veracruz supported Mexican revolutionaries. On July 28, 1915, American troops landed in Haiti and, by treaty two months later, the country became a virtual United States protectorate. During 1916 General John J. Pershing entered Mexico to pursue Francisco (Pancho) Villa, who had raided United States border areas. That same year, the United States established a military government in the Dominican Republic. Some one thousand Marines landed in China in 1927 to protect American property during Chinese civil unrest.

The Marines landed in Nicaragua in 1927 to protect American lives and property. (Marines had been sent there in 1896 to protect United States property and again in 1912 when the country defaulted on American and European loans.) The 1927 intervention gave the United States effective control of Nicaragua for fifty-two years. Control finally ended with the 1979 Sandinista overthrow of Anastasio Somoza Debayle whose father, Anastasio Somoza Garcia, had been the United States' hand-picked dictator during its 1927 intervention.

The Age of Conquests continued for eighty-seven years, three and one-half generations, ending in 1933 when the Marines returned from Nicaragua. This was the last incident constituting conquest or sovereign control by the United States government.

Before, during, and after the Age of Conquests, there were other wars and conflicts in which the United States netted no spoils, territory, or control. In 1798, with forty-five ships and 365 privateers, the Navy captured eighty-four French ships after French raids on American shipping and France's rejection of United States diplomats. In 1801 Tripoli declared war when the United States refused to pay added tribute to Arab pirates. (America had bought peace from Algiers and Tunis in 1795 with $800 thousand, a ship, and an annual tribute of $25 thousand.) Land and naval defeats forced Tripoli to bargain for peace four years later.

Although important factors in the country's development, the American Civil War, World Wars I and II, the Korean conflict, and the Vietnam War produced no new territories or spoils of war for the nation.

In contrast, World War II netted the Soviet Union a huge amount of territory (some of which had been its pre-World War I domain) during its Age of Conquests. Secretary General Stalin insisted that a second front be opened in western Europe; President Roosevelt of the United States and Prime Minister Churchill of Great Britain finally agreed. This action allowed Stalin to "liberate" eastern Europe. He established procommunist "peoples' democracies" in Albania, Bulgaria, Hungary, Poland, Romania, and the Soviet-occupied zone in eastern Germany. North Korea came under Soviet domination in 1945 when the country was divided after Japanese rule ended. Stalin took over Czechoslovakia in 1948 with an internal procommunist revolution.

America's Age of Conquests was long in years but short on conquests and blood spilled compared to the conquests of earlier empires and superpowers. Many United States detractors cry imperialism at every turn, even as concerns American participation in World Wars I and II. Heroic actions in far-flung places, either to assist nations under attack or to defend the United States, are unappreciated by most of the world.

During the Age of Outburst (Pioneers), the United States lauded pioneering efforts. Few found fault with the eradication of the "heathen" Indians. When the Indians lost, the pioneers viewed the battles as victories; when the Indians won, the pioneers tended to call them massacres. The dominance of the pioneers prevailed. During that Age, actions by American citizens and their government appeared correct, proper, and justified to most of the population, and they were regarded in the same way during the Age of Conquests as well. Other countries involved in their comparable ages probably received the same approval and support from their citizens.

⊰⊱ ⊰⊱ ⊰⊱ ♩ ♩ ♩

A prime cause of the Age of Commerce as well as of the Ages of Outburst and Conquests was the favorable balance of dominance in the population. High dominance levels, with needs to achieve and control, were present in both the birth and accomplishing generations during the Ages of Outburst and Conquests, and favorable ratios continued in the Age of Commerce's accomplishing generations.

Population dominance levels affect the success or failure of one country's commerce relative to that of another. The percentages of dominance and nondominance in the adult population are identifiable in each country. These percentages fluctuate year to year, decade to decade, and generation to generation. Although overall dominance levels continually fluctuate on a nationwide basis, annual changes are usually insignificant; changes, if measured, would be easier to detect between generations.

Variables such as the form of government, the importance of social classes, the absence or presence of affluence, religion, educational and job opportunities, and migrations and immigrations are relevant to changing ratios of dominance and nondominance. Nevertheless the dominance and nondominance ratios in a population fundamentally are determined by the numbers of children born to dominant and nondominant mothers and, acknowledged or not, at any given time each nation has definite ratios of dominant and nondominant individuals.

As a civilization progresses, commercial enterprise becomes an enlightened method of putting to work the high dominance levels of individuals, groups of dominant persons, or countries with large numbers of such people. Pioneers often reflect high dominance in their desires for freedom and personal gain, and in high-risk behavior. Similar characteristics are found in those who direct their efforts toward warfare and conquest. During conquest recognizable personality traits such as assertiveness, arrogance, aggressiveness, and belligerence overlap dominance; needs to achieve and to control others are fulfilled by conquest and the acquisition of territory.

Sublimation redirects the more negative aspects of the dominance trait from a detrimental goal toward one of a higher social, moral, or aesthetic nature. Creating outstanding art constitutes aesthetic sublimation in some dominant, aggressive individuals. (Michelangelo and Van Gogh provide two distinctive examples.) Releasing such tendencies in antisocial activities causes mayhem.

Karl Menninger writes of sublimating the aggressive instinct in *Love Against Hate*, "The boy who wanted to chop off his little brother's head becomes a surgeon." The world's greatest surgeons are dominant and aggressive with needs to cut. Sublimation directs such inclinations toward surgical skills, not only furnishing the surgeon with psychological and monetary compensations but providing society with lifesaving rewards. "Sublimation," according to Karl Menninger, "is always a compromise; it is better to love than to sublimate but better to sublimate than to hate." So it is with sublimating dominance and aggressiveness to commerce instead of war.

The dominance trait and its personality components do not change from one age to another—as from the Age of Conquests to the Age of Commerce. Human nature remains the same; the change is in its focus. Enlightenment, much of which comes about through educational advances (often reinforced by religion), redirects dominant, aggressive tendencies; one such redirection leads to the field of commerce. Behavioral patterns stemming from the dominance trait (assertiveness, arrogance, aggressiveness, leadership, risk-taking, and the drive to attain freedom and control) can be guided. With sublimation, dominant individuals can direct their aggressive actions into commerce and bring about results far more acceptable and beneficial to society than are war and conquest.

The economic successes attributed to the Protestant ethic, later called the Protestant work ethic, provide examples of the sublimation of dominance into commerce. The Protestant ethic was first espoused by Max Weber in 1904-05 in *The Protestant Ethic and the Spirit of Capitalism*, but the precepts of the Protestant work ethic began with Martin Luther early in the sixteenth century.

Martin Luther appears to have been reared by a highly dominant mother. By today's standards she seems extremely harsh, beating him unmercifully for the smallest infraction of her rules and terrifying him with stories of demons.

On October 31, 1517, Martin Luther, a professor of theology at the University of Wittenberg, and Johann Schneider, another Augustinian monk, nailed the Ninety-Five Theses to the door at the entrance to Castle Church. The Theses begin, "Out of love and zeal for the elucidation of truth, the following theses will be debated at Wittenberg, the Reverend Father Martin Luther, Master of Arts and Sacred Theology, presiding." Not particularly startling or inflammatory nor meant as a gesture of defiance, these words ignited the Protestant Reformation.

The bulk of the Ninety-Five Theses centered on the sale of indulgences, forgiveness and expiation of sins with limited penances, by Church representatives. Martin Luther's wrath focused primarily on Johann Tetzel, a Dominican with long experience in these sales. Even though he was said to use unscrupulous methods, Tetzel raised large sums of money for the Church. He maintained that neither repentance nor confession, only money, was essential to acquire written indulgences. When Luther criticized some of his parishioners for their wickedness and refused to let them receive communion, they showed him their indulgence letters overriding his authority. Luther believed the whole concept of indulgences needed clarification and should be debated, hence the Ninety-Five Theses.

The Church could have placated or accommodated Luther but instead straddled the issue. While reprimanding the sellers of indulgences for their actions, the Church also attempted to restrict Luther.

The newly invented printing press made copies of the Ninety-Five Theses available to the general public, helping turn the issue into a public controversy. Protestantism was born.

From its inception and primarily because of Luther's assertion that religion was a spiritual relationship between God and sinful man, Protestantism emphasized personal Bible study and interpretation. In contrast to the Roman Catholic tradition in which the clergy interpreted the teachings of Christ and the Latin Bible for the laity, Protestant leaders expected their followers to read the Bible to develop a deeper understanding of their religious responsibilities.

Protestants of all denominations united in their efforts to learn the Bible. The Bible was translated into modern languages, and printing presses made it possible for almost any Protestant household to own one. Copies were distributed to as many ministers and laymen as possible. Since many people could not read, Protestantism deserves some credit for the modern push for worldwide literacy.

Protestantism expected and encouraged women to read and study the Bible. Learning to read was an important step forward for Protestant women, not available to most of their Roman Catholic counterparts. During the first three hundred years of the Protestant Reformation, Bibles became standard Protestant household items and were read by both sexes. This opportunity for personal control would have appealed to dominant women; it gave them a chance to achieve by learning to read and later by teaching their children. Only within the past hundred years (four generations) has society deemed education necessary for women regardless of faith.

The Bible was the only book in many homes. Its teachings, passed down from one generation to the next, mother to child, were an integral part of each generation's upbringing. Even though the mother rarely received any education beyond the Bible, often that sufficed to direct her thinking toward education and learning for her children, not only her sons, but in some degree her daughters.

The German sociologist Max Weber was reared by a Calvinist mother who maintained a Puritan morality in dealing with her children. In *The Protestant Ethic and the Spirit of Capitalism*, Weber presents the theory that modern capitalism resulted from the Calvinistic concern for moral obligation and economic success. Calvinism viewed worldly achievement as a sign of election to salvation and strongly encouraged professional success. At the same time, Calvinism forbade the enjoyment of material gains; profits were to be used to achieve continually increasing levels of success. Protestants viewed the linking of Protestantism, capitalism, and economic success favorably.

The idea behind the phrase the Protestant ethic gained wide acceptance. Protestant male successes, past and contemporary, were often attributed to the concept. Dominance derived from the child-rearing practices of the mother was never considered as a source. Dominant Protestant mothers produced many dominant children; for generations the Protestant birth rate equaled or exceeded that of Roman Catholics in England, the United States, and European countries. Jewish families equaled or exceeded Protestant families in number of children. (The relatively low Protestant and Jewish birth rates today are not religiously mandated but are cultural, resulting primarily from affluence.)

Sons succeeded primarily because of the dominance trait, environmentally created and transmitted from mother to child. Dominant daughters also achieved by producing dominant children. Although high dominance levels can be deduced from the accomplishments of successful men, dominance was not as easily discernible in women since they lacked achievement opportunities outside the home.

The expression Protestant ethic is now relegated to the past and Protestant work ethic is being replaced with simply the work ethic. All three phrases could be misnomers. In the term the Japanese work ethic, not a religious but a nationalist connection is made; it undoubtedly is as misnamed as the Protestant work ethic. Both emanate from dominant people with great needs to achieve, those reared by dominant mothers. Perhaps the *dominance work ethic* is a more apt description.

A high dominance level is traceable as the cause of successful commercial activity not only in the recent past but also in early civilizations. The prehistoric golden age of Scandinavia around 2000 B.C. developed as the area's climate changed, as warm then as southern France is now. With their mastery of the waters and their seafaring tradition, the Scandinavians promoted trade between northern and southern Europe. They developed a sea trade in amber, furs, and bronze weapons and ornaments. The opulent gold and bronze burial accouterments of their princes during that period attest to Scandinavian successes.

Findings from 1700 B.C. indicate that the Minoan (Cretan) civilization in the Aegean was a great trading nation, as was the later Mycenaean culture, and still later Classical Greece. Perhaps the greatest of all early commercial traders were the Phoenicians. They built few major cities but, during their journeys around 1100-900 B.C., spread what became the modern alphabet across the Mediterranean to Greece.

In more modern times, Great Britain's international trading exploits surpassed those of the world's earlier trade giants. The Industrial Revolution, begun in the mid-1700s, was capitalized on and spread worldwide by dominant British traders. Because of diminishing dominance levels in the population, Britain occupies a lesser role in world trade today. A comparison by the International Monetary Fund in 1985 concluded that the average Briton had a poorer status than did the average Italian. Today's great trading countries are Japan, the Federal Republic of Germany, and the United States.

High dominance levels in a large percentage of the population probably occurred in all great civilizations. Their sublimation into commerce moved the societies away from warfare and conquest to the more socially acceptable activities of trade. As commercial battle-grounds became more rewarding to a greater number of its achievement-oriented citizens, a society benefited by widening its sphere of economic influence and increasing its overall wealth.

🙰 🙰 🙰 🙰 🙰 🙰

Such enlightenment, or sublimation into commerce, by dominant individuals in the United States did not take place on a broad scale until 1874. The change spanned several generations. The Age of Commerce overlapped the Age of Outburst for sixteen years from 1874 through 1890 (the end of that Age). Another fifty-nine years after 1874 were required to complete the transition from conquest to commerce. With the end of the Age of Conquest in 1933, the nation gained full commercial maturity. The time span, the generations involved, and the overlapping of myriad endeavors served to hide the sublimation process.

The dry statistics of international commerce, domestic goods sold to foreign countries and foreign goods purchased, become more meaningful when viewed as the result of sublimating dominance into nonviolent competition. Commercial trading activities are competitive. There are winners and losers. Successful competitors view commerce as winning or losing battles and even wars in the marketplace. Individuals, companies, and countries are judged by the thousands of large and small daily battles of commercial adventures and misadventures. These contests are fought by dominant individuals against other businessmen. Sometimes the fight includes governmental assistance in the form of subsidies to companies engaged primarily in international sales.

Countries with large populations that have a high percentage of dominant individuals are the overall winners in international trade competition. Wins and losses become commercial statistics in ranking the year-to-year competitive struggles by dominant groups in different countries. They compete to better themselves individually, and that benefits the country as a whole.

Record-keeping of export-import statistics began in 1790 for United States international trading activities. Figure 1 presents percentage statistics for 1790 through 1988.

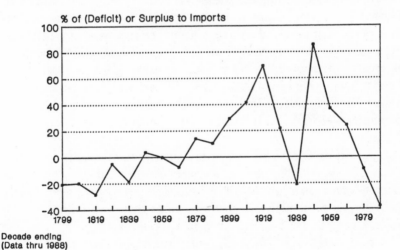

Figure 1. U.S. Trade Balance,
1790 through 1988, Relative Surplus (Deficit)

The first decade's activities, 1790 through 1799, reflected nine consecutive years in which imports exceeded exports with imports and exports being equal in 1799. The trade deficit averaged 20.4 percent for the ten years.

The next decade, 1800-1809, closely resembled the previous one with ten straight years of trade deficits averaging 19.6 percent.

The 1810-1819 decade contained only two years in which the country sold more goods to foreign countries than it purchased. For the remainder of the decade, the United States was a net importer of foreign goods, creating annual trading deficits from a low of 11.1 percent in 1817 to highs of 49.4 percent in 1812 during the war with Great Britain, and 53.1 percent in 1815 in the war's aftermath. The average trade deficit for the decade was 28.1 percent.

The next decade, 1820-1829, showed more balance in the export-to-import ratio. For seven years there was a virtual stand-off in surpluses and deficits with a less than 1 percent annual difference. The remaining three years had trade deficits; the deficit average that decade was trimmed to 5 percent, the lowest to that date.

The decade of 1830-1839 produced an unfavorable trading record. The average annual deficit for the ten-year period was 18.5 percent.

The 1840-1849 decade was similar to that of 1820-1829. It was the most favorable trading decade in the country's history to date. In four of the ten years there were differences, plus or minus, of less than 3 percent annually. Positive trading activity was established in 1840 and 1843 with surpluses of 23.4 percent and 29.2 percent. This became the country's first surplus trade decade, at 3.7 percent.

The following decade, 1850-1859, showed six years of surpluses and four years of deficits. Imports for the decade were $2.739 billion and exports were $2.736 billion, a virtual match between purchases and sales.

The period of 1860-1869 was only slightly unfavorable for international commerce. The deficit averaged 7.5 percent. However, this decade, encompassing the Civil War and its aftermath, was fiscally impaired. The estimated war cost was more than $15 billion, which is much greater in 1865 dollars than in 1988 dollars.

The next decade, 1870-1879, had unusual beginnings. In 1870, imports and exports were almost equal, $462 million and $451 million, a difference in favor of imports of only 2.4 percent. The next year, 1871, exports and imports matched exactly at $541 million. A deficit of 18.1 percent was recorded in 1872, and of 8.6 percent in 1873. In September 1873 financial panic swept the country; many banks failed and a five-year economic depression began. Notwithstanding, the decade averaged a 13.9 percent surplus, the best in the nation's history to that time.

The United States began its Age of Commerce in 1874 with a trade surplus of $57 million (9.6 percent). For the first time in six years, the country sold more goods to foreign countries than it purchased. Since 1790 (the first year of record-keeping), 1874 was only the twenty-second time that had occurred—twenty-two years of surpluses versus sixty-one of trade deficits and two break-even years. Starting in 1874, however, trade surpluses continued for the next sixty years except for 1887 and 1888. That represented a string of successes by American workers greater than those of their contemporaries in any other country.

The decade of 1880-1889 reflected a 10.4 percent average trading surplus. After an even trading year in 1887 and a 5.2 percent deficit in 1888, forty-five consecutive years of surplus trading activity occurred from 1889 through 1933.

There were ten years of surpluses averaging 29.2 percent from 1890 through 1899. This was the first decade in which Americans sold more goods and food to foreign nations each year than the country purchased. The period's international sales were so large compared to foreign purchases that it became the country's fifth most prosperous trading decade. Financial panic beginning in 1893 turned into four years of depression, adversely affecting imports and assisting exports.

The twenty-year period from 1879 through 1899 had a magnificent gain in the aggregate value of all manufactured goods; it more than doubled from $5.4 billion to $13 billion. The volume of industrial production, the number of workers employed in industry, and the number of manufacturing plants more than doubled. The iron and steel industries expanded production from 1.4 million tons in 1880 to eleven million tons in 1900. The United States passed Great Britain in iron and steel production, and had more than 25 percent of the world pig iron market.

The decade of 1900-1909 was even better for the country commercially. There were ten years of surpluses averaging 41.6 percent annually to make the decade the nation's third most successful. Even so, 1907 saw still another bout of financial hysteria and depression.

Improvement continued in 1910-1919, another decade of consecutive yearly trading surpluses. The average annual surplus of 69.3 percent made it the second most prosperous, productive, and successful decade. At the time, that was the highest percentage gain in the country's history. Many see that decade as the "high noon" of America's greatness, although their view is not based solely on the nation's export-import activities.

The first slowdown in the country's Age of Commerce came in the 1920-1929 decade. Despite ten years of surplus trading activity, the average annual percentage slipped to 21.8 percent, a sizable drop from the three preceding decades. In addition, the ratio of exports over imports during the decade was decidedly uneven ranging from 49.8 percent in 1920 to 1.9 percent in 1923. Even though it was the country's seventh most successful trading decade, the downturn in the average annual percentage from the prior thirty-year period was, in retrospect, a portent of the severe economic decade to follow.

Nineteen thirty through 1939 was the decade of the Great Depression. The first four years remained surplus trading years, but the decade averaged a 21.8 percent deficit. The last six years, 1934-1939, produced an average trade deficit not seen in the United States since 1816, some 120 years earlier.

After the Great Depression and its deficit years of 1934 through 1940, there were another thirty consecutive years of trading surpluses from 1941 to 1971.

In the 1940-1949 decade, America reached its commercial zenith. During this ten-year span with four years of warfare against the Axis powers, the trading surplus averaged 85.6 percent and the decade became the greatest of American commerce. The first year of the decade, 1940, had a massive deficit of 45.8 percent. Three years, 1943, 1944, and 1945, had trade surpluses of 271.1 percent, 277.4 percent, and 135.9 percent. They still hold the record for the greatest annual trading surpluses in American history.

The country had consecutive surpluses in foreign trade for the following ten years, 1950-1959. It was the fourth most successful trading decade with an average annual surplus percentage of 36.9.

There was a historical recurrence in the decade of 1960-1969 much like the rise and fall of surpluses in past successful trading decades. It was the sixth best decade of the Age of Commerce. But the average surplus for the decade slipped to 24.1 percent from 36.9 percent for the previous decade. This 24.1 percent approximated the 29.2 percent of the Age's first consecutive yearly surplus decade during 1890-1899. However, the successful trading activity of the 1890 decade was heading up—the 1960 decade was heading down.

The 1970-1979 decade signaled the end of the Age of Commerce. After a surplus of 7.7 percent in 1970, the Age's demise came with the 4.6 percent deficit of 1971. Even though there were two surplus years, 1.9 percent in 1973 and 9.3 percent in 1975, the decade's remaining years had deficits. The average annual deficit for the decade was 9.2 percent.

Trade deficits worsened in the 1980-1989 decade: 9.9 percent for 1980, 10.5 percent for 1981, 13 percent for 1982, 22.3 percent for 1983, 36.1 percent for 1984, 36.6 percent for 1985, 40 percent for 1986, 40.3 percent for 1987, and 37.7 percent for 1988.

The United States reigned commercially supreme during almost the entire ninety-seven years (four generations) of the Age of Commerce. The beginning of the end, heralded by a $2.1 billion increase in imports over exports, came in 1971 when the United States became a net importer of foreign goods. For the first time since 1940, the United States sold fewer goods than it purchased from foreign countries. Nineteen seventy-one was only the eighth deficit year in the four generations since the Age of Commerce began in 1874.

Based on the nation's international commercial feats, a favorable balance of the dominance trait appears to have continued in the accomplishing generations throughout the Age of Commerce. (The accomplishing generation of 1971, age thirty-six through sixty, was born in the twenty-five-year period of 1911-1935.)

Since 1976 increasingly disproportionate trade balances have favored other countries. Just as world wealth moved into the United States for ninety-seven years, it has been leaving the country in ever-increasing amounts for sixteen of the eighteen years beginning in 1971, including thirteen consecutive years—1976 through 1988.

For several years after 1976, optimists forecast that the country was turning the corner and predicted a resumption of American trade surpluses. During 1981-1988 optimism lessened and reducing the trade deficit became a prime goal. In mid-1988 and early 1989, improving trade deficit reports stimulated the stock market. Today, few Americans would agree that the Age of Commerce is over or accept 1971 as its end.

One possible cause for a lack of public concern is government and media methods of reporting trade deficits. Percentage differences between imports and exports are not reported. For example, Paul Duke, Jr., in *The Wall Street Journal* of September 30, 1985, in an article on "Smaller Deficit in Trade Cheers Some Analysts" states, "The seasonally adjusted trade gap narrowed to $9.90 billion in August, a 5.8% drop from the July deficit of $10.51 billion, the Commerce Department reported." One economist was quoted as saying, "It looks good." The article did note that "total imports in August were $27.33 billion" and, in the following paragraph, "exports in August totaled $17.42 billion." The account followed a format similar to that in other newspaper articles reporting the "good news" of the August 1985 deficit decline from the July numbers. Not specifically stated was that the "smaller" August deficit represented imports exceeding exports by 36.2 percent (the $9.9 billion deficit divided by $27.33 billion in imports) and that, if annualized, the percentage deficit would be greater than for any year since reporting began in 1790 except for 1808, 1812, 1814, 1815, 1816, 1935, 1939, and 1940.

The consistency of this reporting is evident in excerpts from the Associated Press release concerning 1985 deficits published January 31, 1986:

The U.S. trade deficit widened to a record $148.5 billion in 1985, as imports in December outpaced exports by $17.4 billion, the government reported.

The 1985 trade deficit was up 20.4 percent from the then-record $123.3 billion deficit of the previous year. U.S. imports have climbed more rapidly than exports since 1981.

In all, U.S. imports totaled $361.6 billion in 1985, up 6 percent from the preceding year. Exports totaled $213.1 billion, falling 2.2 percent from 1984, the report said.

December's trade deficit was up 27 percent from the $13.7 billion of November. Exports during the month fell by 5.3 percent, to $17.0 billion, while imports soared to $34.4 billion, more than double the export total.

The article failed to state that 1985 was the ninth worst trading year since record-keeping began. Though mentioning that December imports were more than double exports, it did not specifically include percentage comparisons. Actually, the December 1985 imports, if annualized, would be surpassed only by the two worst trading years in American history, 1808 and 1815.

ᐁᐁᐁ ᔑᔑᔑ

The United States required four generations, 1763 through 1874, without losing a war to enter its Age of Commerce. In contrast the short time period involved in the sublimation of dominance into international commerce by the German and Japanese populations after World War II was dramatic.

High dominance levels in the populations of Germany and Japan before and during the 1930s were expressed through expansion, conquest, and the instigation and waging of World War II.

Germany's human losses, after unconditional surrender to the Allies in 1945, totaled 3.5 million combatants and 780 thousand civilians; for Japan the figures amounted to 1.3 million military personnel and 672 thousand civilians. Most of the war dead were men; without a war, many would have become the mainstay of leadership in these countries. Male survivors provided that leadership.

Capital and tools for continued warfare were nonexistent in both countries, but capital for rebuilding was made available primarily by the United States. Germany and Japan both repopulated and the dominance trait remained favorably skewed. The male survivors of the war sublimated their dominance into commercial activities. The sublimation, fueled by American capital, brought about the so-called German and Japanese miracles. Attained in the equivalent of one birth and accomplishing generation, 1946-1971, the "miracles" continue.

International commercial success for every country is based on a favorable balance of high dominance in the population and its sublimation into commerce instead of war. The Age of Commerce could be considered the Age of Sublimation or Enlightenment or Great Endeavor or Accomplishment. Perhaps it could even be considered a country's Age of Greatness.

Chapter XV

The Age
of Affluence

Nineteen forty-six, the year after World War II ended, is the logical start of the Age of Affluence. Even though long in arriving, 183 years after the country's 1763 beginning, it will have a shorter duration than the preceding Ages. It is easier and less time-consuming to spend money than to make it.

In the 1920s, the country tried but failed to enter the Age of Affluence. One indicator was the largest percentage drop in the nation's foreign trade surplus for any decade since the Age of Commerce began in 1874. Another sign was financial and commodity speculation by novice investors unfamiliar with the market trading process. The desire for easy money was linked to nationwide euphoria. We notice the grasp for affluence in the style of living, which led to the decade's being tagged The Roaring Twenties.

Following the 1929 stock market crash, any illusion of affluence quickly disappeared. The country drastically curtailed foreign purchases from $4.75 billion in 1929 to $1.70 billion in 1932. Even though exports dropped from $5.77 billion in 1928 to $2.06 billion in 1933, they remained higher than imports during 1928 through 1933.

The Great Depression was drawing to a close before World War II's beginning; from 1934 through 1940, Americans imported much more than they exported. In 1934 foreign purchases rose while exports remained static; in 1940 the United States set an annual import record of $7.43 billion. At the same time, that year's $4.03 billion in exports was less than the annual average for the 1920s decade. From 1934 through 1940 export-import imbalances created a greater percentage of imports over exports than in any other seven-year period since 1814.

Many experts do not believe that World War II ended the Depression (though it is still a popular public opinion) but consider that the Depression ended well before the United States began gearing for war. Employment was rising before 1939, banks were regaining respectability, and Depression-era government jobs were being abandoned for higher pay in the private sector.

Losses in world trading activity from 1934 through 1939 were reversed in the following decade, 1940-1949, the most successful trading decade in the nation's history. This was accomplished even though for almost four of those years the United States and its allies were immersed in war on the largest scale ever waged.

In 1939 the entire armed forces numbered approximately 356 thousand. At the height of the nation's military strength in 1945, these forces were estimated at 12.5 million. Since mostly men joined the service, women replaced them in the war plants. By 1943 more than two million women worked in American war industries, and the number increased until the war's end. By then women made up 36 percent of the work force, up from 28 percent in 1940. Women, working alongside men, made great contributions to the enormous foreign trade gains of the early 1940s.

The United States government sold more than $156 billion in war bonds, certificates, and notes to finance World War II. It levied special excise taxes on luxury items such as jewelry and cosmetics, and imposed an excess-profits tax on corporations. Government spending increased from $8.76 billion in 1939 to $100.4 billion in 1945. Revenues from income, excess profits, and special excise taxes increased from $2.18 billion in 1939 to $35.17 billion in 1945. Meanwhile, the national debt rose from $42.96 billion in 1940 to $269.42 billion in 1946.

Massive government deficit spending during the war effectively transferred large sums of money to the general public in return for work on war and defense projects. Although people worked hard and were paid well, their living standard was low. Deprivation was not new. Having recently emerged from the Great Depression, most people did not resent a low living standard during the war. Sacrifices were made willingly and considered small compared to the price paid by the war dead and wounded.

For the war's duration, rationing was a way of life. Butter, canned goods, coffee, fats, meats, sugar, gasoline, and shoes were rationed along with what seemed a thousand other items. Rationing, price controls, and scarcity limited the availability of merchandise for public consumption. Besides food shortages, there was little new clothing—no new automobiles—no new appliances—no new houses, and virtually no materials for home remodeling or expansion. These years of doing without set the stage for the Age of Affluence.

With few consumer goods available, people were forced to save. A large part of the increased national debt was retained in personal savings derived from good wages and low living standards; America's ratio of savings to income was greater than in any comparable period. Between 1940 and 1945, individual savings totaled $136 billion. *In effect, the citizens financed the war through their low standard of living.*

How did the United States stand as a nation in 1945? It stood alone at the top in wealth, power, and fame. By these three measures no other country approached it. The government owned 60 percent of the total gold held by world governments. The country had a military-industrial complex second to none and was the world's major oil exporter. It was the sole owner of the most powerful weapon in history, the atomic bomb. The work force had power; 36 percent of American workers belonged to unions. Business failures numbered only four per ten thousand firms, the lowest in American history. (The failure rate in 1932 was 154 per ten thousand companies; in 1985, 114 per ten thousand.)

In 1945 citizens, on the whole, were considered honest, moral, ethical, and law-abiding. Good manners were in; wholesale rudeness had not begun. Discipline and integrity were in, and the thought of bankruptcy was humiliating. A man's word was better than a contract. Borrowers and lenders expected loans to be repaid and almost all were. Buyers were treated as customers not as consumers. Personal savings were in. Heroes were in; criminals received little sympathy. Stealing or moral turpitude or plagiarism were called wrong, not a mistake. Malpractice was a seldom-used word. Deferred adjudication was a little-known phrase in criminal justice proceedings. Perhaps 1945 was the true "high noon" of the United States.

With the lifting of controls at the war's end, prices skyrocketed. People wanted to buy; they had money available from savings, but goods were scarce. The lean war years coming on the heels of the Great Depression and the money saved during the war fueled the opening of the Age of Affluence in 1946.

♫♫♫ ♪♪♪

A macroscopic example of the country's affluence can be traced through the game of golf and its spread across the nation. Why golf? It is an old game, not a fad; it originated over five hundred years ago and is international in scope. Naturally, golf does not cause a country's decline. The game is significant only as a measure of a country's level of affluence and how it spends its time, and as a portent of a future decline in world status.

Early in the fifteenth century, the Scots played a game closely resembling today's game of golf. Scotland today barely resembles the Scotland of 1457 when James II and the Scottish Parliament first prohibited the game, fearing that it was weakening the nation's defense by diverting time away from the military sport of archery. The game's growth was slowed, but it was never wholly abandoned.

In 1754 the Royal and Ancient Golf Club was established at St. Andrews, Scotland, and today is the oldest and most famous club in golf's history. That year, no golf clubs existed in the thirteen colonies. The British colonists had little time to pursue such pleasures. One hundred thirty years elapsed before Oakhurst Golf Club, said to be the country's first, was founded in 1884 near White Sulphur Springs, West Virginia. By 1891, the year after the Age of Outburst ended, the Shinnecock Hills Golf Club reputedly became the first to erect a clubhouse and secure a charter. Two years later, the Chicago Golf Club opened the country's first eighteen-hole course. The following year, the United States Golf Association (USGA) was instituted.

By 1893 golf clubs abounded throughout Great Britain as that nation enjoyed its Age of Affluence. The United States was well into its Age of Commerce. Each country's habits reflected the Age it was experiencing. Great Britain was in the pleasure phase of its cycle while the United States was into its achieving stage.

After the game's dramatic growth in the 1920s, by 1931 there were 5,691 golf facilities (4,448 were private clubs) in the United States. Economic repercussions of the Great Depression and World War II, however, shrank total facilities to 4,817 from 1931 to 1946.

Since 1946 the number of golf facilities has increased every year. According to the National Golf Foundation, 1962 represented ''a milestone year for golf because it was the first time the number of public facilities in the United States exceeded the number of private clubs.'' Even the recession years of 1966, 1974-1975, and 1981-1982 did not adversely affect growth, a reflection of national affluence. By 1984 the country had 12,278 golf facilities.

Golf's importance to a great number of people is well stated in ''Statistical Profile of Golf in the United States, 1983 Annual Review'' in a letter by the National Golf Foundation President:

The vitality of American golf in 1983 manifested itself more through its expansion of play and players than in the increase of places for them to play.

More Americans than ever, roughly 17.8 million, are playing golf today. By conservative count the number is up by 200,000 over the start of 1983. . . .

Not only that, the growing legion of golfers is spending more time on the fairways. Between 1979 and 1983, the National Golf Foundation determined in its sampling of typical golf facilities that rounds played increased by 25 percent to 434,000,000 in 1983. An early attainment of a half-billion annual rounds of golf on American courses is the prediction of statisticians.

There are 5.6 courses in the United States today for every 100,000 inhabitants and one 18-hole course or the equivalent for each 23,156 persons. . . .

A flight over Florida or virtually any other populated Sun Belt region makes it easy to believe that some 1.5 million acres of this land are devoted to golf courses. And $1.5 billion is being spent annually to groom that turfgrass for the pleasure of the game's devotees. Golf, indeed, is making America beautiful.

With fifty-six million people, Britain has over eighteen hundred golf courses. The Soviet Union, population 272 million, had one golf course under construction in 1988. The Soviets have little time for golf; they are expanding their international influence. Their Age of Conquests has yet to end; their Age of Commerce is still to come.

The Japanese are in their Age of Commerce but are nearing their Age of Affluence. The first golf facility in Japan was founded in Kobe around 1900, the Tokyo Golf Club in 1914. In 1983 estimates of Japanese courses exceeded fourteen hundred, many having opened since 1973. The population is turning toward leisure activities while continuing economic expansion. Land scarcity there could inhibit golf's growth, but that appears unlikely. Japan, with about half the population of the United States, would require some five thousand additional facilities to match the ratio of courses to population figures that the Age of Affluence brought Americans. Land scarcity can be overcome—where there is a market, entrepreneurs will find a way to fill the need.

According to its proponents, the benefits of golf include relaxation, exercise, personal challenge, competition, and family togetherness. Golf is credited with providing a pleasant environment for making business contacts and deals. The game provides employment and spectator entertainment, and promotes the sale of goods and services. The economic benefits of golf, however, are service-oriented rather than directed toward international manufacturing and marketing, which increase a country's exports.

Golf provides gainful employment for professionals competing for prize money and endorsement contracts, media people covering the sport's events, and those employed by or supplying goods and services to the facilities. But for many participants, time playing golf means time away from work. Other than those players who claim business-related benefits, few can believe the game's spectacular growth is allied to the work ethic.

The game takes time and money. Lack of money and the time spent working for life's necessities severely limit participation in the sport for an overwhelming majority of the population. But in 1988 affluence provided both for an estimated twenty-one million players. When American affluence ends, the number of players and golf facilities and their profits will drop at a faster rate than they ascended.

Another indication of national affluence involves the pet industry, which generates billions of dollars annually. Domesticated animals, of course, are not a recent phenomenon; their fortunes have intertwined with those of humans for millennia. What is new is the country's volume of annual sales accounted for by pets as well as related products and services.

Most American households contain a pet. The country has over fifty million dogs and more than forty-six million cats, and national affluence is obvious when billions of dollars are spent on pet food while people are starving in other parts of the world. The level of affluence becomes even more glaring when we add to the equation other pet-related items. Dog and cat veterinary care alone accounts for over $3 billion annually. There is a market in pet insurance. There are commercial pet cemeteries and pet-to-pet greeting cards. Jogging outfits are available for dogs, and some stores have pet clothing departments. There are even animal therapists to help pets with psychological problems.

A small occurrence in 1975 illustrates the changing values created by affluence. That year, a California advertising man successfully marketed a "pet rock." At the height of the fad's popularity, he shipped three to six thousand rocks per day to prestigious stores across the nation. The package included a "pet rock" and an instruction manual on its care and feeding. Public acceptance was excellent with strong sales at a retail price of $4.00 each. This happened in a year of economic recession when the country's minimum wage was $2.10 per hour and 8.5 percent of the work force was unemployed—7.9 million people.

Still another sign of affluence emerges in the proliferation of licensed attorneys compared to their numbers near the Age's beginning. In 1948 the country had one attorney per 860 citizens. By 1960 the ratio had changed to one per 632. In 1985 there was a lawyer for every 382 people.

Only an affluent society can support the number of attorneys practicing in the United States. Many of their incomes are dependent, some totally, on the problems caused by divisiveness—individuals against individuals, individuals against corporations, corporations against individuals, corporations against corporations, and individuals or corporations against municipal, county, and state governments. According to *The Gallagher Report*, thirteen million civil suits were filed in federal and state courts during 1985. The size of an attorney's fee is usually tied to the affluence of his "host," thus the excessive number in the profession. Is this productive or parasitic?

Contrast the proportionate number of this country's attorneys to those of the nation's major trade competitors. In 1984 Germany had one attorney per 1,290 people. Japan had approximately thirteen thousand attorneys, one per 9,250 people; only four hundred new lawyers enter the profession each year. As these countries progress into their respective Ages of Affluence, they undoubtedly will experience a striking increase in the number of practicing attorneys. This is only one of many barometers of a country's level of affluence.

Even with the waning of America's affluence, the number of attorneys may continue increasing as happened in Britain. During Queen Victoria's reign the British Empire was the wonder of the world. As late as 1933, its global empire included a quarter of the world's population. In the 1950s Britons were still among the richest people in the world, and Britain was Europe's greatest trading nation. By 1985 various international comparisons placed it between tenth and fifteenth in the world ranking of wealth.

The populations of England and Wales approximate 88 percent of the United Kingdom. The ratio of solicitors to this population segment was estimated at one per 2,008 people in 1961, one per 1,526 in 1971, and one per 928 in 1981. From 1961 to 1981, the population of England-Wales increased about 3.5 percent while the number of solicitors grew 123 percent.

Signs of American affluence crop up everywhere. Affluence manifests itself in the numbers of doctors, dentists, and medical institutions, and the large medical field gains as a percentage of gross national product. In 1987 the mean income of physicians reached almost $120 thousand annually.

Traditionally, obesity was a characteristic of the rich, and the amounts of food that some ate at a single meal were legendary; the middle and working classes were lean in comparison. Affluence has reversed the situation.

More people are overweight as a result of affluence today than in earlier years. They eat larger amounts of food rich in fat but perform much less physical labor. In 1987 an estimated thirty-three million American women wore clothes size fourteen or larger. Many in the highest six income categories, however, are weight-conscious and go to great lengths to fight fat with exercise and diet. Obesity is more often found in the lower income categories.

How-to manuals on diet, exercise, and weight loss appear on nonfiction best-seller lists. Companies offering goods and services catering to leisure activities are growing rapidly. Television viewing time has lengthened dramatically, and the number of meals eaten outside the home has increased.

Another example of the nation's affluence and growing preoccupation with leisure is found in the ranks of early retirees. The percentage retiring before age sixty continually increases.

The list could go on and on. Hundreds of other signs of affluence have surfaced since 1946 and are accelerating. Affluence has brought with it a host of social and economic problems. In time affluent values with an emphasis on money and pleasure rather than hard work, declining dominance ratios in the general population, and efforts to maintain the appearance of affluence within the society at all costs will bring the Age of Affluence to a painful close.

rله rله rله ‿h ‿h ‿h

A nation's fall from affluence is more traumatic than the suffering of an individual who must lower his standard of living. The major difference involves the number of people experiencing the change when an entire country is affected.

Union memberships dropped from 36 percent in 1945 to less than 19 percent in 1985, coinciding with job losses in the manufacturing sector. The heavily touted change from manufacturing to service-oriented industries is particularly evident in the phenomenal multiplying of consultants. These individuals, according to the dictionary, give professional or expert advice, but few using the title are experts. Many consultants have never been charged with profit and loss responsibilities. Some charged with such accountability failed and then moved into consulting. The United States government is the world's largest employer of consultants, using their services for an almost infinite variety of purposes. Some major corporations employ sizable internal staffs to manage outside consultants.

Financial advisers, who counsel individuals in the top seven income categories, have also become popular. Many of them have no appreciable net worth and are personally debt-ridden. Often their sole business experience has been advising others.

Affluence supports consultants and financial advisers. But at some point a service-oriented economy will resemble, as someone once described it, a national economy based on each family's surviving by taking in another family's washing.

Affluence, real or imagined, can also be measured by the work week. Fewer working hours leave more time for leisure activities. In France, 91.7 percent of the labor force works a five-day week; in the United States, 85.1 percent; in Japan, 27 percent. The average Japanese currently works three to five hundred more hours annually than an American worker. The Japanese ethic of *senyu koraku*—struggle first, enjoy later—represents earlier American thinking. This is apt to change in Japan to *senraku koyu*—enjoy first, struggle later—as it has in the United States for many born after 1946. As that segment of the American population nears retirement, the struggle may begin. In Japan affluence is arriving. The government now has a Leisure Development Center to encourage leisure activities. It has also introduced the Labor Standards Act and other legislation to compel a five-day work week at large Japanese companies.

Tax incentives do not have long-range effects on a country's productivity levels. People with high dominance are driven to succeed regardless of tax incentives. Such stimulants can direct the flow of capital, but the direction may have little to do with the country's international trading activities or future well-being. Investors direct capital to areas that they consider financially beneficial to themselves.

The American family has changed significantly during the Age of Affluence. One of the first meaningful damage reports came at the peak of American well-being in 1945 with the highest divorce rate ever recorded to that date, 3.5 per thousand population. No alarms sounded, since the marriage rate that year increased to 12.2 per thousand—another record—exceeding the 12.0 per thousand of 1920 and the 12.1 per thousand of 1940.

Even though divorces increased in 1945, the birth rate began escalating in 1946. Between 1946 and 1964, 76.4 million children were born in the United States. However, the number of children born to dominant women decreased. To illustrate, highly successful women attorneys, entrepreneurs, executives, judges, politicians, and physicians, well established in 1987, had the smallest number of children in the childbearing age group (excepting some religious orders), and many had no children. Do the demanding, stressful positions of high-achieving women interfere with having children? Is it a matter of personal choice? Or is it some of both? One thing is clear, neither began in 1987. Both trends have been growing in the United States for several decades.

High achievement and limited childbearing are now accepted as normal. It is unclear whether dominant women, if confined to the home or nonexecutive positions during affluent times, would place similar limitations on having children. I propose that their age group has, increasingly since 1945, done just that. A decrease in births by dominant women relative to nondominant women beginning in 1946 is an unpublished, undocumented, and hard-to-prove statistic. If correct, this could be the most devastating, far-reaching, and continuing blow to the national weal dealt by the Age of Affluence.

The diminishing dominance levels in the population since 1946 resulted from the decreasing number of children born to dominant women, primarily because of the country's affluence. Affluence may also be at the root of the nation's productivity problems; it could be a major cause of the unfavorable foreign trade balances since the 1970s.

Dominance levels are already in place for the current birth and accomplishing generations. Any near-term changes in achievement levels will reside with the tenth generation births beginning in 1988. With the 1946 link to the beginning of the loss of dominant citizens and the shifting ratio since then of dominant and nondominant women who give birth, and with no dramatic change in the dominance levels of the next generation, history may record the Age of Affluence as the twilight years rather than the golden years of the United States.

Although their percentages are smaller than in earlier generations, dominant children born to dominant mothers between 1946 and 1964 are highly visible in the United States. They are making their mark in entrepreneurship, in the executive suites of corporations, in the practice of medicine and law, and in other rewarding endeavors. They are referred to as Young Urban Professionals or Young Upwardly Mobile Professionals. Although these dominant individuals constitute only a small segment of their age group, the media portrays their accomplishments, buying habits, and lifestyles as if they represented the nation's norm. But, according to *Newsweek* in November 1985, of those born during this nineteen-year period, only 2.5 percent of the men and 0.3 percent of the women make $50 thousand or more annually, although working spouses raise family incomes significantly.

Evidence of the changing dominance composition of the population and the country's waning affluence surfaces in the large numbers of nondominant working wives. Most are not pursuing achievement-oriented goals as are many dominant working women, married or single. Nondominant wives work to maintain the family position in the middle class. Without their supplemental incomes, the so-called middle class would have shrunk severely since 1971. Single incomes can no longer sustain most American families in the middle class.

Even with two incomes, middle-class families are losing ground. First-time buyers of new homes were a major market force from 1946 to 1982. In 1946 the average household size was 3.5 persons. Even though household size declined to 2.7 persons in 1987, the average new home increased to a record size approaching 1,850 square feet. In 1983 first-time buyers of new homes curtailed purchases and builders began constructing larger homes catering to the more affluent move-up buyer, elevating the average new home size. Lessening affluence comes to light in statistics on home ownership. More families are renting even though new apartments have been downsized. The increase in purchases of small automobiles in recent years is also income-related as wages remain relatively static in a waning economy.

Changes in the country's debt structure help individuals retain their buying power. Credit came into vogue during the 1920s but was not widely used during the Great Depression or World War II. In 1971 credit use exploded. Repayment periods have been extended to lengths unheard of two generations ago. Down payments are usually only token amounts. Increased purchasing power through high interest credit-card financing is commonplace and a way of life for many families. All these, plus many two-income families, help the country maintain an illusion of prosperity. Government dependence on retail spending and the expansion of consumer credit to maintain jobs and affluence encourages overconsumption.

A long-range problem of national dependence on consumer spending is the resulting consumer debt. A 1985 report by Morgan Stanley & Co., an investment firm, noted that the ratio of outstanding installment credit to disposable income had increased sharply to 18.9 percent, surpassing its record level of the late 1970s. The report further stated that during the previous year, a 2.4 percent rise was the highest gain ever over one twelve-month period and was accompanied by a sharp escalation in the consumer loan delinquency rate.

Not all Americans are participating in the country's Age of Affluence. The handicapped, some of the elderly, the jobless, and those in the lowest two income categories are not reaping the rewards of affluence. Neither are some family farm owners.

The nation's farmers embody one of the last vestiges of the pioneer spirit. Although one of the most hardworking, productive segments of American society, few farm families partake of the good life, and their numbers dwindle. Even in years with high yields, family farmers—the moral backbone of the country—are frequently penalized for bountiful production by lower prices. Continued reductions in the numbers of family farms are likely. Waning affluence dictates that along with other spending priorities government price support levels be reviewed and subjected to reductions.

As the country's affluence continues to diminish, people will focus on maintaining as much personal affluence as possible. Individuals and groups will fight to retain their advantages. State governors already compete for slices of a shrinking pie. Commentators deplore the population's selfishness, yet books abound advocating looking out for one's self, among them: two from the personal side by Robert J. Ringer, *Winning Through Intimidation* and *Looking Out For #1*, and one by Matthew Lesko from a more societal point of view for taxpayers, *Getting Yours: The Complete Guide to Government Money*. This attitude suits the popular mood.

Divisiveness between the haves and have-nots will accelerate as the country's waning affluence leaves fewer funds available for social redistribution. Reduced living standards for broad segments of the population will lie in legislative decisions on whose living standards to reduce. Since great disparities in living standards prevail, it is impossible to decrease them proportionately. As the general public's status continues changing from affluent to less and less affluent, legislative bodies in the United States will be challenged in ways unimagined by past generations.

⚜ ⚜ ⚜ ☙ ☙ ☙

Government spending patterns and policies depend on the degree of national affluence. Federal budgeting becomes more understandable when divorced from political rhetoric and viewed instead in a context of rising or declining affluence. For example, the waning of affluence shows up in the procrastination by governmental agencies in the cleanup of chemical and radioactive sites: it is less a case of callous or uncaring government than a change in priorities for the allocation of diminishing funds.

Foreign aid is rooted in affluence. Reporting on its distribution began in 1946, the same year the Age of Affluence began. An October 25, 1982, report prepared by Theodor W. Galdi, Caleb Rossiter, and Alfred Reifman titled "Costs and Benefits of U.S. Foreign Aid" says:

. . . The major purpose of these programs has been to contribute to the security of the United States—at a minimum to deter instability and aggression—and help build a world in which our values and basic institutions can flourish.

In addition, foreign aid has other functions, notably: to strengthen the U.S. economy by building markets abroad and developing sources of supply and, to help the less fortunate abroad in keeping with American moral or humanitarian values.

How effective foreign aid has been in achieving these objectives is a most difficult question, one which this study will not attempt to answer.

Estimating the costs of foreign aid is also difficult. Actual net economic and military aid outlays (expenditures minus foreign loan repayments) from 1946 through 1980 were $170 billion. If each year's outlays are converted to constant 1980 dollars (to avoid adding dollars of widely differing values), then the total for these 35 years is $391 billion, or $11.2 billion per year.

The broad categories comprising foreign aid are: economic aid, food aid, multilateral development banks (MDB) aid, and military aid. Government taxation or government borrowing finances foreign aid costs. Galdi, Rossiter, and Reifman state:

. . . Borrowing is likely to reduce private investment more than taxation would; the impact of such government action on money markets increases the cost of borrowing for non-government enterprises and, in certain instances, crowds out some non-government borrowing. As a result, borrowing tends to reduce future consumption in favor of present consumption, while taxation has the reverse tendency. In other words, borrowing helps to maintain current consumption because the resources needed for the government program come more from private investment than they would in the case of taxation. As a result, in comparison with taxation, borrowing shifts the burden of reduced consumption from current taxpayers to future taxpayers.

Ignoring its purposes or intended results, foreign aid reflects a nation's affluence and generosity. Without affluence, this bounty cannot prevail. Future spending reductions will not represent America's lessening benevolence, only its diminishing affluence. To many detractors of foreign aid, reduction is long overdue, though for reasons other than waning affluence.

One method governments use to help cover up a decline in affluence is currency debasement. Ten generations before Christ, at the time of the Punic Wars, the silver denarius was the standard of Roman currency. It weighed 1/84 of a pound of pure silver. In Nero's regime, it was debased to 1/96 of a pound of silver and mixed with 1/10 copper. Around A.D. 100 under Trajan, the alloy was increased to 20 percent and the silver cut further. Some one hundred years later under Septimius Severus, the alloy was increased to between 50 and 60 percent and the silver content again reduced. Less than one generation later at the time of Elagabalus, A.D. 220, the new coinage contained only base metal; all silver had been removed.

During the same general periods, the aureus gold coin shrank. It was equal to 1/40 of a Roman pound of gold under Augustus. Although not debasing its purity, Nero reduced the coin to 1/45; Caracalla to 1/50; Diocletian to 1/60; and, during the reign of Constantine, it became only 1/72.

At the time of the full debasement of the denarius, Italy had lost its accumulated treasures. A generation later in A.D. 250, Rome no longer enjoyed high political or commercial status in world affairs.

England's currency debasement was more subtle. In 1299 Edward I reduced the silver content of the penny from 22.50 grains to 22.25. Shortly before the French war, the penny lost two grains, to 20.25. Between 1346 and 1351, the penny's silver content was reduced another 2.25 grains.

Under Henry IV, an additional three grains of silver were removed. By 1470 during the reign of Henry VI, pennies fell to only twelve grains of silver. In 1526 another one and one-half grains of silver were deleted, and the coins became too flimsy to allow any further reduction of silver content without alloy. In 1542 pennies were adulterated with 20 percent alloy; by 1545 they were two-thirds alloy. Near the end of Henry VIII's reign, the penny contained only five grains of silver.

Early in her reign, Elizabeth I fully restored the integrity of the English currency. This action accorded with the stage the country occupied in its ten-generation cycle.

Following the practice of past civilizations of debasing their currency in times of waning affluence, the government of the United

States passed the Coinage Act of 1965. It phased out the traditional 90 percent silver coinage and replaced it with cupronickel-clad coins.

On August 15, 1971, a major political decision further delayed admitting the nation's declining affluence. By legislation the dollar lost its convertibility into gold. Is it coincidental that America's Age of Commerce ended the same year?

Not even the United States penny was overlooked as a candidate for debasement. In 1982 with its purchasing power approaching zero, the penny's composition was changed from 95 percent copper/5 percent zinc to 97.5 percent zinc/2.5 percent copper. The change went virtually unnoticed because the coin's original color was retained.

Although history has witnessed many attempts, debased currency, fiat currency, or any artificial fiscal juggling cannot maintain fiscal confidence, slow the decline of affluence, or restore affluence. Even during prehistory, advanced cultures regarded precious metals as solid standards of wealth. Scarce, therefore valuable, metals may again become the standard non-fiat measurement of value and confidence. Human rationalizations to the contrary notwithstanding, countries must eventually bow to reality.

All currency has become a casino for speculation rather than an accounting standard for the settlement of debits and credits. Fiat money does not provide a stable monetary standard and is especially hard on working people, the poor, and the elderly on fixed incomes.

For the first time in several centuries, no major nation has a currency convertible to gold or silver. Currency convertibility into precious metals has been replaced by a sophisticated evaluation process of currencies floating against each other. The value of each country's money is set and reset on a day-to-day basis by human judgment, subject to human error and contrivance. World leaders meet often to make additional adjustments.

As a proportion of disclosed world government holdings, the gold the United States government held dropped from 60 percent in 1945 to 25 percent in 1985. It would be virtually impossible for the country to buy sufficient gold to restore the nation to its 1945 position. The certainty of a massive reduction in the dollar's value and the resulting astronomical dollar cost per ounce would render the attempt useless.

Only the governments of a few countries, most importantly the People's Republic of China and the U.S.S.R., do not report their gold holdings. Gold reserves and respective world positions of eighteen governments in 1945 and 1985 appear in Tables 7 and 8.

Table 7. Gold Reserves - 1945

Government of Country	Gold Holdings Millions of Ounces	Percentage of World Governments' Disclosed Holdings
United States	573.80	60.33
United Kingdom	56.31	5.92
France	44.23	4.66
Switzerland	38.34	4.03
Argentina	34.20	3.60
South Africa	26.11	2.75
Belgium	20.46	2.15
Sweden	13.77	1.45
Portugal	12.43	1.31
Brazil	10.11	1.06
Canada	10.11	1.06
Mexico	8.40	.88
Netherlands	7.71	.81
Spain	3.14	.33
Japan	2.00	.21
Italy	.69	.07
Austria	.14	.01
Germany	0.00	0.00
	861.95	90.63
International Monetary Fund	0.00	0.00
Remaining Countries	89.05	9.37
All Countries and International Monetary Fund	951.00	100.00

Table 8. Gold Reserves - 1985

Government of Country	Gold Holdings Millions of Ounces	Percentage of World Governments' Disclosed Holdings
United States	262.65	24.95
Germany	95.18	9.04
Switzerland	83.28	7.91
France	81.85	7.78
Italy	66.67	6.33
Netherlands	43.94	4.17
Belgium	34.18	3.25
Japan	24.23	2.30
Austria	21.14	2.00
Portugal	20.23	1.93
Canada	20.11	1.91
United Kingdom	19.03	1.81
Spain	14.65	1.39
Sweden	6.07	.58
South Africa	4.84	.46
Argentina	4.37	.42
Brazil	3.10	.29
Mexico	2.36	.22
	807.88	76.74
International Monetary Fund	103.43	9.82
Remaining Countries	141.47	13.44
All Countries and International Monetary Fund	1,052.78	100.00

These countries owned 90.63 percent of world government gold in 1945. The same countries with the addition of the International Monetary Fund owned 86.56 percent of world government gold in 1985, a change of only 4.07 percent in forty years. The gold reserves of all reporting central banks and governments increased only 10.70 percent during this forty-year period, less than three-tenths of one percent per year.

The forty-year redistribution among these countries tells a different story. Seven governments squandered their gold reserves: Argentina (–87 percent), South Africa (–81 percent), Mexico (–71 percent), Brazil (–69 percent), the United Kingdom (–66 percent), Sweden (–55 percent), and the United States (–54 percent).

The countries whose governments increased their gold holdings ranged upward from Portugal's 62 percent increase to Belgium's 67 percent, France's 85 percent, Canada's 98 percent, and Switzerland's 117 percent. The largest percentage gainers from their 1945 bases were: Spain, 4.7 times its base; the Netherlands, 5.7 times; Japan, 12.1 times; Italy, 96.6 times; Austria, 151 times; and Germany, from zero to 95.18 million ounces, now second in world ownership with 9 percent of world government gold reserves.

Table 9 presents still another picture. The total gold reserves of each country converted to dollars at the rate of $336 per ounce were divided by the estimated 1985 population figure of each country to determine a per capita allocation.

Table 9. 1985 Government Gold Reserves at $336 per Ounce on a per Capita Basis (1985 Population Estimates)

Switzerland	$4,333.60
Belgium	1,164.99
Netherlands	1,019.53
Austria	953.30
Portugal	676.62
Germany	524.70
France	499.66
Italy	392.20
United States	369.82
Canada	266.03
Sweden	244.31
Spain	126.77
United Kingdom	113.32
Japan	67.43
South Africa	50.09
Argentina	47.82
Mexico	9.95
Brazil	7.72

Governments that have decreased their gold holdings since 1945 or that have holdings not commensurate with their population numbers and living standards would probably strongly resist efforts toward gold convertibility. The countries most likely to oppose the fiscal restraint of currency convertibility to gold in order of resistance are Brazil, Mexico, Argentina, South Africa, Japan, and the United Kingdom.

Japan's small gold reserves relative to its commercial strength is apparently a temporary aberration. Profits from international sales and the Japanese custom of saving a high percentage of personal income provide the government with funds for deficit spending without the necessity of devaluing the currency by printing additional money or raising interest rates. Unless increased Japan's gold holdings will be extremely low to support affluence, when the population's saving trend reverses to consumer spending and the country's international profits decline. With its small gold cushion, Japan will not be able to cope with those occurrences as were the United Kingdom and the United States. Both countries sold gold to sustain affluence and its accompanying consumer spending and to postpone the day of fiscal reckoning. Without substantial gold reserves, rapid changes in consumer spending versus saving could wreak havoc in Japanese financial institutions. Considering its strong international position, Japan is likely to dramatically increase its government gold position soon.

Those countries that have increased their gold position since 1945 and that have gold holdings commensurate with their population numbers and standards of living would be little affected by having their currencies become convertible to gold. These fiscally responsible countries, in order of responsibility, are Switzerland, Belgium, the Netherlands, and Austria.

The lack of size and breadth of any foreign currency has assisted in the partial stabilization (nondeterioration) of United States currency since 1971. The only international replacement large enough to equal the present breadth of the United States dollar is gold—or a combination of gold and silver.

No continued manipulation by those responsible for the well-being of United States currency values can offset the nation's lessening competitive levels. Overaffluence can be altered, but the changing composition of population dominance levels has placed the currency's future value outside the long-range manipulation of monetarists.

Those who contend that precious metals have outlived their purpose as a standard for the settlement of debits and credits should consider one question. Why do the most fiscally responsible countries increase their gold holdings whereas the least fiscally responsible decrease theirs? The same question applies to individuals who own precious metals. Perhaps it is because fiscally responsible countries and individuals understand the vagaries of inflation and the repetitive nature of history. The derisive 1896 political label "gold bug" does not deter either one from acquiring the financial protection derived from gold ownership.

Gold ownership has been debated for decades. Even though many people worldwide are financially capable of acquiring gold, it could be a poor choice in some countries at certain times while offering financial protection to citizens of other nations.

In the past, logic provided a simple formula for the personal ownership of precious metals: a country's fiscal responsibility or irresponsibility coupled with timing. While a government amassed gold or maintained high gold reserves, gold purchases by its citizens were not advantageous; they had little need to own gold. When a government began to deplete its gold reserves, its citizens had a signal to buy gold; they had a need for personal ownership. The individual's need for the financial protection of owning gold grew in inverse relation to the diminution of his government's gold reserves; a lack of gold reserves and fiscal instability often went hand in hand.

The Mexican government owned 5.03 million ounces of gold in 1970 when 449 pesos would buy one ounce. In 1976 government ownership dropped to 1.6 million ounces and 1,806 pesos were needed to purchase an ounce of gold. The following year, 1977, an ounce cost 3,348 pesos. In 1987 over six hundred thousand pesos were required to purchase an ounce of gold.

The United States government owned 316.34 million ounces of gold in 1970 and thirty-six dollars bought one ounce. (Although it was illegal at that time, many American citizens owned gold.) In 1976 government holdings fell to 274.68 million ounces and 125 dollars were required to purchase an ounce; during 1987 the cost was in the vicinity of four hundred dollars.

Those pushing for a return to the gold standard by the United States are actually advocating a return to fiscal discipline and responsibility, since there has been a world gold standard for some twenty-five hundred years. Contrary to conventional wisdom, the gold standard exists today. Almost all countries operate by the gold standard, because their national currencies have ongoing relationships with the United States dollar so that their gold costs can be computed daily.

As most world governments now seem to be awash in their respective paper currencies and to print additional fiat money at will, gold appears to fluctuate widely. It may be that only paper currencies have extensive swings and gold fluctuates little. Gold and silver cannot be created by politicians. Politicians can create fiat money, but not one has mastered the art of alchemy.

♪ ♪ ♪ ♫ ♫ ♫

Consumers, businessmen, and politicians are acting in concert at great cost to the country to extend the Age of Affluence. The greater part of the general public, albeit subconsciously, participates in this effort.

Few major political actions benefit all the people they affect. For every credit there is a debit; for every action, a reaction; for every reward, a penalty. A sword cuts with both edges, and both edges can be sharp. Politicians are human and subject to human error; evaluating all sides of an issue is an arduous process. With reelection pressures weighing heavily during most of their political careers, politicians have little time to study long-term consequences.

Legislators mirror the consensus of the population. Their primary concern is reelection. Human nature lends itself to our seeing only one side of an issue, the side which benefits ourselves. When large numbers of us, the voting public, value integrity, honor, and service to the country, most politicians exhibit similar concerns in their lawmaking. When a sizable proportion of voters sets a high value on greed, many politicians tend to reflect the same value. This represents reality as opposed to rhetoric.

Lawmakers who recommend tax increases and reduced government spending may be insightful regarding the nation's welfare; however, they are not being prudent if their goal is to remain in public office. On the other hand, those advocating tax cuts without reducing government spending are not heedful of the national well-being but are certainly perceptive regarding the voters' wishes to extend the Age of Affluence. Politicians recommending legislation to cut government spending quickly lose support from special interest groups and voting blocs when such cuts affect the spheres of affluence and self-interest of these groups.

Massive tax cuts in mid-1981 reduced government revenues. Already operating in red ink, deficit spending soared to a historic high. Fiscal integrity would have mandated spending cuts greater than the tax revenues lost. That did not happen. Instead, based on "supply-side" economics, a gigantic bubble is building. The public, especially those who invested some years ago and stand to profit from present stock market values, seems pleased with federal deficit spending. This scenario has played out before; individual investments using borrowed money inflated each disastrous bubble in history. Deficit spending propels the country's supposed well-being. When "supply-side" economics fails, it is unlikely that government officials will be held criminally negligible. Other sources can be blamed— possibly the world economy. More than likely, it will be charged off as an experiment that failed.

In 1985 one presidential cabinet member opined that the country's huge trade deficits were a testimonial to the country's economic growth and stability. Only one state governor challenged his state- ment; little other notice was taken. A 1988 presidential aspirant took a stand on government spending versus tax revenues: "I think it's better to have a big deficit at a low level of federal spending than a balanced budget at a high level of federal spending."

Are these men knowledgeable? Do they believe these statements? Are they simply saying what they believe people want to hear? These statements would not have been made in the 1950s or earlier; they would have been ludicrous to the media and to informed voters. Even with these efforts to soothe and a collective attitude of burying one's head in the sand, the bubble is nearing the point of bursting.

October 19, 1987, Black Monday or Meltdown Monday, was the most unusual day in stock market history. A percentage decline record nearly twice as large as that of October 28, 1929, was established. Computerized "program trading," tightening of the money supply, and increasing interest rates were blamed. The trade figures released the week before also contributed to the massive decline. After years of indifference, investors are finding an unsettling relationship between trade figures and United States equity markets. The markets have recorded new highs since October 19, 1987, but even though improved, the trade figures continue to reflect high American consumption and a lack of competitiveness in international trade.

The Age of Affluence will weaken rapidly once foreign countries acknowledge America's deteriorating international trade status. Unfavorable trade disparities represent consumption as opposed to competition. High imports versus low exports put a lower value on a consuming country's currency and a higher value on its successful competitors' currencies.

In 1985 Third World debtors, Brazil, Mexico, Argentina, Venezuela, the Philippines, Chile, and Nigeria, owed $348.4 billion to creditors in other countries, particularly to American banks. Who in the United States truly believes that these loans will be repaid? Loss reserves of major American banks for Third World debts were hailed as prudent since each was expected to be a one-time occurrence.

Even though now the world's largest debtor nation, the United States must give others hope that financial stability exists. Foreign banks increased their loans to American businesses from $13 billion in the mid-1970s to an estimated $100 billion in 1985.

United States credit is without question; loans to foreign banks will be repaid. What is questionable is the exchange rate at the time of repayment. The fiscal significance of America's continuing consumption versus its lessening competitiveness is that foreign lenders will eventually demand that the United States borrow in their currency—borrow marks and pay back marks, borrow yen and repay yen. New? For United States borrowers, yes, but not for American lenders. United States lenders instituted this model for Mexico and Central and South American countries. As their currencies lost value, these countries were unable to arrange financing repayable in australs, bolivars, cruzados, or pesos; the countries borrowed dollars from United States banks with repayment due in dollars.

Perhaps the greatest influence on the nation's near future rests with legislative decisions on whether to inflate or deflate the economy to compensate for the country's dwindling affluence. Perils exist with either decision. Danger also lies in maintaining the status quo and allowing the problem to grow.

Deflating the economy through large tax increases and massive reductions in government spending would accelerate the end of the Age of Affluence. The resultant unemployment would parallel what happened in earlier periods, such as the Great Depression.

Inflating the currency by printing unprecedented amounts of money would also hasten the Age's end. Many of the problems that result from massive inflation, other than unemployment, are without precedent in this country. It happened in Germany in the 1920s. Inflation and the following deflation set the stage for Adolf Hitler's ascent to power. A similar chain of events in China in the 1930s and 1940s contributed to the rise of Mao Tse-tung, who retained power for three decades.

Congressional actions on government spending increasingly favor a future of inflation over deflation. In mid-1988 more than a dozen new domestic programs with a five-year price tag of over $100 billion were pending in Congress. Impending inflation is also discernible in actions of the Federal Savings and Loan Insurance Corporation (FSLIC). Potential savings and loan losses in 1988 were estimated variously at $22.7 billion, $26 billion, and $64 billion. When opinions cover a range this wide, losses could be double or even triple the highest estimate. More importantly, Congress aids and in some cases openly encourages the FSLIC to address the problem by consolidation instead of liquidation.

"Texas has some of the best-managed insolvent institutions in the country," according to the chairman of the Federal Home Loan Bank Board in January 1988. Apparently this statement was given and accepted as sincere, not tongue in cheek. Could this open the door for more dubious honors? "Iowa has the best-managed insolvent farms?" "New York has the best-managed insolvent brokerage houses?" "Oklahoma has the best-managed insolvent oil companies?" Worse yet, "The United States is the best-managed insolvent country?"

When the FSLIC foreclosed on a few looted savings and loan institutions, it did not require that all their assets be liquidated for cash. It consolidated problem savings and loan facilities into larger institutions, thereby only postponing a solution to the problem. Meanwhile, anticipating no day of reckoning, poor lending practices by some large savings and loan institutions may surpass past excesses.

In early 1989 the Federal Deposit Insurance Corporation (FDIC) was given jurisdiction over the troubled savings and loan industry. The FDIC greatly expanded foreclosures of insolvent savings and loan institutions, but it followed the FSLIC's course of asset consolidation rather than asset liquidation.

The problem may eventually destabilize national financial security. If that occurs, losses will be moved to the Treasury and added to the national debt. Eventually that shift to distant taxpayers will contribute to the dollar's decline in purchasing power. Popular American thinking equates inflation with an expanding economy and low unemployment. A currency can decline in purchasing power in a stagnant economy, as is happening in Argentina, Brazil, Mexico, South Africa, and many other countries. Many Americans seem to have forgotten the term "stagflation."

A depression caused by a money shortage is unlikely. The United States seems to have a greater fear of an American 1930s-type depression than of the hyperinflation Germany experienced during the same period.

The collective attitude of the Japanese people may provide a clue to America's future financial condition. Japan has assumed the financial superiority of a 1920s America and is experiencing a heady euphoria just as the United States did. A bursting Japanese stock market bubble will greatly influence United States well-being. The Japanese may follow the example of America during the 1930s, internalizing the blame for their market folly and shouldering all responsibilities for the resulting depression. Americans may follow the German example and inflate beyond logic or reason. It is not whether but when Japan's bubble will break; not how much it will affect the United States, but how America will respond.

America's ten-generation cycle will end in the vicinity of the year 2012. The Age of Affluence will end much earlier.

Chapter XVI

The Age
of Intellect

After World War II, college campuses experienced a massive influx of new students, many educated at federal government expense. Approximately 2.2 million veterans attended college under the Servicemen's Readjustment Act of 1944, popularly called the GI Bill. By 1956 almost all the educational benefits of the 1944 Act had ended. The 1952 Veterans' Readjustment Assistance Act helped more than a million Korean War veterans attend colleges and universities.

Colleges and universities absorbed and educated the World War II and the Korean War veterans in addition to the normal flow of high-school graduates. Though the swollen student numbers necessitated crowding, the education was superior. Even with the additional war

251

veteran students, the number of institutions of higher learning declined from 1,891 in 1952 to 1,850 in 1956, since state and federal subsidies had not yet made the large shift from elementary and high schools to colleges.

The Age of Intellect began in 1964 with a record number of 136 new colleges and universities opening during the 1963-1964 school year. That growth resulted from the Age of Affluence and the baby boom, both having begun in 1946.

Great intellectual achievements began in 1964 with that period's accomplishing generation. From 1964 forward, outstanding achievements linked to intelligence reflected the flowering of the Age of Intellect.

Advances followed quickly one upon another, achieved almost entirely by those born between 1904 and 1945. (The accomplishing generation—age thirty-six through sixty—of 1964 was born between 1904 and 1928; of 1974, between 1914-1938; of 1981, between 1921-1945.) Enough time has not yet elapsed for those born after 1945, the accomplishing generation of 2006, to have achieved outstanding feats as earlier accomplishing generations have. How well will the accomplishing generation that grew up during the Age of Affluence perform?

Even though dreams of making forays into space are as old as intellect, the United States was not spurred to serious space exploration until after the Soviet Union launched Sputniks 1, 2, and 3 in 1957 and 1958. A shocked country reacted by launching Explorer 1 in January 1958, inaugurating the nation's space program. The competition for achievements in space technology was on.

The Orbiting Solar Observatory was first launched in 1962 to gain knowledge of the Sun. A Pioneer series of spacecraft began operating in deep space in solar orbit. Additionally, there are Explorer spacecraft collecting a wide variety of data, an Orbiting Astronomical Observatory, a Pegasus series of three satellites used in 1965, and the large earth-orbiting Geophysical observatories. The first recoverable scientific satellites were the Biosatellites used to test the effects of weightlessness, radiation, and the absence of the Earth's twenty-four-hour cycle on biological specimens. The unmanned flights helped prepare the way for man's physical entry into space.

The space race received another competitive push on April 12, 1961, when the Soviet Union put the first man, Yury Alexseyevich Gagarin, in space. In May 1961 President John F. Kennedy captured the nation's enthusiasm by committing the country to land a manned spacecraft on the moon within the decade. That year, Alan B. Shepard, Jr., became the first American in space aboard Freedom 7.

In June 1965 Edward H. White II became the first American to float free in space (three months after Aleksey Leonov of the Soviet Union). The United States placed the first man on the Moon on July 20, 1969. Neil A. Armstrong stepped onto the Moon's surface where he was joined by Edwin E. Aldrin, Jr. The third crew member, Michael Collins, remained in orbit aboard Apollo 11. Manned space flights continued; astronauts explored the Moon's surface and collected lunar samples.

On May 14, 1973, America launched its first space station, Skylab. Three crews of three members each made trips to Skylab later that year. They successfully made repairs to the station and conducted experiments, spending 171 days, thirteen hours aboard. A cooperative U.S.-Soviet manned space mission, the Apollo-Soyuz Test Project, was launched in July 1975.

In 1981 the United States space program began a new era with the first flights of the reusable Space Shuttle. The Orbiter, the central unit of the Space Shuttle system, can be reflown for up to one hundred missions. The boosters can be recovered and refurbished for additional flights.

Accomplishments became so consistent that journeys into space the public once followed with bated breath began to seem routine (an exception being the Challenger's ill-fated launch of January 28, 1986) and were no longer viewed with amazement.

The world gained a wealth of new knowledge through the space program. Experiments were conducted on the Moon and at orbiting space stations. Photographs were taken of the Moon, Mars, Mercury, Jupiter, and Venus. The Earth and its weather have been studied and new inroads made in communications and navigation. The nation produced new materials and manufacturing techniques, and expanded the related technology. New industries developed based on space technology.

The program provided direct economic benefits to man. Satellites became a significant factor in global communications, handling telephone circuits and television channels. Almost a thousand inhabited islands in the Indonesian archipelago are linked via satellite. Improved ship-to-shore communications assist in emergency rescue operations. Communication satellites allow direct-broadcast classroom and community educational programing in isolated communities like many in the Appalachian and Rocky Mountain regions. Isolated areas receive improved health services, for example, by linking rural clinics in Alaska with medical advisers in major hospitals of the Northwest. Communication satellites are used jointly with India to broadcast agricultural, health, family-planning, and other educational programs to remote Indian villages. Two Satellite Business System satellites, launched in the early 1980s, provide high-speed networks for large business organizations in the United States and the southern part of Canada.

Satellites operating globally allow continuous monitoring of weather and its movement, improved forecasts, and advance hurricane warnings. The Geodynamics Experimental Ocean Satellites help improve world maps. Measurements of the Earth's movements are recorded to study continental drift, tides, fault motions, and earthquakes. Landsat 1 studied the land, allowing crop acreage to be estimated and urban development monitored. Now it is possible to plan future land use and to locate air and water pollution. Strip-mine and forest-fire scars are mapped, geological formations studied for indications of the presence of minerals and petroleum, maps and navigation charts updated, glaciers' advances monitored, and flood hazards and water resources studied and managed.

Some believe that today's satellites are in their initial stage of development, and will improve and change as aircraft changed from the days of the Wright brothers. Others are optimistic about future unification of the entire Earth's people via satellite communications. Ardent proponents of the space program believe interplanetary travel is part of America's future.

Not everyone sees worth in the country's space program. Criticisms have been voiced since the program's inception and a few troubled operations have proved some criticisms just. Today there are opponents who advocate dismantling the program or selling it to the private sector and diverting the funds saved or recovered to the country's social needs. However, critics and backers alike must agree that the program is a tremendous intellectual achievement.

During this Age, amazing strides have also been made in the medical field. The following highlight a few among innumerable examples. In 1964 Muriel Roger, a geneticist, successfully transplanted individual genes from one cell to another. In 1968 Norman Shumway performed the country's first successful heart transplant. By 1978 scientists realized that chromosomes exist in parts of the cell other than the nucleus. Since the Age of Intellect began in 1964, doctors and scientists have advanced toward the goal of extending life and have dramatically increased survival rates for patients, particularly children, with some forms of cancer believed terminal as late as the 1940s and 1950s. So it continues; Americans make significant medical discoveries annually. The state of the art in medicine in the United States since 1964 is without equal.

Since 1964 Americans have initiated research and excelled in almost every field of intellectual achievement, and have made major scientific breakthroughs. These include applying new knowledge in concrete ways to existing knowledge (as in the hybridization of seeds for increasing food crops and the miniaturization and sophistication of electronic devices) and producing entirely new inventions. This is only the tip of a dazzling iceberg of American intellectual achievement from 1964 forward.

The Alfred B. Nobel Prizes, awarded annually since 1901 except in 1940, 1941, and 1942, symbolize the world's highest recognition for intellectual achievement. The awards reflect individual achievement, national accomplishment in producing and backing such individuals (or attracting them from other countries), and the ascent and decline of various countries based on the prevalence of achievement-oriented individuals. The first two factors are universally recognized, but little attention has been paid to the third.

By 1985 the United States' Age of Intellect covered twenty-two of the eighty-two Nobel prize years. The eighty-two years can be divided (although not equally) into four periods: 1964-1985 (twenty-two years), 1939-1963 (twenty-two years, excluding 1940, 1941, and 1942), 1917-1938 (twenty-two years), and 1901-1916 (sixteen years).

For this analysis, only individual awards were counted; institutional awards for the Peace Prize were excluded. An award in a specific category to two or more countrymen was counted as one; if given to individuals from more than one country, it was counted separately for each country. The country designated as having a prize winner was determined by the citizenship of the recipient at the time of his award.

Figure 2 indicates the intellectual achievements of nations based on the Nobel prizes from 1901 through 1985.

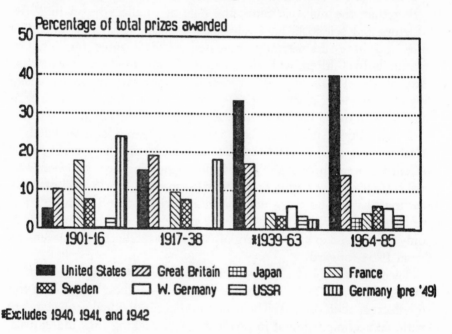

Figure 2. Trends of Nobel Prizes Won

For 1901-1916 United States citizens garnered one prize each in Physics and Chemistry, and two for Peace. During that sixteen years, the country was not represented in either the Physiology or Medicine category or in Literature. The awards to citizens of other countries presented a contrast. Germany received nineteen awards; France, fourteen; Great Britain, eight; Sweden, six; and the Netherlands, five. Italy and Switzerland won four awards each, while Austria and

Belgium won three each. Denmark, Spain, and Russia (before the 1917 Revolution) collected two awards each. Three other countries received one award each. For the period, the United States equaled Italy and Switzerland and was surpassed by the Netherlands, Sweden, Great Britain, France, and Germany.

The 1917-1938 period had a different winning line-up. Citizens of the United States received sixteen prizes. Awards to citizens of other countries were: Great Britain, twenty; Germany, nineteen; France, ten; Sweden, six; Austria, five; Denmark, Norway, and Switzerland, four each; Italy and the Netherlands, three each; Belgium and Ireland, two each; six other countries received one award each. Only Great Britain and Germany surpassed the United States.

Over the 1939-1963 period the United States more than doubled its Nobel awards, receiving thirty-nine awards in all. The prizes to citizens of other countries included: Great Britain, twenty-one; West Germany (after its division in 1949), seven; France and Switzerland, five each; Austria, Sweden, and the U.S.S.R., four each; Italy and pre-1949 Germany, three each; Denmark, Finland, and South Africa, two each; and one award each for sixteen additional countries. United States citizens now led in receiving the world's most prestigious award for intellectual achievements beneficial to mankind.

During the twenty-two years of 1964-1985, American citizens dominated the awards more strongly than any country had in previous periods. In a strict comparison with former periods, Americans won fifty-two Nobel prizes. The Nobel Prize for Economics, begun in 1969, went to United States citizens in all but four years, adding thirteen more awards. In the first twenty-two years of the Age of Intellect, citizens of the United States collected sixty-five prizes. The awards to other countries were: Great Britain, twenty-three; Sweden, eleven; West Germany, eight; France, seven; the U.S.S.R., six; Japan, five; Argentina and the Netherlands, three each; Austria, Belgium, Canada, Ireland, Israel, Italy, Norway, and Switzerland, two each; fifteen other countries, one each.

By analyzing the four periods and the percentages of prize winners from the United States and other leading nations, an ebb and flow of intellectual achievement can be charted.

In the 1901-1916 period, German citizens made up 24 percent of the prize winners; French, 17.7 percent; British, 10.1 percent;

Swedish, 7.6 percent; Dutch, 6.3 percent; Italian, Swiss, and United States citizens, 5 percent each.

For 1917-1938 Great Britain showed the greatest achievement with 19.2 percent of the awards. Germany received 18.3 percent; the United States, 15.4 percent; France, 9.6 percent; and Sweden, 5.8 percent.

The United States won 33.3 percent of the awards in the 1939-1963 period. Great Britain won 17.9 percent; West Germany (after its division in 1949), 6 percent.

For the 1964-1985 period, citizens of the United States received 40.1 percent of the prizes. Great Britain won 14.2 percent; Sweden, 6.8 percent; and West Germany, 4.9 percent.

A review of the eighty-two-year period is striking. Germany (including Germany before its division in 1949 and both countries since) slipped from 24 percent in the first period to 18.3 percent in the second, 6 percent in the third, and 4.9 percent in the fourth. France fell from its high of 17.7 percent in the first period to 9.6 percent in the second and less than 5 percent in the third and fourth periods. Great Britain rose from 10.1 percent in the first period to 19.2 percent in the second period then slipped to 17.9 percent and 14.2 percent in the third and fourth periods. Sweden dropped from 7.6 to 5.8 to 3.4 percent during the first, second, and third periods but rose to 6.8 percent in the fourth. Italy and Switzerland each achieved 5 percent of the prizes during the first period but fell below that ratio in the last three periods. The United States moved from a 5 percent rate in the first period to 15.4 percent, 33.3 percent, and 40.1 percent during the following periods.

Studying earlier distributions makes future allocations of the awards somewhat predictable for incremental periods of twenty-two, forty-four, sixty-six years, or longer. In the past four periods, only nine countries received 5 percent or more of the awards. They included France, Germany (before its division in 1949), West Germany, Great Britain, Italy, the Netherlands, Sweden, Switzerland, and the United States. The ebb of these countries can be seen; the flow of the United States in the opposite direction is just as obvious.

With the exception of the Nobel Peace Prize, there has been quite a lag from the time an individual completed the work for which the prize was awarded to the year Nobel recognition was actually received. From 1964 through 1985, the average age of Nobel laureates (excluding Peace Prize winners) was sixty.

If the lapse between the date of accomplishment and the receipt of the award remains fairly constant, America's leadership in Nobel honors could continue until 1998. The United States is then likely to experience slippage in the number of prizes received, with the decline accelerating after 2005 until the country finally loses its preeminence in award distribution. This is calculated by subtracting twenty-five years from the last year before the Age of Intellect began, 1963, thus identifying a specific accomplishing generation whose births began in 1938. Therefore, the culmination of wisdom in the United States (as expressed by the Nobel prizes garnered) could occur around 1998. The country's massive intellectual achievements might continue about seven years after that—representing Nobel recipients born between 1938 and 1945 (the year before the Age of Affluence began).

Presumably, Great Britain's percentage slide in Nobel awards will continue. It may lose ground even faster in the next twenty-two-year period.

Japan will be a new candidate for first place when the United States takes fewer Nobel honors. That country's citizens received prizes only six times during the eighty-two-year award history and none during the first forty-seven years. However, Japan is entering its Age of Affluence, the precursor of the Age of Intellect. During its forthcoming Age of Intellect, Japan's intellectual achievements could exceed those of the United States, just as America's surpassed those of Great Britain, who had previously superseded Germany.

At a much later date, another country is likely to replace Japan. Although Russia, later the Soviet Union, had small award percentages of 2.5, 1.0, 3.4, and 3.7 for the first four periods, that is not necessarily indicative of the future. If the Soviet Union moves successfully through the Ages of Commerce and Affluence to Intellect, it could surpass Japan as the premier intellectual center. Farfetched? Not if that progression occurs. When a country devotes its time to survival, makes intensive use of manual labor, is involved in conquests, or pursues commercial growth, only a tiny portion of its population can afford purely intellectual pursuits. After a great nation attains affluence, intellectual endeavor follows.

"The spread of knowledge," writes Sir John Glubb, "seems to be the most beneficial of human activities, and yet every period of decline is characterised by this expansion of intellectual activity."

One can see the link between intellectual achievement and cultural decline in the United States by examining the accomplishing and birth generations as separate entities from 1964 forward. Both generations have been highly active during the Age of Intellect, but the achievements of the accomplishing generation and the problems of the birth generation are poles apart. Possibly the same dichotomy held true in earlier successful societies.

According to Landon Y. Jones in *Great Expectations: America and the Baby Boom Generation*, Carl Harter of Tulane, a demographer, referred to persons born during the Great Depression as the "Good Times Generation." That could be expanded to include the first eight years of the eighth birth generation. Shared group characteristics include a less affluent upbringing, indoctrination in the work ethic by parents, and demanding elementary and secondary school teachers. In addition, the low birth rate in the seventh and the first eight years of the eighth birth generations created a high percentage of first-born children. Although having had a more frugal beginning than later birth generations, this group on the whole achieved rich personal rewards in middle life, and for most life continues to improve. Almost the entire group could appropriately be labeled with Harter's "Good Times Generation" tag.

Many born in 1946 through 1962, the eighth birth generation's last seventeen years, and those born in 1963-1987, the ninth birth generation, will live a reversal of the Good Times Generation. In spite of their comparatively affluent beginnings, they are less likely to have a bountiful middle period, especially those born past the halfway mark of the baby boom—1955. Most will experience less prosperity during later life than they did growing up.

A cause of the generational dichotomy in the Age of Intellect hitherto overlooked can be established by relating the beginning of affluence in 1946 to the changing dominance ratios in births that year. The accomplishments during the Age of Intellect are counteracted by problems in the opposite direction.

American levels of intelligence and achievement have dropped dramatically among those born during the Age of Affluence. As posited earlier, once affluence started in 1946, dominant women began having fewer children than nondominant women. From that year forward, the imbalance in children's dominance levels increased. At the same time, the greatest baby boom in the country's history was taking place. Therefore, the ratio of children born to nondominant mothers is probably greater than in any previous period of the nation's history. Those born in 1946 became eighteen in 1964, the year college educators first recognized problems in student achievement. Coincidence? Since then, education has become the focus of national attention, concern, and derision.

The media constantly reports that public education is in shambles. Citizens from every walk of life—from the poor to the very rich—agree that children are receiving an inferior education. They lament the falling away of the high quality education provided past generations. On the whole, the system's end results as measured by student aptitude appear sadly lacking. Today's learning deficiencies look particularly unsatisfactory compared with student achievements only two generations ago.

Teaching in public schools should not be considered grossly inadequate for nondominant pupils. Taking the country's declining overall dominance level into consideration, the learning environment for nondominant pupils may not be as bad as depicted. Pupils contribute to problems in the system that cannot be directly attributed to superintendents, teachers, or the schools.

The attitudes and actions of many students indicate low dominance levels. They are fatalistic; some students feel they have no individual control over the outcome of forces or demands with which they must contend such as achieving an acceptable grade. An overriding reliance on luck has surfaced. If you are lucky, good things happen in your life; if not, then bad things occur. Lucky or unlucky, the attitude is that one's life is manipulated by influences beyond one's control. Fatalism combined with a lack of ambition fosters the sentiment that it really does not matter how hard a person tries; he can have bad luck just as easily as good, so, why bother? Some adopt the cliché, "I'd rather be lucky than smart."

These students attach little importance to meeting school timetables. Tardiness is often excused with reasons defying logic. Absenteeism is not necessarily an act of rebellion; it could be indifference to attending class or the desire to do something more enjoyable than going to school. They might choose to attend college simply because it appears to be something more enjoyable than the alternative—employment with pay commensurate with ability and having to meet another and more rigorous timetable.

To some students low grades are not particularly disappointing since they are considered unavoidable, just another form of bad luck. Disobedience is not necessarily a form of defiance but may be a subconscious effort to distract a teacher from criticizing the student's academic performance. Thus disobedience can be handily used to shift attention to the possibility of a personality conflict with the teacher as the reason for failure. The issue of the failure in academic performance may be forgotten if both concentrate on the specter of disobedience.

Softness and affluence are closely allied. The relatively new practice by schools of using counselors and psychologists in the aftermath of "catastrophes" combines both. For example, a teacher or student commits suicide or a heinous crime, is raped, accidentally killed, or murdered. Even a school destroyed by fire with no loss of life qualifies as a "tragedy." Extensive publicity usually accompanies such occurrences. Psychologists and counselors are rallied to provide "coping" assistance to students to prevent "emotional scarring." Affluence enables schools to pay for such services; thus few taxpayers and no parents begrudge the costs. Such counseling was nonexistent a few decades ago. Students were hardier, taxpayers stingier, and less prosperous parents were not overly concerned with shielding their children from reality.

Children of dominant mothers constitute a student minority, and their percentages are likely to continue shrinking. Since public school enrollment is made up largely of nondominant students, the system is inadequate for many dominant students. Considering that the majority of teachers may also be nondominant (and possibly the product of an inferior education themselves), their failure to motivate dominant pupils to excel becomes understandable. This situation does not confine itself to particular geographical areas nor does it exclude private schools. Some schools, public and private, do better than others; but all fail if one judges them by across-the-board student excellence.

As discussed in Chapter X, Discrimination, until recently dominant women were basically confined to the home, teaching, or nursing. They had few opportunities to achieve in other fields. From the political founding of the United States in 1776, 144 years passed before women acquired the right to vote in 1920. Although successful in gaining voting rights, they learned that those rights alone were not enough to appreciably change their status. Dominant women continued teaching because they found little acceptance in business, finance, or other traditionally male careers. That state of affairs continued for more than a generation after Women's Suffrage.

With the advent of the Great Depression, few opportunities for economic progress existed for either sex. In reality fewer achievement-oriented jobs were available than the number of dominant men to fill them. Consequently, the work opportunities of dominant women remained limited for the Depression's duration. Economic circumstances during the 1930s kept dominant women in the places they had long occupied: homes, schools, and hospitals. However, the relative affluence of the 1920s coinciding with Women's Suffrage gave an inkling of the future awaiting dominant women beyond the Depression.

There is outrageous irony in past discrimination against dominant women, particularly in limiting their achievement opportunities to teaching. Confined to teaching, these dominant women were major contributors to producing the best educated children in sheer numbers the world had ever known.

Dominant teachers with high expectations for their students demanded excellence of them. Students with high dominance levels responded and excelled in their studies. It was taken for granted that these teachers should expect obedience and should get it, and they did. Disobedience was handled quickly by dominant teachers and just as quickly by parents. The overwhelming majority of teachers were competent in their fields, and they had the confidence, determination, and sheer willpower to transfer knowledge to their students.

During World War II, large numbers of women entered the work force for the first time. The necessities of war made jobs available, and this set the stage for a different future for women in the world of work. Dominant women teachers were not directly affected. They had tenure, retirement benefits, dedication, and the pull of the status quo to keep them at their posts. They continued teaching; consequently, the quality of education did not deteriorate during the 1940s.

The decline of the school system resulted from a combination of factors. One was the changing ratio of teacher dominance. As a greater variety of opportunities became available to women, a sizable number of nondominant men and women filled the void created by younger, dominant women avoiding the teaching profession or leaving after a few years for higher-paying careers in other fields. At the same time many dominant teachers reached retirement age. This combination of occurrences weakened the system. Perhaps those making plans to revitalize the schools should consider these circumstances and their ramifications.

Dominant women are active in today's work force. They are physicians, politicians, and upwardly mobile executives in all branches of commerce and finance. These women are achieving the successes denied their mothers, maternal grandmothers, and maternal great-grandmothers, many of whom were the schoolteachers of yesteryear.

The increasing scarcity of highly dominant men has helped eliminate the blatant job discrimination of the past. With fewer dominant men, competition faced by dominant women for higher-paying careers has been reduced. The loss of dominant women to teaching means that their traditional teaching roles are being filled chiefly by nondominant men and women. The trend in the dominance levels of public school teachers is downward and is contributing to the less than desirable results we are seeing in our educational system.

Nondominant teachers are not always successful at imparting knowledge to dominant students. Unless highly knowledgeable in their subject, they may be unable to gain and keep these students' interest or respect. Some nondominant students meet a lack of demand for excellence with favor; some dominant students experience frustration. They are left unchallenged, their need to achieve unstimulated. Without the stimulus of something to strive toward or someone to look up to, which the nondominant teacher is not always able to provide, a dominant pupil's mind may be barely engaged. His dominant mother's early demands for excellence exerted from birth forward may be thwarted.

Talented students whose mothers encouraged them to develop early reading skills sometimes realize that they are more conversant with certain subjects than their instructors. That can foster disdain and, at the least, a lack of interest in the course work. Lack of interest in or challenge by the subject matter undoubtedly contributes greatly to the diminishing number of students with scores in the very highest range on the Scholastic Aptitude Test, a widely used national college admissions test. Another problem involves the effectiveness of the schools of education responsible for preparing teachers to teach.

Under the right circumstances, dominant students can excel from instruction by nondominant teachers. A highly intelligent nondominant teacher, well informed in a subject, can fire the interest and imagination of a dominant student and motivate him to excel in that subject. Such a teacher can exert a positive effect on the achievement levels of all students including nondominant ones. (A dominant teacher making continuous demands often alienates rather than challenges nondominant pupils.)

In the face of the country's diminishing dominance levels, many problems in the public school system are affected by public expectations of education, particularly that education means intelligence. The idea that education alone creates intelligence seems to have taken root. That encourages the false conviction that the greater a person's educational level, the greater his intelligence. It creates and fosters the belief that if one is not smart, it is because he did not apply himself. Because of a lower intelligence level, one may be penalized throughout life for something over which he has little or no control.

ᏒᏒᏒ ᏕᏕᏕ

Cyclical timing differences between Japan and the United States appear in each country's educational system. Several factors cause the Japanese system's superior results as compared to the less favorable results of the United States public school system. Japan's educational superiority is the outcome of the work-ethic level which presently prevails there, the large numbers of dominant students reared without affluence, the job discrimination against dominant women, and the birth rate by dominant women. Nowhere in the world today are dominant mothers more visible or more discussed. They begin making demands on children in infancy. Massive pressure and intense coaching continue until the adolescent enters college.

As Japan's affluence increases, these factors will almost certainly change in the way they changed in the United States. Over time, a decline much like that in the American public school system will materialize.

Currently, teachers are in the top 10 percent of all Japanese wage earners, and four out of five high-school teachers are men. In time Japan will realize a high level of affluence, negatively affecting childbearing by dominant women. The need for dominant men and women will pull dominant teachers into the executive suites of business, finance, and government. Less dominant men and women will fill the vacuum created by the exodus of dominant teachers. The Japanese public school system will weaken, and its quality will become noticeably lower.

Even Japan's current educational controversy resembles that in America beginning in the late 1950s, when misbehavior and disobedience began to be increasingly tolerated in American public schools. Similar behavior is appearing in the junior high segment of Japanese public schools, but it is attributed to the bullying of some students by others.

Bernard Wysocki, Jr., in The Wall Street Journal, "Hazing of Schoolmates Rises Sharply in Japan, Alarming the Public," of November 12, 1985, quotes Shinsaku Nojyu, a student counselor: "We're trying to make school more fun for students with singing contests, class trips, and special free-time periods. We're trying to make things brighter here." Wysocki notes that Japanese skeptics say the problems won't truly subside until Japan overhauls its educational system, offers more freedom to its students, gives them more interesting classwork, puts less emphasis on the all-important entrance-exam system, and decreases parental pressure for academic success.

Do these solutions have a familiar ring? They should. These were America's answers to disobedience and misbehavior beginning with students born after 1945 when they reached junior high in the late 1950s and early 1960s!

ᘯᘓ ᘯᘓ ᘯᘓ ᘍᖾ ᘍᖾ ᘍᖾ

Secretary of Education Terrel H. Bell created the National Commission on Excellence in Education in August 1981 because of his concern about "the widespread public perception that something is seriously remiss in our educational system." Chaired by David P. Gardner with Yvonne W. Larsen as Vice-Chair, the eighteen-member panel in April 1983 delivered a scathing report to the President titled *A Nation at Risk*. Rejecting bureaucratic language, the report was concise, understandable, and explicit in describing problems in education.

Among the findings and conclusions, the following especially stand out:

. . . the educational foundations of our society are presently being eroded by a rising tide of mediocrity that threatens our very future as a Nation and a people. . . .

If an unfriendly foreign power had attempted to impose on America the mediocre educational performance that exists today, we might well have viewed it as an act of war. As it stands, we have allowed this to happen to ourselves. . . .

Some 23 million American adults are functionally illiterate by the simplest tests of everyday reading, writing, and comprehension.

About 13 percent of all 17-year-olds in the United States can be considered functionally illiterate. Functional illiteracy among minority youth may run as high as 40 percent.

Between 1975 and 1980, remedial mathematics courses in public 4-year colleges increased by 72 percent and now constitute one-quarter of all mathematics courses taught in those institutions.

. . . More and more young people emerge from high school ready neither for college nor for work. . . .

. . . In some colleges maintaining enrollments is of greater day-to-day concern than maintaining rigorous academic standards. . . .

Twenty-five percent of the credits earned by general track high school students are in physical and health education, work experience outside the school, remedial English and mathematics, and personal service and development courses, such as training for adulthood and marriage.

A 1980 State-by-State survey of high school diploma requirements reveals that only eight States require high schools to offer foreign language instruction, but none requires students to take the courses. Thirty-five States require only 1 year of mathematics, and 36 require only 1 year of science for a diploma.

One-fifth of all 4-year public colleges in the United States must accept every high school graduate within the State regardless of program followed or grades, thereby serving notice to high school students that they can expect to attend college even if they do not follow a demanding course of study in high school or perform well.

. . . During the past decade or so a large number of texts have been "written down" by their publishers to ever-lower reading levels in response to perceived market demands.

In many schools, the time spent learning how to cook and drive counts as much toward a high school diploma as the time spent studying mathematics, English, chemistry, U.S. history, or biology.

Too many teachers are being drawn from the bottom quarter of graduating high school and college students.

The teacher preparation curriculum is weighted heavily with courses in "educational methods" at the expense of courses in subjects to be taught. . . .

Half of the newly employed mathematics, science, and English teachers are not qualified to teach these subjects; fewer than one-third of U.S. high schools offer physics taught by qualified teachers.

Particularly insightful and portentous is the Commission's statement, "For our country to function, citizens must be able to reach some common understandings on complex issues, often on short notice and on the basis of conflicting or incomplete evidence."

A Nation at Risk presents problems and forcefully suggests solutions for those interested in educational reform. The report stirred action. Political concern about education moved up a few notches; twenty state legislatures passed new educational packages and spending on schools rose. But five years later, reforms continued to be debated, and the consensus was that the nation was still at risk.

Additional information about the public school system's problems comes from the College Entrance Examination Board, the organization responsible for the Scholastic Aptitude Test (SAT). These and similar tests have been administered since June 1926. The SAT was designed to be an unchanging measurement. Its primary purpose, today as then, is to provide college admissions personnel with a measure of academic potential that is not based on a specific secondary school curriculum. The SAT is used in conjunction with high-school grades and other qualifications as evidence of ability to perform college work. It is also used to aid in scholarship selection and guidance counseling.

Published SAT results became available beginning with the academic year 1951-1952. That year, the median for all test scores was 476 on the Verbal and 494 on the Mathematical test sections (perfect scores being 800 in each). That reflected test results principally for students born in 1933 who completed high school and started college in 1952.

A dramatic difference exists between the SAT results for the academic year 1962-1963 (most participants born in 1944) and 1983-1984 (most born in 1965). The 1962-1963 period reflected primary and secondary education's zenith in the SAT scores: Verbal, 478 and Mathematical, 502. (The SAT scores of the academic year 1955-1956 for those born primarily in 1937 matched those of 1962-1963.) The 1983-1984 scores fell to 426 Verbal and 471 Mathematical.

The decline from 1962-1963 to 1983-1984 is unequaled. In only twenty-one years, slightly less than one generation, Verbal scores dropped fifty-two points and Mathematical scores dropped thirty-one points. Even though both scores showed a small upturn in 1984-1985, the annual declines resumed with the 1985-1986 academic year.

The downward trend in the number of highly talented pupils with SAT scores of 700 or above is particularly disturbing. These figures are not affected by the increased number of students, minority or otherwise, taking the SAT today compared to earlier periods. These numbers represent specific students achieving specific scores. In 1962-1963, 19,099 students scored 700 or above on the Verbal scale, and 40,644 made 700 or above on the Mathematical scale. In 1983-1984 only 9,392 met that level on the Verbal section and only

32,469 on the Mathematical. This drop occurred even though the country's population had increased markedly during those twenty-one years, and the number of students taking the SAT had risen from 914,204 in 1962-1963 to 964,684 in 1983-1984.

Little or no attempt has been made to rationalize the severe drop in the very highest scores. At the same time they are not widely publicized. In the 1962-1963 academic year, a very high score of 750-800 was achieved by 2,673 participants on the Verbal portion and by 8,628 on the Mathematical. In 1983-1984 only 1,588 and 7,002 scored in the 750-800 range on the Verbal and Mathematical sections. Can the number of high-scoring students decline further? In 1988 only 986 students scored 750-800 on the Verbal section of the SAT. The numbers of the country's most brilliant high-school graduates plummeted. Alarming? Yes. The cause determined? No.

Large baby boom families have been advanced as one reason for the drop in SAT scores from 1964 forward. At the peak of the 1946-1964 baby boom, the average was 3.8 births per woman. The thinking was that with larger families, parental attention must be shared among several siblings and thereby diminishes. That is exposed as a rationalization when one compares baby boom family size with earlier American periods when families were considerably larger. (Interesting although unusable for comparison, the first United States census in 1790 implied just under eight births per woman, more than double the baby boom birth rate. The mortality rate of live births was considerably greater than now, but in some families the survival rate surpassed current ratios.)

Many of the world's achievers and intellectual leaders came from large families. George Canning had ten siblings; Charlemagne, six; John Churchill, Duke of Marlborough, eleven (seven died in infancy); Francis Galton, six; John Stuart Mill, eight; Washington Irving, seven; George Herbert, nine; Oliver Cromwell, fifteen (three died in infancy); Benjamin Franklin, nine; Lord Nelson, ten; Jacques Benigne Bossuet, nine; Charles Darwin, five; William Shakespeare, at least seven; Michelangelo, four. In addition, contemporary achievers such as John F. Kennedy and Nelson A. Rockefeller had considerably more siblings than the baby boom average. Family size, large or small, has little to do with SAT scores; it is the mother's influence and early efforts that contribute to scores—high or low.

In 1977 the College Entrance Examination Board's publication *On Further Examination* states, in Part Three—The Two Score Declines, "Fourteen years of uninterrupted decline in the SAT scores create the illusion that there is some single force or closely related set of forces at work here. This isn't the case."

Actually, that could be the case. A *single force* to consider is dominance: the dominance levels of students taking the SAT combined with the teacher dominance levels during the pupils' twelve-year school experience. The *closely related set of forces* could be the changing dominance level ratios that coincided with the country's realization of affluence in 1946.

In Part Four—Circumstantial Evidence, the Board notes:

Searching for the causes of the SAT score decline over the past six or seven years is essentially an exercise in conjecture. So much has happened that may have affected this record that there is no way of telling what did; the only evidence is circumstantial, leaving it hard to distinguish cause from coincidence. Most of the 50 or so theories brought to the panel's attention have in common only three assumptions; first, that since the problem has been reduced to a single statistic—the drop in these averages—there must be a single answer; second, that what has happened is in every respect bad; and third, that whatever caused it is somebody else's fault.

Perhaps all three assumptions are correct!

Although most adults agree that the public school system has been producing inferior results since 1964 compared to earlier periods, few concur on the causes or on methods for improvement. Opinions proliferate on the changes needed to improve the system. The only unanimity seems to be the desire to produce better educated children in the future than are being produced today.

One recommendation suggests eliminating the SAT and similar tests. Proponents argue that creative abilities cannot be measured by these tests; others, inferring cultural bias, accuse the tests of unfairness to ethnic groups. Some simply conclude that there is no need for such testing, since of over two thousand four-year colleges, less than one hundred remain highly selective in test score requirements. The overwhelming majority consider virtually all applicants.

Unless other standardized achievement tests are substituted, eliminating the SAT and similar tests only hides deficiencies of the public school system. That could dilute and postpone perception of the need for change. However, nothing would be solved. Students will have the same mental aptitudes whether measured or not. Successes or failures in college and later careers will be identical with or without test scores to sound the alarm. Eliminating testing cannot eliminate deterioration in the educational system. At least with testing, classroom learning problems will continue to have exposure.

Although most of the country's leading educators understand the direct correlation between intelligence (as presently measured) and SAT and similar test scores, few would willingly bring that information to the public's attention. Informed politicians also know of this strong relationship. Both recognize the strength of parental concern as to the intelligence of their children. Educators realize that they would be publicly condemned for focusing on the correlation of test scores with intelligence. Most people are unwilling to acknowledge the linkage between SAT and similar test scores and intelligence, even though their common sense makes the connection.

Even though students take general aptitude tests every few years, these are not comparable to the Scholastic Aptitude Test. The College Board, in cooperation with public school systems, could render the country a valuable service by administering the SAT to all graduating high-school seniors without regard to future educational plans. A comparable exam could be designed for all sixth grade students, thus assessing the mental abilities of those who drop out before completing the twelfth grade. This could help gauge the nation's future intellectual resources. Equally important, as public school system changes are implemented, these assessments can measure whether the changes are positive or negative. There is little doubt that dramatic and costly changes will be made. Had we had some such testing program during the past twenty-five years, we could have prevented costly mistakes in effort and money.

Other less extreme ideas have been suggested to improve the public school system; however, many have offsetting debits. One frequently heard involves pay increases for teachers tied to higher competency requirements. Since the proposed monetary increases have not been particularly large, it is questionable how much the competency requirements could be raised. In any event, teacher pay raises come from increased taxes. Income or property tax hikes to support public education are often resented by those in the upper six income categories. More and more of this population segment do not have school-age children or, if they do, have them in private schools. If teacher pay increases were funded through a sales tax, the lowest three income categories would have their real income reduced, requiring them to cut personal spending—something they would surely resent.

Raising taxes addresses only one side of the equation. Assume that the problems of taxing special interest groups were overcome and that a fairly large tax increase to fund a substantial teacher pay increase were passed. Higher competency requirements, the reason for the tax and pay increases, could then be instituted. Dramatically increased teacher pay combined with the country's diminishing dominance levels could set in motion a bidding contest for these professionals. Business firms, financial institutions, and entrepreneurs would definitely up the ante rather than cede great numbers of these achievers to public schools. On the other hand, how would the teachers who fall below the new competency standards be removed? How could this be done fairly? How would their unions react? How could potential improvement in the schools versus lost jobs be justified?

These questions are not new. Many government, education, and civic leaders and parents know the problems. What is not realized or understood is the degree to which changing dominance levels in teachers and pupils have already influenced and will continue to influence the public school system.

Private school enrollments may rise even in institutions no better than public schools as parents seek a better education for their children. However, the solutions to the pervasive problems of education may well lie outside the province of existing private schools.

ᏧᏩᏧᏩᏧᏩ ᏑᎲ ᏑᎲ ᏑᎲ

Affluence was primarily responsible for the proliferation of universities, colleges, and junior colleges. Higher education has been affordable since 1964 because of parental, state, and federal largess.

Only an affluent society can afford to spend public money on such endeavors—building, funding, staffing, and maintaining these institutions—since tuition at public colleges and universities is relatively low compared to operating expenses. (Government-guaranteed student loans are an indirect subsidy, since they are available to students at public and private institutions.) Without affluence neither governments nor parents could afford this level of formal education for so many.

The growth of institutions of higher learning was intended to produce an outstanding advanced education system. Society now espouses a college degree as necessary for success; that became a greater propellant for higher education than either intellectual ability or a desire for knowledge.

Since 1964 and society's decree that every individual can and should obtain a college diploma, the expression "not college material" virtually disappeared from popular usage. At some universities where minimum entry requirements using tests such as the SAT were still employed with other screening to admit only bright students, another adage became common: "There is a college for every IQ."

The baby boom ended in 1964; the last baby boomers were seventeen years old in 1981. From 1964 through 1981, 1,114 new institutions of higher learning, including community and junior colleges, opened, an increase from 2,139 to 3,253. Another twenty-seven were added in 1982, bringing the level to 3,280 institutions at the time the last baby boomers became eighteen. In 1983 there was a slowdown with only four new institutions. The expansion has now virtually ceased; soon a constriction will begin. As the country's affluence deteriorates, college closings will become commonplace. The growth of new institutions failed to improve the country's overall intelligence level or to prevent its decline.

America reached the high-water mark for new colleges and universities between 1968 and 1970 when 151 were opened, a 6 percent gain to 2,525 from 2,374. The largest growth took place in junior and community colleges.

From 1964 through 1985, two-year colleges provided a place for even more students wanting higher education. In 1985 there were 1,274 junior colleges with about five million students. The general public does not seem to realize that much of that growth was only indirectly related to advanced studies in the standard college or university curriculum. Even though some highly successful, late-maturing individuals who want a second chance go to community colleges as a prelude to starting university work, much of what these colleges offer is closer to that formerly provided by the extension divisions of universities and called "adult education," courses which did not result in a degree but at most a certificate. Business and industry use community colleges for technical and refresher training, senior citizens for later life enrichment, and deficient students for remedial work. These pursuits are commendable, but few taxpayers directly benefit from them although they bear the costs of such secondary benefits.

Considering the expense involved, the large number of institutions of higher learning has produced different results from those intended. Two are adverse. One involves taxes: higher taxes coupled with unsatisfactory results tend to foster taxpayer animosity. The other is in false expectations: of the society that paid for the institutions, of the educators employed there, of the parents of the children attending them, and of the students and graduates themselves.

The elevated expectations of a nondominant person with below-average intelligence who obtains a college diploma may well prove unrealistic as concerns his future accomplishments and thereby detrimental to his happiness. Spending several years in college does not necessarily increase a person's success potential as society currently defines success. Without the prospect of a diploma, some of these individuals would perhaps be more content. Without a degree, they might be less concerned with acquiring the trappings of success that many times fail to materialize. Of course they might still believe that they could have done better had they obtained a college degree.

At the same time, the average annual income of college graduates is considerably higher than the average of those who do not attend college. Two generations ago, a similar earning gap existed between high-school graduates and those who completed only the seventh grade. In addition there is a general perception that college attendance turns students into wage earners and taxpayers rather than leaving them dependent on the nation's social services.

That a person with below-average or even average intelligence without a strong achievement orientation can receive an under-graduate degree reflects the good intentions of society—perhaps incorrectly focused on higher education. Possibly that is the culmination of an affluent society's educational philosophy: that attendance alone entitles one to a college degree regardless of ability.

The number of colleges still could have increased somewhat with affluence but without a baby boom. And the national intelligence level might still have dropped.

The growing number of college freshmen and even college seniors who barely have a speaking acquaintance with English though born and reared in the United States is a sign of lower achievement needs. Another indication is the number of those who, before entering college, came close to matching their TV viewing time with their sleeping time.

Many blame public school superintendents for the poor general performance of students. A close look reveals that the position is underpaid and superintendents are caught in the middle, sandwiched between federal and state laws, school board members, teachers and their unions, parents who have opted out of their responsibilities, and in particular, early child-rearing practices over which superintendents have no control.

Enculturation, affluence, and the modern expectation of a higher education have enabled educators, parents, politicians, and students to ignore the high predictability of future college performance which SAT and similar test scores provide. These indicators are available to all students and parents. Affluence has elevated society's expectations and enables students mentally unequipped for a college curriculum (some 30 to 35 percent of total enrollment) and their parents to look the other way in the face of such portents of college performance. As A Nation at Risk suggests, administrators and teachers at marginal colleges may foster the willful disregard of these indicators to sustain enrollment and retain their jobs. Affluence could be described as the ability to afford something of marginal or questionable value.

Today we have a surplus of at least one thousand advanced education facilities, including community and junior colleges, representing billions of dollars in expenditures. Only affluence, as in an affluent society, affluent state and federal governments, and affluent parents, can continue to support such an educational structure.

In May 1988 The Wall Street Journal noted a comment in a recent College Board study that about 45 to 50 percent of all college students are age twenty-five or older. The *Journal* also quoted findings from another study that serious interest in college is being shown by adults through age forty-five. Some students are working full time and taking night courses. Others are on sabbatical leave to acquire a higher degree in order to attain a better paying position. A sizable number, however, make college attendance their profession and continue in this "career" for years. Might affluence also be described as allowing one's children to delay maturing and accepting responsibility in the society?

In earlier decades the pejorative term "professional student" applied to a minuscule percentage of students. Since their dramatic increase, the phrase seems to have been dropped from common usage. Facing closure and in desperate need of enrollments, some colleges are exploring day care and family housing to attract older students. Some colleges even publicize those well past retirement age who obtain college degrees.

Many a "mature" college graduate today, with degree in hand, has unrealistic expectations about the kind of job he is eligible for and the money he will earn, especially as compared to his same age group a generation ago. He does not realize that before 1964 a college degree had greater value because of the smaller number of graduates and the superior education it represented.

In 1952 only half of all students completed high school. (Some educators believe that an average 1952 eighth grade education equaled an average 1987 twelfth grade education.) By 1964 the number increased to two-thirds and by 1970 to three-fourths. About a quarter of high-school graduates went to college in 1952, about a third in 1964, and almost half by 1970.

Telling questions could be raised about the 25 percent who attended college in 1952 and the 75 percent who did not. Were the 25 percent better educated than they would be today? Were the 75 percent who did not attend college in 1952 worse off than many who have gone to college since the 1970s? Answers might lie in the intellectual and achievement distribution in the United States population.

One avowed purpose of education is to balance or equalize the distribution of wealth and social power. Increasing the number of years each student attends school and decreasing the drop-out rate have not contributed greatly to meeting this goal. For example, less than four generations ago in 1900, only 6.3 percent of the seventeen-year-old population finished the eleventh grade (the final year of high school in many communities) and graduated from high school, compared to the 75 percent in 1988 who received high-school diplomas.

Harry Truman was one of those graduating from high school in 1901, finishing seven years of grammar school and three years of high school. He did not attend college; at age thirty-nine he enrolled in the Kansas City Law School for evening classes and dropped out after two years. Yet Harry Truman became the thirty-third President of the United States. Is it likely today that someone who did not attend college could become president?

Increased high-school graduation often followed today by college attendance has not changed the unequal distribution of wealth and power. Higher education of the less intelligent merely instills false expectations for success.

It is possible, although not probable, that we could address the problem of too many under-educated people holding degrees from inadequate educational institutions by changing the idea of worth. If individual dignity, for example, could become a value honored in our society, we might then come to consider a person's spirit of social duty and service and his goodness as a human being as worthy as high intelligence and a high educational level.

Dignity of work at all levels could come to be regarded as valuable, as it once was when children were taught, "anything worth doing is worth doing well." The efforts and accomplishments of people who are not, and never can be, highly intelligent could come to be appreciated as contributions to society. Unless dignity is restored to those of less-than-average intelligence, any democratic efforts for dramatic change in the public school system will fail.

We could try to restore faith in the quality of education on the elementary and high-school levels and to discourage the idea of a college degree for all, especially if an inferior degree. In any case, however much we can improve our educational system, it cannot increase or maximize intelligence if child-training practices have not laid the foundation for intellectual stimulus. If society reassesses and emphasizes the value of the person—his dignity and self-worth—

separate from his intelligence, the public school system might then respond. After such a change of attitude, the system could be modified to serve the needs of individual students.

๙๒ ๙๒ ๙๒ ฌ ฌ ฌ

The demise of the Age of Intellect will occur when: (1) dominant individuals born before 1946 grow too old or dwindle too much to contribute to new national intellectual achievements (members of the accomplishing generation of the year 2006 will be those born exclusively from 1946 forward) and (2) the country's wealth is so diminished that parents and taxpayers cannot support mass higher education along with other, more crucial financial demands.

These two conditions have little or no relationship, yet it is highly probable that they will transpire only a few years apart. An identifiable downturn in the nation's intellectual achievements will coincide with a dramatic drop in the number of colleges and college enrollments. At that time, the number of colleges and universities and their enrollments may well drop to the population percentage levels of the 1950s and eventually even lower. As in past empires, reductions in formal educational facilities will seem to be the cause of reduced intellectual achievements. Despite one appearing to cause the other, both conditions are ultimately traceable to the change in dominance levels resulting from the withholding of children by dominant women, in combination with waning affluence.

The Ages of Affluence and Intellect, beginning eighteen years apart, are inexorably tied together. As affluence wanes, so will the educational problems associated with the Age of Intellect. At the end of the Age of Intellect, new educational problems will arise more serious than those of today. As Will Durant notes in *The Life of Greece*, "Science and philosophy, in the history of states, reach their height after decadence has set in; wisdom is a harbinger of death."

Chapter XVII

The Age
of Decadence

What is decadence? The dictionary defines it as the process of decay or decline. To understand it however we need to compare: Decaying or declining from what? Falling from what superior condition to what inferior condition? Like beauty, decadence is in the eye of the beholder. A religious conservative over age sixty can readily define decadence; in a lifetime, he has witnessed drastic changes in social and moral values. On the other hand, the average American teen-ager's definition would probably be vague, but though poorly understood by the conservative it would be easily understood by his peers. An understanding of the concept of decadence can only be arrived at by considering it as a process rather than as a series of specific behaviors.

Every society can be defined by the formal structures through which it expresses its preferred values in such areas as the family, commerce, law, and government. Over time, changes in these structures mark the evolution of the society. As long as such changes are modifications of the traditional structures, the "new" society still retains its identity. A society can be said to decay when large segments of its population seek not to adapt its defining structures but to abandon them wholesale as irrelevant to the way they choose to live.

In 1964 Beatlemania, protests, riots, and other cultural cross-currents signaled the arrival of the Age of Decadence (coinciding with the Age of Intellect). The rise of the counterculture had at its core the ideal of repudiating the "system" in favor of "doing your own thing." The growing numbers of long-haired "hippies" wished either to overthrow the "establishment," by violence if necessary, or simply to "tune in, turn on, drop out." This group differed sharply from past rebellious generations, who had decried mediocrity and commercialism in the masses but continued to live within existing social structures. Where earlier rebels often used the arts as the medium for expressing their criticisms and ideals, many members of the Sixties era believed that they could make a new and better world if they destroyed existing social structures.

Although many young people, including a great number with high dominance, followed traditional paths and remained outside the movement, other dominant youths became counterculture leaders in search of social change. Large numbers of nondominant young people, unable to compete with their more dominant contemporaries or simply uninterested in achievement of any sort, provided an enormous base of followers helping to bring the counterculture into being. The first Pied Pipers mobilizing and leading these youths were older and more dominant than they. In 1964 those born between 1938 and 1945 and aged nineteen to twenty-six formed the vanguard of the opposition to conventional culture. They were the "pioneers" of the Age of Decadence.

৩৫ ৩৫ ৩৫ ৯৮ ৯৮ ৯৮

How did this movement, unparalleled in American history, come about? What caused so many young Americans to spurn the structures of their society? The Age of Decadence occurred as a result of two factors: changing dominance levels and the effects of the Age of Affluence.

The world's then-largest baby boom began in the United States in 1946. Only three other countries, Australia, Canada, and New Zealand, experienced similar baby booms but on a smaller scale. Past baby booms had differing causes, beginnings, and end results. (The introduction of wire window screens in Africa dramatically decreased infant mortality and, in effect, created a baby boom.) The magnitude of the American baby boom, lasting nineteen years and ending in 1964, was without equal.

As previously posited, dominant women began having fewer children than less dominant women in 1946. This was a decision taken by a sizable percentage of dominant women in contrast to their nondominant counterparts, although their actions were hidden in the sheer numbers of children born between 1946 and 1964. This nineteen-year period produced 76.4 million children, approximately 31 percent of the 1988 population and 42 percent of the eligible electorate.

The changing composition of dominance only minimally affected the period in which the first baby boomers grew up. In retrospect, the effects of changing dominance levels among young people were recognizable by 1964. Reaching early adulthood that year, they began influencing events across the country.

Were these children reared differently from those of earlier generations, or did the magnitude of the baby boom highlight child-training practices?

Dr. Benjamin Spock's *Common Sense Book of Baby and Child Care*, first published in 1946, is the all-time best seller specifically addressing child-rearing practices. Dr. Spock's book has been identified as an important source of today's adult permissiveness. Although incorrect, one can support that contention by selected excerpts from the 1946 edition:

He doesn't have to be sternly trained. You may hear people say that you have to get your baby strictly regulated in his feeding, sleeping, bowel movements, and other habits—but don't believe this either. In the first place, you can't get a baby regulated beyond a certain point, no matter how hard you try. In the second place, you are more apt, in the long run, to make him balky and disagreeable when you go at his training too hard. Everyone wants his child to turn out to be healthy in his habits and easy to live with. But each child wants, himself, to eat at sensible hours, and later to learn good table manners. . . .

The same thing goes, later on, for discipline, good behavior, and pleasant manners. You can't drill these into a child from the outside in a hundred years. The desire to get along with other people happily and considerately develops within him as part of the unfolding of his nature, provided he grows up with loving, self-respecting parents.

Suggestions for sensible training. If you want to be *completely* natural, you can leave bowel training almost entirely up to your baby. . . .

Some mothers who have been bitten ask if they should bite back. . . . The only thing you really need to do is to keep from being bitten again, by drawing back when he gets that gleam in his eye.

In general, remember that what makes your child behave well is not threats or punishment but loving you for your agreeableness and respecting you for knowing your rights and his. . . .

That brings up the question of teaching a bright child to read and figure at home before he starts first grade. It often does harm, and it never helps. It will only put him out of step with the other children, and may make it more difficult for him to catch onto the school's system of teaching these subjects. . . .

Michael Seiler in the *Los Angeles Times* quotes Dr. Spock in 1986: "My book's main effect was that parents realized they didn't have to intimidate their children the way I was intimidated as a child by my sternly disapproving mother." Few Americans in their eighties are as dominant and outspoken as Dr. Spock, still striving to achieve and influence people. His qualities of leadership and independence, fostering his later crusades and varied achievements, can be directly attributed to his dominant mother. What child-training practices did his mother use? If Dr. Spock had written a book in 1946 detailing how his mother reared him, it might not have gained as wide a readership.

Dr. Spock did not create permissiveness in child-rearing practices, and it is doubtful that his book materially influenced dominant mothers. With more than thirty million copies sold, *Baby and Child Care*'s timing fit the country's collective attitude and the changing dominance ratios produced by affluence from 1946 forward.

James Dobson's *Dare to Discipline* (1970) fits well with dominant mothers' child-rearing practices. Even though over a million copies have been sold, the book is unlikely to materially influence non-dominant mothers.

The Age of Affluence caused the Age of Decadence. Affluence provided the fuel for continuation and acceleration of the Age of Decadence after 1964; it paid the bills. The Haight-Ashbury subculture of San Francisco in 1967, for instance, was supported to some extent by indulgent and, more importantly, affluent parents. Communal living, a fad from the 1960s and the 1970s, has faded. Nevertheless, the counterculture's lessening influence and a move toward more traditional values did not stem the tide of decadence. Though made up of somewhat different components, decadence was greater in 1989 than in 1964.

Communal living did not originate recently. Experiments in utopian lifestyles have a long and varied history. Charles Fourier's ideas were influential in the United States during the 1840s; an estimated twenty-eight Fourierist communal colonies were established between 1841 and 1859. They failed because of financial problems and public outcry, as did several communes in Illinois, Missouri, and Texas established by Etienne Cabet. The Oneida Community of Oneida, New York, founded in 1848 by John Noyes, was another early attempt at communal living and was unique since all husbands and wives were physically shared. The goal of such sharing was to create superior offspring.

Even though the hippie communal lifestyle was not new, its scope was unequaled; yet no great public outcry resulted. On the contrary, much of the money necessary for the livelihood of its members, and in some instances for drug habits and later rehabilitation, came from affluent parents. The communes did not support themselves.

The affluent federal government contributed to the Age of Decadence. It spent vast sums in efforts to eliminate poverty.

Through the 1970s work, particularly low-paying work, was plentiful. During this period the government augmented the income of those who were able but chose not to work, often because they believed the available jobs to be unworthy of them, or who chose work that they found more meaningful (and less arduous) but unavailable.

In the United States before 1946, neither great parental largess nor bountiful government subsidy was available to support those who chose not to work or those whose career expectations exceeded their competence levels. Parents and government could ill afford such financial assistance to able-bodied adults.

Only an affluent country could or would adopt such policies. Only affluent parents in an affluent nation can dispense this largess to their children and support them indefinitely. In the Soviet Union and many other countries during the same period, most parents could not afford to be so generous to their children, nor could the governments support such subsidies. In an unaffluent country, each generation must work.

If one considers decadence to be the decay of existing social institutions because of affluence, one may see the events from 1964 onward more clearly. Since affluence did not extend to all population segments, resentment developed. In 1965 there were riots in the Watts section of Los Angeles, and Malcolm X was murdered. During 1966 the Ku Klux Klan attacked blacks and civil rights workers in the South, and massive rioting spread through the slums of several large cities. Deprived of opportunities to participate in the affluent society, some members of minority groups concluded that their only solution was to tear down the institutions of the society that excluded them. Meanwhile, some affluent young people relied on the very wealth they claimed to despise to support their "alternative lifestyles," a commonly used phrase. They refused to participate in the society that supported them, claiming instead a degree of personal freedom little short of anarchy.

Most of these young people as well as many members of previously excluded minorities eventually entered the mainstream of society, but the Age of Decadence continues. Since 1964 increasing numbers of people consider themselves free from any need to conform to the social norms.

In a society steeped in the tradition that freedom is one of its most cherished assets, it is difficult to understand that maximum personal freedom, freedom of choice, represents a society in decay. (The actions of Adam and Eve when tempted by the serpent represent the first Biblical incident of free choice.) But freedom, like decadence, lies in the eye of the beholder. Nathan Hale, Patrick Henry, George Washington, and countless other heroic defenders of freedom from the country's beginning would have shared with citizens born before 1946 a consistent definition, a common understanding, and a continuity of agreement about the meaning and purpose of freedom. Beginning in 1964, freedom began to develop other connotations, many of which earlier heroes would have called license. The ideal of freedom has been extended to unparalleled lengths for both dominant and nondominant citizens. Used in the most popular fashion, decadence represents freedom at its finest hour.

Before 1964 freedom generally meant the right to pursue socially encouraged and usually constructive goals within the framework of existing social institutions. Since 1964 freedom has instead come to mean freedom to pursue material gain and self-gratification regardless of the rules and values traditional in the society. If these goals conflict with the overall good and cohesiveness of the country, how many care?

Some new "freedoms" enjoyed virtually without penalty even before 1964 included the public use of formerly taboo words, taking the name of God in vain, not keeping the Sabbath holy, and not honoring one's mother and father. Since 1964 coveting, stealing (if limited to small sums or items), and bearing false witness have been tolerated. Sexually explicit or violent material is common and widespread and no onus is attached to consuming it by viewing, reading, or listening. Compared to earlier eras, little is now considered pornographic.

Many advertisers capitalize on the Age's sexual revolution by using innuendo and double meaning in words and pictures to sell their products. Some are more honest; Decadence Parfum was advertised with the phrase "Welcome to the age of Decadence."

In 1987 over two million unwed couples lived together openly and were accepted socially. Many couples postpone marriage, a trend that appears to be increasing. The divorce rate in 1979 and again in 1981 was 5.3 per thousand, the highest in the country's history. (In 1960 the divorce rate was 2.2 per thousand.) Living with only one parent, most often the mother, is now a way of life for many children.

"Freedom" to amass and exhibit enormous wealth is also more acceptable than it once was. Perhaps the most ostentatious flaunting of wealth in the United States occurs via the pages of *Forbes* magazine. In August 1982 the magazine began an annual listing of the four hundred richest Americans and their estimated net worths. The scale, rather than the idea of such a list, is new. According to the Fall 1983 edition, *Forbes* published a list of "America's 30 Richest" in March 1918, two years before the Roaring Twenties. The October 1, 1984, issue noted that other periodicals published similar articles during the 1840s and 1850s. (That was the time of Fourier's and Cabet's communal living experiments.)

Although exhibitions of wealth do not totally break with American tradition, no precedent exists for detailing in this way the numbers of individuals, the amounts of wealth, and whether it is earned or inherited. It is hard to credit that a plutocratic group of the size of the *Forbes* 400 would allow such full national disclosure of its position. Even in the ostentation of Imperial Rome and pre-1789 France, such detail about the wealth of the richest was not publicly circulated.

Disclosures of wealth are popular; newspapers, radio, and television quote from the *Forbes* articles. During the 1960s such disclosures might have provoked additional civil disruptions. In the 1950s they probably would have been considered boorish and pretentious. The list would have been far less dramatic in the 1940s, since the Revenue Act of 1944 imposed the highest income tax in United States history. The surtax on individual incomes exacted a 91 percent tax on any amount over $200 thousand, so that the richest would have made great efforts to avoid publicity. Throughout the Great Depression, such disclosures may have been embarrassing to all but the most crass.

By 1985 these four hundred families had accumulated enormous wealth, even though they represented only a tiny fraction of one percent of the estimated 238.6 million population. According to the

October 1985 *Forbes*, each family averaged 3.08 children. This totaled approximately 2,032 individuals or about one family member per 117,421 Americans. If the cumulative assets of these families, estimated at $134 billion, were converted to gold at the then-current market price, the amount would be more than 398 million troy ounces, 50 percent more gold than owned by the United States government. Further, that wealth in gold would have exceeded the combined gold holdings of central banks and governments of 166 of the world's 173 independent countries.

Even when compared to riches of the past, such wealth is amazing. The amount can be compared to the gold taken by Hernando Cortez and Francisco Pizarro from Mexico and Peru. From 1503 through 1560, the New World sent Spain 101 metric tons of gold. The combined wealth of the *Forbes* 400 measured in gold at the 1985 market price would be over 125 times greater than that amount.

We can make another comparison by converting the $134 billion to silver at the 1985 market price; it would equal over 21.5 billion ounces or 27.1 million talents. For more than two thousand years in the ancient world, the talent was used as currency for the settlement of large transactions. The Persian talent weighed approximately sixty-six pounds and was usually cast as an oval or disk. Had a small group like the *Forbes* 400 living in Old Testament times owned 27.1 million talents of silver (or 502 thousand talents of gold) and it was known that they did so, they may well have been noted in the Bible!

Are the *Forbes* articles decadent? Or are they just one more manifestation of freedom of the press? Apparently *Forbes* does not publish this information to accord honor or recognition of achievement, since it stated in 1985 that 181 members of the *Forbes* 400 controlled fortunes that were mainly or entirely inherited.

"It is easier for a camel to go through the eye of a needle, than for a rich man to enter the kingdom of God." (Matthew 19:24) The clergy in the United States has always been in the forefront in identifying and combating decadence. Since 1964, however, many apparently no longer consider amassing great wealth a form of decadence; some popular spiritual leaders ask their followers for great amounts of money which they put to often flamboyant personal use. Perhaps they are so busy combating less subtle and more obvious aspects of decadence that they overlook Biblical teachings on wealth. Still, some ministers express concern about the use of wealth by religious organizations. Dr. Sam Cannata, missionary-in-residence at Baylor University, criticizes Baptists for building multimillion dollar "Christian country clubs" and neglecting mission work. Cannata declares, "We say these buildings are built for the glory of God, but they're basically for us—it's for ourselves."

"For the love of money is the root of all evil." (I Timothy 6:10) Collective attitudes change after a country realizes affluence; the pursuit of money and the cachet it brings become more important than duty, service, and personal honor. Affluence has caused the gap between the wealthiest and the poorest in the United States to widen since 1964, and it is now greater than at any time since Imperial Rome.

When the pursuit of money becomes all-consuming and great deference is given its owners, societies become increasingly vulnerable to the have-nots from within and without.

◦◦◦◦◦◦

Religious organizations in the United States are being transformed by changing dominance levels in the population. There are dozens of subtly different Protestant sects with liberal, moderate, and conservative factions.

An early strength of Protestantism was its ability to accommodate dominant leaders. Leaders founded new religious sects that were accepted under the Protestant banner. During the first hundred years after its beginning—four generations, 1517 to 1617—there was a worldwide explosion of new denominations. The freedom resulting from Martin Luther's protest set the stage for all the rest.

Sects formed in recent years, whether or not under the Protestant name, have the same beginnings as those since Martin Luther. The way they were created and established, enforce their rules, and convert new members follow the same pattern. Even so, these sects depart drastically from Martin Luther's protest and from the groups founded during Protestantism's first three hundred years.

The most striking difference among new sects and cults in the United States lies in the dominance level of the members. In Martin Luther's case and for generations, the majority of adherents exhibited leadership abilities through religious or secular successes, thus indicating high dominance. Founders of religious groups are still judged dominant because they are leaders, but members of cults formed during the last generation are not strong achievers and so are judged to be primarily nondominant. The same now holds true for established Protestant denominations; the numbers of dominant members appear to be decreasing. In addition, most followers of Roman Catholicism appear primarily nondominant.

Beginning with Luther, the high dominance levels of many members of the sects that came into being produced the Protestant ethic of the past. Many of today's cults, even some under the standard of Protestantism, exploit the nondominant individuals who most often become followers. Possibly one of the worst of these cases was the tragedy of Jonestown, Guyana, during 1978 when more than nine hundred followers of Jim Jones died at his order.

ᵣᶩᵉ ᵣᶩᵉ ᵣᶩᵉ ᵧᶩʰ ᵧᶩʰ ᵧᶩʰ

The triad of affluence, softness, and lack of will contributes to decadence. This triad affects the outcome of battles and wars. It becomes a leash on a great nation's armed forces until enervation replaces the need for restraint. "Civilized" becomes a code word for softness, "barbaric" for hardness.

The lack of will is most evident in political leadership. When affluence and softness prevail in a citizenry, public outcry is directed against warfare and toward maintaining the status quo. Political leaders lack the will to move contrary to such public opinion and those who forcibly do so stand the risk of public disaffection.

Courage and cowardice appear neutral in relation to dominance; both are found in dominant and in nondominant people. In spite of that, military personnel of an affluent nation seem to have less incentive to fight in a poor foreign country than do the natives, perhaps because those who can return to affluence feel they have more to live for. In contrast, the soldiers of the poor country, with less to lose and more to gain, exhibit a will to win made patent by their willingness to die.

In February 1898 the battleship Maine was blown up and 260 crewmen lost their lives. Even though those responsible for the disaster were never clearly identified, the hardened, unaffluent United States blockaded Cuba and went to war with Spain.

In October 1983, 241 Marines lost their lives in a truck bombing in Beirut, Lebanon. Intelligence and evidence on the perpetrators was better established than in the Maine explosion. Yet a soft, affluent United States retreated and abandoned Lebanon.

The 260 who died aboard the Maine and the 241 who died in the Beirut bombing are numerically close and their lives equally precious. Further comparisons are possible, but the major difference lies in the collective attitude of Americans living in 1898 and 1987. Only three and one-half generations apart, valor and offense made the shift to affluence and defense.

The Old Testament mentions property distribution by lot several times. The Roman Emperor Nero used lotteries to make gifts of property and slaves during feasts and entertainments. Lotteries were popular in France for years before the 1789 French Revolution. They were abolished in 1836, opened again in 1933, closed shortly before World War II, and reopened after the war.

Lotteries have a checkered past in the United States. Lottery money provided part of the building funds for several universities— Brown, Columbia, Dartmouth, Harvard, Union, William and Mary, and Yale. Even Thomas Jefferson said, "The lottery is a wonderful thing; it lays the taxation only on the willing."

In 1868 Congress banned lotteries through a law prohibiting use of the mails for such purposes. The Supreme Court upheld the restriction in 1878. The Court's opinion said that lotteries have "a demoralizing influence upon the people." But neither Congress nor the Supreme Court deterred Louisiana from operating its lottery continuously for another generation.

Large-scale entry of state governments into lottery operations became significant after 1964. The earliest popular support originated in the eastern states. New Hampshire held its first sweepstakes in September 1964, the first year of the Age of Decadence. Coincidence? The movement tracked westward, gaining larger markets with novel and sophisticated advertising. Even when sanctioned or operated by the state, lotteries are gambling. Is this a manifestation of decadence or merely taxation directed primarily toward those in lower income categories?

There are other areas of deterioration, whether construed as decadence, degeneration in people or product quality, accidents, or acts of God. While great strides were being made after 1964 in intellectual fields, day-to-day commercial operations deteriorated. Drilling near Santa Barbara, California, created a massive oil leak in 1969 and caused extensive property damage, water pollution, and destruction of wildlife. Since then destructive technological accidents have happened regularly. Profit-conscious businesses sometimes ignore legally mandated safety guidelines and pollution controls.

Meanwhile, employees who focus exclusively on receiving a paycheck ignore their obligation to earn their money by providing quality work. Employee theft is a major problem for many businesses. One opinion survey estimated that *time theft* cost American employers $160 billion in 1985. Major forms of time theft by employees include arriving late or leaving early, excessive socializing with other workers, using the telephone for personal calls, taking long coffee and lunch breaks, and working at a slow pace to create overtime. Before 1964 the problem was not serious enough to have warranted such a survey.

Greater "freedoms" with relatively small penalties are seen in the astronomical increases in white-collar crime and nonviolent theft. First offenders can expect deferred (withheld) adjudication or, if sentenced, probation. Cheating, as in reporting to the Internal Revenue Service, is considered smart.

The government has similar problems. J. Peter Grace, an American business leader, chaired the President's Private Sector Survey on Cost Control (the Grace Commission). In January 1984 he and other business leaders submitted an in-depth account of wasteful government spending. A massive indictment, the report contained specific recommendations to eliminate government squandering of billions of taxpayers' dollars. Grace used personal funds trying to explain, convince, and instigate a change in American thinking toward reducing government expenditures and the national deficit. Who listens? Who cares? Congress ignored and belittled the Grace report. The general public seems unaware of J. Peter Grace; he cannot compete with popular celebrities. (Even though faddish celebrities enjoy only brief interludes of intense publicity, since 1964 their numbers increase dramatically from year to year.)

Nor can the government command the loyalty it once did. Expressions of patriotism raise sophisticated eyebrows. During the Vietnam War, it was excusable to avoid the draft by moving to another country. Some Americans openly supported the North Vietnamese. Definitions of treason became blurred.

In September 1780 General Benedict Arnold, commander of the fort at West Point, secured a place in American history by instigating a plot to turn West Point over to the British. Reasons he gave for his action included disillusionment with American leaders, lack of promotions, and a conviction that the American cause was lost. His justifications fall by the wayside, however, because he proposed selling his services to the British. The rarity of the act of treason placed him in United States history books.

In February 1950 the British arrested Klaus Fuchs, a German-born scientist who had worked on the American Manhattan Project building the first atomic bomb. He and others admitted complicity in relaying atomic secrets to the Soviets, enabling the Soviet Union to build its own atomic bomb and opening the door to future Soviet nuclear technology. Julius and Ethel Rosenberg, both Americans, were implicated in the plot, tried, found guilty, and executed in 1953; many history books record the event.

During 1985, the twenty-second year of the Age of Decadence, thirteen American citizens were arrested and charged with treason for spying. All had a common motivation, the transfer of national security information to a foreign power for money. Thirteen in one year! More to come? Duty, honor, and service become archaic words when the pursuit of money reigns as a pervasive social force. Although Benedict Arnold and the Rosenbergs may remain in American history books, it is doubtful that all thirteen from 1985 or future American traitors will be mentioned or their names remembered—how could so many in such a short time be explained?

This Age can be described further with page after page of statistics. Drug use presents a particularly fertile field. It now appears acceptable for members of the higher income categories to use controlled substances (such as marijuana, LSD, cocaine, amphetamines, and barbiturates) so long as they obey the law in other areas. In these income groups, there are fewer felony convictions than in the past and, in the event of conviction, more cases of probation. How many people today have experimented with marijuana, LSD, cocaine, heroin, MSDA, or uppers and downers? How many are steady users? How many users are there among adults, teen-agers, preteens? What is the tonnage of marijuana confiscated each year by law enforcement agencies? (In December 1985 Edward Barnes and E. Graydon Carter, "Into The Night With The Real Miami Vice" in *Life* magazine, wrote that: "Vice cops say that the Drug Enforcement Agency has a warehouse filled with cocaine worth more than all the gold in Fort Knox.") How many tons of marijuana are cultivated annually? What is its percentage of the cash agricultural crops of each state? What percentage of criminal activities are directly or indirectly attributable to the use or sale of controlled substances? What is the scope of organized crime's profit from the sale of illicit drugs? Drug-related statistics appear in almost every daily, weekly, and monthly news publication in the country and are constantly on radio and television.

Decadence is closely related to crime. Violent crime increased 57 percent between 1960 and 1968. In 1971 there were four days of rioting at Attica Prison in New York State, and a store in Wilmington, Delaware, was firebombed. Indeed prison riots and inmate violence have become commonplace, and bombings of public and private buildings are not unusual in the nation's major cities. During this Age the number of inmates in state and federal penal systems has grown significantly. In 1963 there were 217,283 prisoners. Each year the number increases. Federal and state prisoners in 1985 totaled 481,393, an increase of more than eight times the overall population percentage increase. The costs of enlarging and maintaining the prison system during this severe increase in crime have plagued state governments since 1964.

The magnitude of criminal activity reflected in prison population growth is grossly understated because of the inability of state govern-ments to cope with the problem. If prisoner space requirements used in the past still prevailed; if more new prisons had been built; if juries had continued to give traditional penalties for crimes com-mitted; if legislative and judicial forces had not initiated deferred (withheld) adjudication, conditional releases, early releases, and new probation guidelines; and if the states had followed earlier prison practices with regard to sentencing and paroles; then today's prison populations would be quadruple or even quintuple the stated figures.

Proportionately, there are probably as many dominant people involved in crime as their less dominant counterparts. Much dominant criminal activity centers on white-collar crimes, primarily financial thefts, frauds, and scams. Even though crimes involving the theft of money and goods from individuals, businesses, and the government cost billions of dollars annually, the criminals involved are often treated leniently by judges and juries since they do not threaten human life. The Privacy Act of 1974 offers all criminals, particularly sophisticated criminals who specialize in white-collar crimes, a degree of future anonymity, with the potential to continue their criminal careers. Agencies may not legally show their files on an individual to other agencies without that individual's consent. Since 1974 private businesses, corporations, financial institutions, and broad segments of American endeavor have been forced to make hiring decisions based on incomplete and unverifiable information.

Softness also links affluence, decadence, and crime. In eras when most of a society struggles to make ends meet or to survive, its collective mind does not turn toward rationalizing criminal activities; the public is neither tolerant nor forbearing of lawbreakers. The first colonists in America were not mild or sensitive when meting out criminal justice, and this in a day when crime was more a nuisance than a serious problem.

Although the early harsh treatment of criminals in America diminished with each succeeding generation, the overall unforgiving public attitude against crime prevailed until 1964. The eighteen years of affluence since 1946 were sufficient to introduce softness into American views toward crime. During riots in the late 1960s, police were instructed not to shoot arsonists and looters. For the first time in United States history, rights to the protection of property were subordinated to the right of the criminal to life.

In 1988 a tender-hearted, humane, and merciful American society appeared aghast at actions taken by the Israeli government to quell civil disorders. They also viewed conditions in certain foreign prisons, particularly those in the Soviet Union, as reprehensible.

Israel is in the fortieth year of its ten-generation cycle, comparable to the United States in 1803. At that time in America civil disorders were not tolerated. Slaves were still legally imported, and five years would elapse before their importation became illegal. The Soviet Union, now in the seventy-first year of its current ten-generation cycle, is at the stage the United States had reached in 1834. Prison systems in the twenty-four American states then were harsh, no better than Soviet prisons today. Once released, United States criminals were strongly motivated not to return, much like Solzhenitsyn's prisoners in *The Gulag Archipelago*.

Since 1964 criminal rights have expanded toward boundaries not yet determined. Softness in the general public has been translated into leniency and mercy toward criminals. Elected and appointed political leaders capitalize on this tender-hearted public attitude. Prisoner "rights" now approach the rights of law-abiding citizens and exceed those of the homeless. Adequate food has been replaced by highly nutritious meals. Each prison is legally required to maintain a law library for inmate use. Arduous physical labor is limited, and self-mutilation to avoid work has long since ceased. Television and entertainment rooms are provided to combat the boredom of idleness; weekend passes and week-long vacations reward good behavior. Prison overcrowding is reduced, many times by premature releases. False equality is fostered as negotiations between leaders of prison riots and leaders in state governments become commonplace.

Criminals have in turn interpreted public softness and compassion as fear and weakness. To criminals weaknesses exist to be exploited, and lawbreakers express little anxiety about arrest, conviction, or prison. The inability of the current system to prevent or curtail criminal activities will have serious consequences in the future as the social structure continues to decay.

ᚾᚢᚾᚢᚾᚢ ᚷᚻ ᚷᚻ ᚷᚻ

Decadence feeds on society's acceptance of greater and greater freedoms. Freedom's zenith will herald the beginning of repression. As certain freedoms begin to infringe on the rights of more and more law-abiding citizens, then suppression of portions of these freedoms will occur. Repression, in turn, grows from its success in restricting liberties. More and more freedoms will be suppressed, until even freedoms cherished by past generations are lost. Nor is this necessarily the end of repression.

Historically, decadence ends when a country fails from within and is conquered by another nation or when affluence is exhausted and a dictatorship emerges. Events playing out either scenario entail financial crisis and civil disorder. If the United States follows the course of past great nations, decadence could continue for some time after our Ages of Affluence and Intellect either diminish or cease.

If the Age of Decadence should end with conquest by a foreign power, the United States would begin a new ten-generation cycle, its direction predicated upon the generosity of the conqueror. With benevolent peace terms and humane assistance, the beginning of the new cycle would be different than if the conqueror were vindictive and punitive.

It is highly probable that, coincidental with massive social unrest and large-scale civil disorder, an individual or group will assume dictatorial powers to bring order to a society out of control. The new ten-generation cycle would then begin under different circumstances.

In 1980 thirty-five consolidated metropolitan areas with a combined population of 107.8 million contained 47.3 percent of the nation's population. The country has experienced an almost continuous movement from rural to urban areas since 1940. There are no significant reasons to suppose that this movement will reverse itself. During a protracted economic downturn or a financial crisis of magnitude, the stresses and tensions of city living would intensify. Any resulting civil disorders would not be new, but the gentle methods of coping used since 1964 will change drastically.

Crime has escalated on an unprecedented scale. Since 1964 Americans have increasingly been subjected to infringement of their rights by criminals. The suppression of criminal activities could become one catalyst to activate governmental repression.

Soon, enough time will have passed so that every honest citizen will personally have been or have a relative or friend who has been assaulted, wounded, robbed, burglarized, raped, murdered, or victimized in a financial fraud or scam. Once that happens, law-abiding citizens may categorically demand that elected officials stop crime.

When elected officials are unable to cope with crime, private citizens step in; lack of lawful protection fuels individual and vigilante actions.

The inhabitants of small towns usually exhibit high tolerance for the idiosyncratic behavior of their neighbors. That there are limits to such toleration however is demonstrated by the July 1981 murder in a Missouri town with less than five hundred people. According to news accounts, a man known as a scrapper and livestock thief was killed. He was also known as a bully and was feared for his guns and violent physical intimidation. His actions had gone virtually unpunished by the county's law enforcement officials. As time passed, his actions touched the lives of almost all the community's citizens. They finally became incensed when the troublemaker was freed on bond despite his having been convicted for wounding an aged local grocer. An estimated sixty townspeople surrounded him. Someone in the crowd shot and killed the man with a deer rifle. No one in the crowd of witnesses acknowledged seeing who fired the fatal shot.

Incidents in which individuals take the lives of others to protect life and property increase dramatically year to year. Even though sporadic, vigilante actions have also been increasing nationwide since 1981.

Adolf Hitler was born in 1889, not the worst of times in Austria/Germany's history. Napoleon Bonaparte, born in 1769, grew up during an era often considered an enlightened period in France. Most would agree that these periods also coincided with national decadence. When Napoleon and Hitler gained power, France and Germany desperately needed strong leadership. Each initially brought internal stability to his country.

Is it possible that America's first president to assume dictatorial powers has already been born and will emerge within the next twenty-five years as the nation's leader? If, following historical precedent, a dictator of the right emerges, he is likely to use the country's military capabilities domestically to protect the life and property of the then-diminished middle class and the wealthy. As rightist suppressions become increasingly unfair to the general population, the stage would be set for a dictator of the left to champion the interests of the less fortunate masses against the wealthy minority.

So-called domestic crises seem to encourage and even necessitate resolution by the military. Armed might under trained leaders easily dispels undisciplined rabble. The military, historically, enjoys success in putting down insurrections. They fail however against a later revolution.

The greatest potential danger from dictatorial powers lies in a rebirth of national expansion—a reenactment in a new cycle of the country's Age of Conquests. Although rapidly declining, United States dominance levels should still be higher at the time of a dictator than those of most countries. Present weaponry if still available and used for expansion would have frightening consequences.

Such a new Age of Conquests might occur at about the time the Soviet Union enters its Age of Commerce. If that happens, one can draw his own conclusion as to which country would be the more dangerous to world peace.

If the United States manages to avoid profound domestic crises and the emergence of a dictatorial president, it might follow the rare path of the United Kingdom in stepping down as a world power. That nation is following a gentle, decade-by-decade transition toward accepting its lessening world status. Ibn Khaldun (1332-1406) in *The Muqaddimah* anticipated a nation like the United Kingdom today, ". . . the dynasty shields itself by holding on to pomp as much as possible, until everything is finished." Even when affluence is greatly diminished, a nation desires to cling to its trappings, as with the retention of the monarchy by the British. Its citizens seemingly do not begrudge the cost of maintaining the royal household. The pomp and ceremony, held over from the country's past majesty and might, provide an illusion of power in world events and tie the population to the Empire's past glories.

Khaldun presaged events such as the United Kingdom's sea battle to regain control of the Falkland Islands/Las Islas Malvinas from Argentina: "At the end of a dynasty, there often also appears some (show of) power that gives the impression that the senility of the dynasty has been made to disappear. It lights up brilliantly just before it is extinguished, like a burning wick the flame of which leaps up brilliantly a moment before it goes out, giving the impression it is just starting to burn, when in fact it is going out."

The ease of Britain's transition downward is a world-class aberration. It peacefully relinquished its position as the most powerful nation on earth to the United States. A common language and heritage smoothed the transition; assistance from the United States during World War II cemented the transfer. The language barrier and lack of a common heritage kept Spain from forfeiting its world position to Britain so easily. Peaceful transitions of power did not occur among other past superpowers in part because of cultural and language differences.

The United States could follow the United Kingdom's path of quietly accepting a more humble status, but it is highly doubtful. The United States does not share a common language or heritage with any world power except the British. Considering its large population base and sizable number of dominant individuals, it would be hard pressed willingly to emulate the United Kingdom's peaceful decline.

The United States still has the dominance levels necessary to institute change. If it can recognize the role played by dominance levels and can use them to change course, it can avoid becoming either a subject nation or a dictatorship.

The United States is governed by the oldest constitution in use in the world. Even so, it is barely eight generations old, a record that points up the relatively short life of written constitutions. None are everlasting.

Thomas Jefferson was insistent that self-government meant the sovereignty of the present generation. "We may consider each generation as a distinct nation," Jefferson writes, "with a right, by the will of its majority, to bind themselves, but none to bind the succeeding generation, more than the inhabitants of another country."

Jefferson's concern of two centuries ago has gone unheeded by the seventh birth generation. That generation is responsible for profligate government spending beyond rational belief. It has bound the eighth generation to debt greater than that left by the six previous generations combined, far exceeding the eighth's ability to repay. Worse, the eighth generation joined the seventh in spending recklessly and creating debt. The huge eighth generation is not exercising its generational right to stop the fiscal excesses of the seventh.

The seventh generation is nearing the end of its time on earth and appears to have successfully foisted the invoice for its "good life" onto the eighth to repay. The eighth generation, taking a page from the seventh's book, apparently believes that such a transfer can be done one more time—to the ninth generation. This perilous game of fiscal musical chairs will severely punish the generation left without a seat. It appears likely that the eighth generation along with a few shards of the seventh will bear the brunt of reform and the resulting havoc brought on when the ninth generation demands a reckoning.

If the will to change suddenly manifested itself in members of the seventh birth generation, those age fifty-one to seventy-five in 1988 and the ones currently with the greatest control, they would face large drawbacks. One is in their small numbers; between 1913 and 1937, the birth rate was low (1933 marking the nadir). Another is a severe time limitation; they will die off in a few years. Leaders from the eighth birth generation, born before the Age of Affluence and aged forty-four to fifty in 1988, are also few compared to those born after 1945. Leaders from these two groups prospered immensely during the Age of Decadence. Who among them would want change?

In 1988 that leaves the last two-thirds of the eighth birth generation, age twenty-six to forty-three, just becoming a part of the accomplishing generation, and the ninth birth generation, age one through twenty-five.

One possibility for change may lie with the coming tenth birth generation. Yet to be born, they could constitute a hope for those who want a return to the values of the first 183 years of the United States. An immediate, sustained increase in births to dominant women, now and in the foreseeable future, or an infant adoption program as outlined in Chapter X, Discrimination, could create a dramatic change in the dominance ratios of the country's population. If coupled with child-rearing practices directed toward honor, duty, and service to the nation, startling changes could begin to appear in only eighteen years. In addition, this change in attitude could accelerate for an additional forty-plus years during that group's accomplishing period. However, today's dominant women are experiencing a heady gain in wealth, power, and fame. Why should or would they discard or lessen these advantages for additional children? Dominant men have the same opportunity to devote themselves full time to rearing dominant children. How many would trade position and power for work that heretofore has generally been thankless?

Since 1964 drugs, crime, homelessness, and nuclear weaponry have escalated. But for an overwhelming majority of Americans, the years since 1964 have been the best of times. There appears little incentive for this majority to effect change.

But! Change is possible.

Table 10. Ages of the United States

Age of Outburst	1763-1890	(127 years - 5 generations)
Age of Conquests	1846-1933	(87 years - 3.5 generations)
Age of Commerce	1874-1971	(97 years - 4 generations)
Age of Affluence	1946 and continuing	
Age of Intellect	1964 and continuing	
Age of Decadence	1964 and continuing	

PART IV
Considerations

Chapter XVIII

Considerations

Human behavior is unique, varied, and complex. Cognizance of maternal dominance and its influences could generate new insights for improving understanding of oneself and others, as individuals and in the context of society. This awareness may help people to live happier, more fulfilling lives. Recognition of people's diverse needs and phobias could lead to greater tolerance and in turn greater social harmony.

Perhaps you have begun to reassess yourself and your family from the perspective of dominance. Whether you are a young adult, spouse, or parent, employee or entrepreneur, I hope that, as you continue to reflect on the consequences of personal dominance in your life, you may gain new and useful understanding of yourself and those around you. Possibly you have also evaluated the dominance levels of your siblings, aunts, uncles, grandparents, in-laws, and even your high-school and college friends and their mothers. If so, you may see some reasons for their attitudes and the degrees of success they have attained.

Perhaps you have also thought about your field of expertise or interest in the light of the ideas outlined here. If you are an entrepreneur beginning or expanding your business, you may be considering the use of IQ tests and personality surveys to improve personnel selection. If you are in the work force, you may more fully understand the problems dominant and nondominant individuals, especially dominant women, face on the job.

If you are a history enthusiast, you may be reevaluating your area of particular interest, whether that be specific political systems, mass persecutions, wars of independence, or the spread of empires. The dominance factor can also shed new light on historical figures; you can gauge the dominance levels of monarchs, their families, and their descendants by their behavior and by tracing maternal dominance. As a concerned citizen, you may now be questioning certain political decisions or have suddenly understood the rationale behind them.

Whatever your vantage point, I hope that you will find applications for this information far beyond anything I have covered. A knowledge of the principles of dominance, its transmission, and its consequences can assist in efforts to bring about positive changes in one's life or in society as a whole. This chapter suggests some possibilities for change. I hope you will use these ideas as a springboard to develop new outlooks and personal goals.

๙๔ ๙๔ ๙๔ ๙ภ ๙ภ ๙ภ

Because of differing dominance levels, people have a diversity of attitudes. Each person has his own perspective about his past, present, and future. The desires and expectations of individuals for themselves and others vary greatly. Most of the time, highly dominant individuals have strong needs to achieve and to control their destiny. They have greater-than-average needs to succeed and to attain power, fame, or wealth, or a combination of the three. Many are task-oriented and pursue high goals despite all obstacles.

The most ambitious individuals in any country are the most dominant. The great discoveries, inventions, medical breakthroughs, and advances of knowledge to better mankind's lot are made by dominant individuals. These beneficial accomplishments give the world an ever-increasing number of advantages.

Although most of us are self-centered, this trait is often glaringly evident in highly dominant people. Since they are psychologically driven to succeed, they may not be particularly tolerant of those with lesser achievement needs. There is a darker side of dominance, most evident in unchecked power. War, a calculated political undertaking by those in power for political and economic gain, causes perhaps the greatest suffering directly attributable to man. Won or lost, wars are instigated by dominant individuals.

Some people with lower dominance levels are more accepting and tolerant of others than their more dominant counterparts. As posited earlier they are, in many ways, the salt of the earth, the backbone of a nation. Those with lower dominance levels often function as stabilizers in conjunction with highly dominant individuals in marriage, business, industry, and political and social situations.

Parents should be wary of those who say, Do not expect too much too soon. Individual dominance levels develop early. The desire to achieve, to accomplish, to lead begins in a mother's arms. Her early demands, encouragement, and praise motivate a child to accomplish. During the formative years, the dominance level of a child is molded under the supervision of his mother (or the person who rears the child) according to her expectations, the constancy of her attention, and the rigor of her demands. Only by tackling ever larger and more difficult tasks can a child continue to grow and achieve. The more successful his endeavors, the more confident he becomes. In sum, the individual becomes dominant to the degree that the mother makes and enforces demands. The more demands enforced, the more dominant the adult; the fewer demands enforced, the less dominant the adult.

Highly dominant women are a key element in the prosperity of nations. Their child-rearing practices are most evident in the leadership and success of sons. On the whole, the social value of dominant women who rear dominant children has gone virtually unnoticed. Even though unnoticed, child-rearing practices of dominant women and their effect on the leaders of each nation will continue to influence world affairs just as they have in the past.

Perhaps owing largely to a lack of understanding of their role, highly dominant women have been badly treated by societies throughout history.

A mother with a low dominance level has fewer expectations of her child than her highly dominant counterpart; she is therefore unlikely to make substantial demands of him. Not pushed to achieve, but rather accepted as he is, the child has few high achievement needs as an adult. To foster an atmosphere of relaxation and tranquillity is apparently a conscious child-rearing goal in many world cultures today, including the United States. If no strong demands for achievement are made on this person in adulthood, he can be among the most content and satisfied members of society. If strong adult demands are made, he is many times unable to cope and will experience stress, tension, and frustration.

ᒧᒧᒧᕫᕫᕫ

Age is an important factor in understanding one's behavior and its predictability. *Know thyself* appears easier at sixty than at thirty and easier at thirty than at eighteen. Self-knowledge is seldom attainable at age eighteen or younger.

Whether dominant or nondominant, a high-school graduate rarely understands his dominance level relative to his age group, although high-school and college students and graduates as well as job applicants of every dominance level commonly claim to aspire to high success. Parents who have a realistic understanding of their children's abilities and true aspirations could help them avoid many false starts and make appropriate career choices, knowing that guidance for a highly dominant eighteen-year-old would be different from that for a less dominant one.

Career concerns preoccupy many people's thoughts during their late twenties and early thirties, when a considerable number of high achievers make major life changes. Thirty appears to be a pivotal age for making long-range employment decisions. The age-thirty transition period affects many success-driven people; decisions at this juncture in an individual's life are crucial to future success. If one were able to evaluate personal achievement needs—for wealth? for power? for fame?—one might gain the insight needed to make a superior career choice at a decisive time. Using the information in this book, perhaps decisions on career changes can be made earlier.

Large American corporations hire executive trainees directly from college campuses. Executive turnover by high achievers at the age-thirty crisis is scarcely ever recognized as such but is attributed to "the seven-year itch." Without change or a significant promotion during this compelling time, dissatisfaction may develop into a lifetime of job frustration.

Leaders building a business or political organization need a cadre of dominant, energetic, intelligent employees for rapid growth. A combination of intelligence tests and personality surveys can identify and assess those attributes as well as other positive and negative personality traits and thus assist in personnel selection. As yet, no instrument can successfully forecast personal integrity.

The three-year mark with one company is significant for employers and employees alike. Three years of learning the rudiments of a business or a specific part of it could be sufficient to start an employee on the road to entrepreneurship. An employee can also adequately judge the promotional opportunities at a firm after three years. (As an employee, bear in mind that repetitive employment cycles of two years or less, whatever the cause, carry job-hopping connotations and normally restrict advancement.) In the same period, a company can determine an individual's current worth and estimate his future value to the firm.

Guidance counselors can use this book to develop diverse possibilities for long-range job opportunities and career satisfaction. In 1988 a disproportionate number of the most energetic, dominant, and brightest college graduates were becoming lawyers, investment bankers, consultants, and financial advisers. When this group reaches their mid-forties in 2012 and are at the midpoint of their most productive years, will they find that these fields still satisfy their needs for wealth, power, and fame? Or will major career changes be necessary in later life? Engineering as a long-range career, for example, might coincide with a scarcity in that occupation by 2012.

Foresight and an unconventional view of future American society could guide smart, energetic, and success-driven college graduates into the military. Possibly the greatest leadership opportunities in the United States will be offered by the military in the year 2012: Air

Force, Army, and Marine colonels and generals, Navy captains and admirals.

For those with average achievement needs, early employment in a congenial job at a large organization or in civil service could help lessen work tension and increase job satisfaction. Employment with a single organization can also enhance future retirement benefits. A thirty-year pension from one organization should be considerably larger than the total of five-year pensions from six firms. An individual who is not highly dominant has the capacity for happiness and freedom from stress if he can avoid succumbing to societal demands for high achievement.

By age forty to forty-five, lifetime achievement patterns are set for most. Talk of attaining success when the right opportunity comes diminishes for low achievers. Those with little success are often weary of planning for it. Late bloomers whose first notable successes came after forty-five, though few, receive considerable attention; perhaps their successes rekindle hope in others of their age. Research on successful late bloomers should show characteristics similar to those of early bloomers; they have been pursuing achievement-oriented goals for many years, probably most of their adult lives. Understanding that certain characteristics lead to achievement, whether early or late, may spare low achievers who lack those characteristics the suffering caused by unfulfillable expectations.

Possibly more beneficial knowledge could be gained by studying highly successful individuals who later fail. They are many, and they appear to share common failure characteristics. Some failures that follow outstanding early successes result from excessive greed and overreaching. Other failures result from overconfidence; having succeeded in one field, they think themselves infallible and capable of success in any area. Perhaps success dulls the cautionary nerves connecting fear with failure in people as well as in countries.

Scientists accept that genes control physical characteristics such as eye and skin color and height. Many sociobiologists agree with Edward O. Wilson that "genes hold the culture on a leash" and postulate that genes govern intelligence and also materially influence personality traits and human behavior. Those sociobiologists will be hard pressed to find genetic origins for dominance, leadership, and success. If they were looking in the right place they would find that all three originate in maternal dominance. *Maternal dominance advances a culture.*

Once dominance and intelligence are no longer accounted for by heredity but rather credited to child rearing, research on child-rearing practices can yield new knowledge on the formation of personality traits. Strong psychological needs, good or bad, are associated with phobias of the same magnitude rooted in childhood fears. Success stems environmentally from maternal dominance, not from genes.

ᎴᎴᎴᎲᎲᎲ

Every nation is composed of individuals with varying dominance levels. A wide spread of dominance levels appears necessary for a society to function well, and its proportions affect a nation's degree of success. When a country maintains an adequate balance of dominance levels, it grows and prospers. If the ratio becomes greatly skewed toward low dominance, a great nation tends to falter and to lose its status among world powers. This trend toward lessening dominance appears to have passed the initial stage in the United States. Unless steps are taken to reestablish a favorable balance of dominance in the country's population, the decline will continue.

Population dominance levels affect political stability. When an imbalance exists in favor of the highly dominant, as was the case in the United States before 1964, some nondominant individuals suffer at their hands. When a significant imbalance toward nondominance occurs, highly dominant citizens frequently suffer at the hands of the nondominant majority.

Dominant, successful ethnic and religious groups in the United States may face increasing hostility in less than one generation, and persecution in less than two generations, or perhaps they may face these conditions even earlier. Success combined with minority status elicits envy and anger from many who wrongfully blame their dissatisfactions on small, easily identifiable groups. There are many who do not covet wealth but only desire that the wealthy become poor, and there are those who do not aspire to success but wish the successful to fail.

Persecutions may well coincide with dramatic social disruptions caused by fiscal deterioration and its accompanying civil discontent. If highly dominant, successful ethnic or religious minority groups such as the Jews are singled out as targets, it is not difficult to imagine that highly dominant individuals of every background will eventually face similar prospects.

Humans too often are ruled by emotion, not logic. If reason prevailed among men and women, they would view successful ethnic and religious groups as valuable human resources whom they should encourage to succeed, thereby increasing the well-being of entire societies (the United States included). If logic held sway, successful minorities would not be envied, feared, and hated.

Studying history from the perspective of dominance levels suggests that the best and possibly the only political climate that will foster and maintain democracy requires some specific minimum, but no apparent maximum, proportion of dominant people. Conversely, there may be some percentage of nondominant individuals that when reached precludes the formation of a democracy or that when reached in a democracy in conjunction with affluence contributes to its failure.

Never in recorded history has a political system provided so much for so many as has democracy during its brief interludes of existence. A democracy benefits all citizens, although to an imperfect degree. Still, the human rewards under democracy are greater than under any political system yet devised.

Some sense that American democracy is in danger, others have misgivings about the direction in which the country appears to be heading, and many others harbor intuitive feelings that things simply are not right. Concerned citizens range across the nation's spectrum: from poor to rich, from those of average intelligence to brilliant scholars, from political activists to silent thinkers, and from pro-testers to detached observers. There can be no comfort in the thought that future generations may look back with awe on the accomplishments, the benefits, and the freedoms of those who lived during the American democracy that once was.

The failure of a democratic society is a loss to virtually all its citizens of every dominance level. The United States can still avoid the fate of ancient Greek democracy and Republican Rome. The preservation of American democracy is a worthy goal. Just as in its ascendancy United States democracy was built by individuals, its decline can be reversed by individuals. Individuals can consciously choose to consolidate their energies and direct them toward the country's well-being and away from divisiveness.

When considering how democracy can be preserved and enhanced, bear in mind that patriotism and democracy are not synonymous. The word patriotism can describe those defending democracy in the United States or those defending a religious dictatorship as in Iran. The average Soviet citizen is presumably as imbued with patriotism as an average American. Under patriotic banners, policies have been made to enslave as well as to free mankind. Even in the United States not all who espouse patriotism also promote democracy.

An imbalance in the country's percentages of dominant and nondominant citizens has been increasing rapidly in recent years. The future well-being of every nation rests with its young, its most important resource. Hopes for future prosperity and greatness are embodied in the country's children. If one believes that dominance is the primary contributor to individual, group, and national successes, increasing the ratios of dominant people may extend the ten-generation cycle. Highly dominant men and women can effect changes in the nation's future dominance levels.

Dominant men have reared highly dominant children, as did the fathers of John Stuart Mill and Wolfgang Amadeus Mozart. To succeed, a dominant father must be wholly responsible for child rearing, not a part-time father leaving primary care to a nondominant person. As noted later in the discussion of child-rearing schools, dominant men can help increase the numbers of dominant children.

Dominant women can rear dominant children by setting high standards and requiring excellence in achieving them. They can demand, encourage, and praise accomplishments. Successful adults reflect their mothers' firm leadership during childhood. To many unsung dominant mothers, the adult accomplishments of their offspring, especially males, have been the primary measure of their own successes. Just as they were expected to excel, dominant daughters can expect the same of their children. But what can be done to encourage dominant women to have or rear more children?

Suggestions made in Chapter X, Discrimination, for an increased birth rate and an adoption program by dominant Jewish women could be used by other dominant women to benefit the United States. An adoption program becomes more meaningful when one considers world population figures and the numbers of unwanted children. If reared by highly dominant women, adopted children could provide many future leaders for the country. To be successful, the program needs to be predicated on adoption at or soon after birth and, for long-range national benefit, to consist of at least twice as many female as male adoptions.

Reforming the country's educational system would produce brighter adults but would not necessarily increase the number of dominant ones. Though the problems associated with meaningful reform are massive, they are not insurmountable. The United States educational system is firmly entrenched; vested interests in higher education alone could block reform. In 1950 the country spent $8.8 billion on education: $6.7 billion (76 percent) for elementary and secondary education, and $2.1 billion (24 percent) for colleges and universities. By 1985 expenditures had increased to $247.7 billion: $149.4 billion (60 percent) for elementary and secondary education, and $98.3 billion (40 percent) for higher education.

Since 1950 federal and state governments have allocated proportionately more funds for higher education than for elementary and secondary schooling. By looking at these spending patterns, one can see that the country's educational priorities have changed. In the past, teachers educating the nation's youth in elementary and secondary schools were expected to be outstanding. Today, many seemingly attach importance to exceptional teachers only at the college level. Perhaps they have forgotten that Aristotle taught Alexander the Great as a youth.

A return to the educational values of 1950 at the 1985 spending level would move $38.9 billion annually from higher education to elementary and secondary schools. In all probability, vested interests in higher education would work extremely hard to stop such a move. Besides, time is short; when affluence diminishes, few if any additional funds will be allotted to education.

Any contemplated reforms necessitate reviewing all aspects of education in the light of reality. Two educational goals are in direct conflict: providing quality education and eliminating student dropouts. In this instance, one cannot have it both ways. The goal of quality education entails faculty demands for student excellence, thus increasing the drop-out rate. To curtail drop-outs means to discourage teacher demands, sanction boosting grades and grading on the curve, condone social passing and misbehavior, encourage school entertainment, and in some instances pay drop-outs to return to school. Regardless of educational goals, child-rearing practices have already set the stage for school performance.

Day-care centers are geared basically for physical child care, and few attempt actual child training. (Project Head Start attempted early childhood training, but it was costly and its gains were short-lived. Dominance was not considered when hiring instructors, and the children did not begin the program early enough.) Day-care facilities offering highly dominant, intellectually demanding instructors and supervisors are rare at best. The average pay of those supervising and instructing children at day-care centers ranks among the lowest in the country; most centers are used by mothers who cannot afford the fees needed to provide salaries that would attract highly dominant supervisors and teachers.

Day-care centers could provide a fertile environment for altering dominance levels if administered by dominant surrogate mothers. Instructors then could encourage and make intellectual demands on infants and provide a disciplined setting for interaction with others. The children who participated from infancy to age five would show significant achievement. From that age forward, any unfavorable elements such as an undisciplined home life or uninspired public schooling would have to be evaluated. It is well to be aware that realistically the costs of such instruction would far exceed current day-care wages or the financial capabilities of most parents.

♪♫♪♫♪♫♪♩♪♩♪♩

Many assume that the words and insights of past great writers have been thoroughly sifted, and all kernels of useful knowledge have been gleaned. Only a few advocate reading and studying the ideas of past great thinkers in order to bring a fresh perspective to today's problems.

It behooves us to reevaluate the works of great thinkers of the past for ideas adaptable to rearing and educating our children in the modern world. Many of them have proposed systems for rearing and educating children. Some of their ideas have already been successfully incorporated into educational systems.

Plato was one of the earliest Western thinkers who detailed the child-rearing methods that would achieve the goals he thought important. He recognized that what a child sees and hears early in life is as much a part of his education as is any formalized process; he knew that early experiences involving the interpretation of the moral beliefs of adults who are significant to the child influence the child's attitudes as an adult. Though taken out of the full context of the earliest utopia ever proposed in European literature, Plato's *Republic*, these excerpts present the flavor of his ideas on education.

What is this education to be, then? Perhaps we shall hardly invent a system better than the one which long experience has worked out, with its two branches for the cultivation of the mind and of the body. And I suppose we shall begin with the mind, before we start physical training.

Don't you understand, . . . that we begin by telling children stories, which, taken as a whole, are fiction, though they contain some truth? Such story-telling begins at an earlier age than physical training; that is why I said we should start with the mind.

And the beginning, as you know, is always the most important part, especially in dealing with anything young and tender. That is the time when the character is being moulded and easily takes any impress one may wish to stamp on it.

. . . A child cannot distinguish the allegorical sense from the literal, and the ideas he takes in at that age are likely to become indelibly fixed; hence the great importance of seeing that the first stories he hears shall be designed to produce the best possible effect on his character.

So far, then, as religion is concerned, we have settled what sorts of stories about the gods may, or may not, be told to children who are to hold heaven and their parents in reverence and to value good relations with one another.

Nor again must these men of ours be lovers of money, or ready to take bribes. . . .

Next, the upbringing of our young men must include physical training; and this must be no less carefully regulated throughout life from childhood onwards. In my view, which I should like you to consider, it is not true that a sound and healthy body is enough to produce a sound mind; while, on the contrary, the sound mind has power in itself to make the bodily condition as perfect as it can be. . . .

Plato maintained that both mind and body must be developed and disciplined, and that moral integrity can be instilled through religious training. He believed an effective educational system benefits a country and prevents the growth of lawlessness. Once an educational system proves its effectiveness and superiority in developing students to their greatest capacity, Plato asserted that the system must remain unchanging. He recognized that knowledge will continue growing and changing, but thought that once a system demonstrates its practicality, it would be foolish to alter a proven process for the sake of change or variety. Plato designed his program for a group he termed the Guardians.

The rulers of the Ottoman Empire developed an educational system strikingly similar to that which Plato proposed for the education of the Guardians. No concrete proof exists that the Ottomans borrowed their ideas from him, but there is evidence that their rulers had great respect for Plato and his teachings. Plato divided the Guardians into Rulers (legislative) and Auxiliaries (executive); the Ottomans differentiated between public officials and an elite military force.

The Ottoman system evolved some 1,700 years after Plato, around the time of the reign of Murad I (1360-1389). A new name surfaced in armed warfare, *Yeni Ceri* (new troops), or Janissaries, as the Europeans called them. Since Holy Law forbade the enslavement of fellow Muslims, Christian boys and young men were captured, converted to Islam, and made the sultan's slaves. They were extensively trained to serve the sultan. When a lull in the Ottomans' European conquests ended the flow of young Christian captives, a new source for recruits was found: the *devsirme* or levy of boys.

Every four or five years as needed, one thousand to three thousand boys were collected from the poor rural Christian sections of the sultan's regional possessions. Though it sounds cruel, many families welcomed this opportunity of advancement for a child. (Other Christians preferred converting to Islam rather than facing the sentimental and financial loss of a son.) Children were taken from near poverty on drab farms and elevated to life in the palace, undergoing training to become public officials or members of the elite Janissary Corps. Strict measures were taken to keep out undesirables; those selected were judged for physical and mental aptitude, good moral fiber, and physical attractiveness. They came from the provinces, not the sophisticated cities; the idea was to obtain raw material that could be molded.

Although slaves the children were educated in the sultan's palace schools (which were far superior to the Ottoman public schools) in Istanbul, Bursa, Edirne, and Galata. Mehmed II (the Conqueror) and Suleyman (the Magnificent) are credited with elevating the palace schools to remarkable heights as institutions for training superior military and administrative minds.

The students studied liberal arts as well as the arts and sciences of war and government, and they received rigorous physical training. Courses included calligraphy, music, architecture, painting, sculpture, history, mathematics, horsemanship, and weaponry. Pupils also learned a craft or trade. Future sultans underwent the same training.

Discipline and competition were intense. Those who excelled physically joined the Janissaries; those who showed superior mental capabilities continued training for civil and political careers. After years of schooling, the graduate was theoretically a scholar-athlete-gentleman and, most importantly, a sincere Muslim and devoted servant of the sultan.

No stigma attached to royal slavery; the sultan himself had a slave mother. The *devsirme* system based promotion on merit alone. Each step on the way to power and success was earned. The captives were often treated as the sultan's adopted sons and brothers; they were his companions. These sons of ignorant farmers and herders formed a huge slave family and became rulers of an immense, powerful, and prosperous empire. They were allowed to own property, had many individual rights, and received lavish rewards for outstanding service. The rigid discipline and rich educational curriculum motivated them to achieve, and many made outstanding contributions to the Ottoman Empire. During the same period, their biological Christian brothers who remained with their parents followed and perpetuated the family's drab existence.

Initially, only men born into leading Muslim families held high positions such as grand vizier. By the time of the conquest of

Istanbul, the *devsirme* had taken control; until the Empire's decline, the palace schools provided almost every court official, provincial governor, and military officer. Those in the highest positions were proud, not ashamed, of their humble beginnings. They believed the ability to succeed had nothing to do with birth; education and success were God's gifts to reward their zeal and hard work.

৵৻ ৵৻ ৵৻ ৵৸ ৵৸ ৵৸

The success of the *devsirme* is in complete contradiction to the theories of the heritability of intellectual achievement. Why have Francis Galton, H.J. Eysenck, and their followers never dealt with this contradiction? Perhaps their schools (British or American) taught them nothing about the Ottoman Empire; even so, it is certainly a researcher's responsibility to investigate all large areas of information relevant to his field. And the scope and time span of such an extensive and successful environment-shaping program is too large to have entirely escaped the attention of prominent hereditarians. Assuredly, those Ottomans charged with the collection of boys had no "genetic wand" to aid their selection. Neither heritability nor "intellectual regression" explains one Christian boy's rise to success under this Muslim regimen while his brothers remained ignorant herders. Common sense dictates that a disciplined, rigorous, and rich educational forum insured success for the one, whereas its lack meant a continued dreary existence for the others.

৵৻ ৵৻ ৵৻ ৵৸ ৵৸ ৵৸

The Ottoman Empire began to decline after it reached its Age of Affluence; the end of the Age overlapped the Empire's Age of Decadence. Beginning with Suleyman, Turks with outside interests gained admittance to the Janissaries. The Janissaries married and enrolled their sons in the Corps, neither of which had previously been allowed. The levy of boys ceased, and the Janissaries deteriorated from a tightly disciplined, elite force of fifteen thousand to a self-perpetuating, pampered, and unruly guard of more than two hundred thousand.

Israel's kibbutz educational system also reflects the educational program Plato outlined in *The Republic*. The adult achievements of its students correspond with the adult successes of Ottoman palace students.

Zionist immigrants to Palestine founded the first kibbutz in 1909 at Degania on the Sea of Galilee. The movement's basic principle, then as now, is that set forth by Karl Marx: From each according to his abilities, to each according to his needs. Its structure is based on equality in all areas: work, housing, and child care. Even though the kibbutz embraces socialistic principles, it seems to function essentially as a democratic institution.

An estimated 270 kibbutzim contain about 3 percent of the country's population. By the mid-1980s, some one hundred thousand kibbutzniks were cultivating 42 percent of the available land and producing 50 percent of the country's agricultural output. Today high technology is replacing agriculture at many kibbutzim. Kibbutzim make half of Israel's industrial robots, produce solar-energy collectors used to heat Israeli homes, and even run hotels to take advantage of the tourist trade.

The kibbutz movement creates no waiting list for enrollment; quite the contrary. Even in the early days of the movement the socialistic principles and communal existence proved too harsh for most. In 1921 a splinter group formed the moshav, a less demanding experiment in collective living, in which homes and land are privately owned and farmers receive the profits from their labors. By the early 1980s, the moshavim had increased to about 350 with approximately 130 thousand members.

Contributions to Israel by individuals from the kibbutz movement far exceed their small population ratio. Of Israel's first six prime ministers, three came from the movement. About a third of all Cabinet members between 1949 and 1967 were kibbutz members. During the Six Day War, 22 percent of the country's army officers and 30 percent of its air force pilots came from kibbutzim. Individuals from the kibbutzim are an elite. They enjoy good living conditions and can expect to secure the best jobs.

Perhaps the individual successes of kibbutz members, disproportionately large in comparison to their small numbers and percentage of the population, lie in the dominance levels and child-rearing practices of the movement. The dominant members of the kibbutz share child care responsibilities along with equal sharing of all other tasks, thus influencing their young charges for dominance.

The kibbutz educational system was begun for practical and economic reasons, but over time ideology and education gained importance. The system was based on four major formulations: Kibbutzim allowed equality of the sexes. The kibbutz movement stood its best chance of self-perpetuation by educating children in special children's houses. Collective schooling was more scientific than leaving education in the hands of children's parents; children would be reared and trained by expert nurses and teachers, away from any family tensions. Lastly, a collective education would be more democratic than a traditional family education.

The system appears to have been strongly influenced by Sigmund Freud's ideas. It focuses on child management and discipline, the use of rewards and punishments, and a particular attitude toward the child's impulses and bodily desires and the attempt to sublimate them. No religious instruction is given.

At their inception, some kibbutzim required that the children spend day and night under the supervision, direction, and instruction of kibbutz teachers. The children visited their parents' home for a few hours daily. By 1986 this changed; even children from the most zealous kibbutzim now spend their nights at home. But from infancy through high school they spend their days together. (Again, the similarity to Plato's Guardians appears.)

The kibbutz takes responsibility for child rearing. Since kibbutzniks are not concerned with individual job remuneration, they can select child care personnel from among those best qualified to supervise, instruct, and discipline the children (corporal punishment is not used).

Changes beginning in 1984—debt and new government policies—bode ill for the kibbutzim. According to Daniel Williams in "Down on the Kibbutz, Israelis Face a Financial Crisis" in the *Los Angeles Times* of May 19, 1989, "About a fifth of the kibbutzim are considered to be in deep and chronic financial trouble." Williams estimates the debt of all kibbutzim at $4.25 billion. These changes are likely to affect child-rearing practices at kibbutzim.

Plato, the Ottoman palace schools, and the kibbutz schools have a common denominator in the transfer of knowledge in a disciplined environment by intelligent and demanding teachers. Another common thread is the age of the pupils—from birth as expounded by Plato and practiced in many kibbutzim to prepuberty and older in the Ottoman palace schools.

꙰ ꙰ ꙰ ♒ ♒ ♒

Perhaps one can draw from Plato, the Ottoman palace schools, and the kibbutz educational structure in forming a new, dynamic approach to child rearing and education today. Conceivably the application of such a program on a large scale could restore a favorable dominance balance in the United States. Depending on its scope and success, such an educational system could pave the way for an economic, political, and moral resurgence in the country.

Youth and education are growing national concerns. Would it not be possible within the framework of democracy to found special child-rearing schools? Only a few general aspects of such programs are offered here; the logistics and mechanics of implementing them would take the combined dedication and effort of educators, religious leaders, and many others. A basic goal would be to rear children in an environment specifically designed to produce dominant, energetic, and intelligent children who would carry these success-oriented traits into adulthood, and in whom the values of discipline, duty, honor, morality, physical fitness, and service would be instilled from infancy onward.

At the risk of invoking paranoia in the poor, it is suggested that these schools could be used as a partial solution to one major social problem: illegitimate children of poor adolescents. These infants could be a national treasure rather than a national tragedy. These children often become part of a vicious cycle with little chance for escape. When grown, they usually follow in parental footsteps. What life will these children have? What achievements and successes will they enjoy? What miseries will they suffer? They will not live and suffer in a vacuum; even if society accepts no moral responsibility for them, it is still involved through vast welfare outlays or the incalculable costs of crime.

Do not conclude that special child-rearing schools should be solely for illegitimate children or those from any particular ethnic group.

Quite the contrary! Limited only by the availability of funds, facilities, and personnel such as nurses, surrogate mothers, and teachers, they could be offered to every child regardless of circumstances of birth. At its inception, the program would have little appeal to parents in the top seven income categories; early interest should develop among families in the lowest two income categories.

The appeal would be simple and direct: Do you want your child reared and educated specifically for achievement and success? Do you want your child to have opportunities far beyond your greatest expectations and imagination? Parents almost always want the best for their children. If the program became available, I believe there would be enough affirmative answers to the above questions to provide a foundation for radically altering the country's future as early as thirty-five years after the program's beginning. These children as successful adults would provide the impetus for a popular renewal of determination to achieve for oneself and for the country and to provide an economic environment in which the less fortunate can cope.

Undoubtedly the schools would create elitism and the problems inherently associated with advantage. Still, the benefits would offset drawbacks; rich and poor alike would be hard pressed to fault the adult successes of infants with humble beginnings.

Since they would benefit society and democracy, funding for the special schools should come from private sources—individuals, corporations, and foundations. Private sources stand to benefit greatly from the preservation of democracy; should democracy fail, they are among those with the most to lose.

Indeed, corporations and foundations voice concern about education in the United States, and both have money available for contributions. However, the truth is that many corporations and foundations, although stating otherwise, are short-term oriented (a few years) and are not likely to commit huge sums to permanent charitable funding needed for the proposed child-rearing schools.

Corporate actions to date in support of educational reform at the elementary and secondary levels have been minimal. According to Nancy J. Perry in *Fortune*, "The Education Crisis: What Business Can Do," July 4, 1988, "Less than 10% of the money corporations voluntarily contribute to education goes to elementary and high schools." Perhaps corporate executives see more glory attached to the ripening grapes than in the planting and fertilizing of young vines.

Even though corporations and foundations would probably not be eager to fund child-rearing schools, they may have an interest in establishing such schools for the children of their employees.

It is important that these programs not be funded by federal or state taxpayers. Governmental intervention or control at any level would dilute the dynamics of the educational process (as the Soviet communal educational system demonstrates) or direct the results toward federal government service (as was done in the Ottoman Empire).

Religion is important to a country's well-being. Philosophy through the ages, arrived at with careful reasoning and logic, has provided mankind with an unending flow of increased wisdom, yet every attempt to supplant moral theology with a philosophical doctrine has failed. Human needs and understandings have not been fulfilled by philosophy alone without some form of religion.

Possibly funding and administration of the special child-rearing schools rightfully belong to religious organizations. Many religious groups stand almost alone in working for the preservation of traditional values, and one aspect of these schools would be to instill the nation's traditional values into the young charges. In addition, religious organizations are adept at raising funds, and they have been successful in retaining their direction without being unduly influenced by their contributors. The competition among religious groups could well benefit the concept of special child-rearing programs. Religious associations would surely understand the future benefits in having reared children who later become successful adults in the private and public sectors and who also retain the moral values instilled by their instructors. The special child-rearing educational system would be vastly different from existing parochial schools.

In a democracy, no single religion can preempt rights denied to others. The school children would come from diverse backgrounds and religious heritages; it would be nearly impossible to provide meaningful uniform and universal religious instruction. Yet, with its stress on moral values that have withstood the test of time, religious grounding should be an important component in rearing the children. It follows naturally that those funding each school should choose the religion to be taught. Having different religions taught in separate schools would help develop tolerance and sensitivity toward all religions, thereby benefiting democracy.

The successes of some parochial schools are well documented. The Jesuits (Society of Jesus) provide the oldest continuous Christian example of parochial education. Ignatius of Loyola founded the order in 1534 and drafted the order's organizational plan in 1539; Pope Paul III approved the plan in September 1540.

As a former military officer, Loyola believed in discipline and expediency. While sublimating his aggressive tendencies to saving souls, he retained his militant bent. Some Roman Catholic men admired Loyola's take-charge attitude and the order's militaristic inclination, and the Society of Jesus attracted many dominant followers. No other religious order held such promise for individual achievement. The Jesuits apparently became a magnet for those with high achievement needs.

Unlike other Roman Catholic groups of the time, the order had not only a dominant leader but also many dominant members. Loyola and the Jesuits influenced the Catholic Reformation of the sixteenth century. The order instituted changes that were opposed and criticized by the Church hierarchy. Ironically, during this period Loyola and the Jesuits were opposed both by elements within the Church and by the Protestant leaders who viewed them as their chief opponents. The latter believed the Jesuits were an obstacle to their success in converting Roman Catholics.

Still today, we see that the Society of Jesus continues to attract dominant followers aspiring to lead. Selection of the order's Superior General from within its ranks guarantees that high dominance is a part of the personality of its leader. A similar process, in the choosing of the Pope from among the Cardinals, ensures that he also is highly dominant. The trials and tribulations of meshing two dominant leaders and two dominant groups into one fold continues, even though all Jesuits pledge obedience to the Pope. Over four hundred years after the founding of the Jesuits, present problems appear little different from those they have always faced.

The Jesuits have the largest membership, over twenty-six thousand, of any Catholic order. Because Loyola directed a major portion of his efforts toward education and the Jesuits continued that work, there are approximately 1.5 million students attending 504 Jesuit schools worldwide. ("Give me the child until he is seven, and I will give you the man," is a maxim attributed to the Jesuits.) It is altogether possible that the Jesuits may take advantage of their large educational base to expand and grow faster than they have in the past.

In the future, a variety of religions could play a larger role in teaching and educating young children. The Jesuits pioneered such efforts, and their success sets one example for religious involvement in education.

The standards for implementing special child-rearing schools must be high. An early obstacle would be the limited supply of nurses and surrogate mothers who could meet the job specifications. The same would be true for primary and secondary teachers. Yet there are Americans of all ages who fit the requirements and fit them well. Many highly dominant men and women are searching for something worthwhile to which they can dedicate themselves—their time, energy, and effort. The match can be made.

The prerequisite of the dominance trait alone would necessitate paying considerably above the average for these positions. In addition, it is impossible to place a value on loving care, devotion, and the desire to inspire and help children succeed in every undertaking.

This educational consideration is offered as a guide, not a blueprint. There are educators with the abilities to design and implement these programs. The United States still has action-oriented individuals, leaders, and educators with vision who could bring the programs to fruition.

Could such a program be abused? Of course. Humans, being imperfect, cannot always prevent that from occurring. (Child-rearing practices designed to mold dominant adults to serve the will of a dictator or an oligarchy would be among the worst abuses of such an effort.) Private funding, individual integrity in administration, and healthy distancing from and distrust of governmental interference would go a long way toward preventing abuses.

rle rle rle sh sh sh

In recent times in the U.S.S.R., the State has claimed some credit for individual success. This has been most pronounced in the creation of Olympic winners, such as Nadia Comaneci, who were reared by State instructors for the specific purpose of winning Olympic gold medals. Along with many other children in the U.S.S.R. and Soviet bloc countries, Nadia Comaneci was taken from her home at the age of five and moved to state-operated housing and educational facilities. She received a state-supervised education, without parental intervention, to develop her mental and physical abilities for eventual Olympic competition.

Were the Soviet Union ever to disabuse itself of its present communal educational system, and to conform to the new program outlined above, it would have profound effects internally and externally. A dominant staff, a rich educational curriculum, and instruction in diverse religions could dramatically change the dominance level, future attitude, and direction of the Soviet Union. If an enlightened Soviet leadership implemented such a special child-rearing program, even if only to enhance its world position by increasing the number of individuals with the achievement needs necessary for the country's development and growth, it would provide a large base for Soviet democracy. Once a country's dominance level ratios shift upward, the environment ripens for democracy.

With its 1.1 billion population, China could follow the same path. The 360 million born there between 1962 and 1975 eclipsed the 1946-1964 United States baby boom of 76.4 million. In only three years Chinese births equaled the nineteen-year American total. In 1979 China set a policy of one child per family and began rigorously enforcing population control. Fairly successful in cities, the program met resistance in the 80 percent peasant population. Even with population control measures, a minimum of twenty-two million births are projected each year for the foreseeable future. The mass installation of special child-rearing schools would make China the future home of the largest number of achievement-oriented citizens in the world.

Two areas might be of special concern to those considering the merits of this child-rearing educational system. Some may believe that no child should be reared away from parents and home; others may fear the system would produce robots.

Many children attend boarding schools and return home during holidays and vacations; they do not appear to suffer. Parents could visit their children at the special schools or vice versa, even though they did not live together daily. Children destined to be physically or mentally abused at home would certainly fare better in the more favorable environment of a special child-rearing school. Consideration of the abject poverty in which many children exist leads one to believe that the setting of a child-rearing school would constitute an enormous improvement in the lives of future siblings.

The kibbutz movement in Israel certainly promotes uniformity in that nearly all its graduates exhibit strong leadership skills. It produces a disproportionate number of leaders in relation to its share of the country's population. Even though slaves, the grand viziers, ministers, provincial governors, administrators, and generals in the Ottoman Empire were leaders, not robots. Child-rearing practices of dominant mothers create dominant, independent, achieving adults and leaders, not human robots.

One threat to establishing child-rearing schools might come from those who believe, or wish to believe, in biological determinism. What are their motives? Are they bigots? Do they wish to maintain the status quo? John Stuart Mill, an exemplary product of a dominant upbringing, wrote, "Of all the vulgar modes of escaping from the consideration of the effect of social and moral influences upon the human mind, the most vulgar is that of attributing the diversities of conduct and character to inherent natural differences."

A dominant child-rearing environment aimed at mental, physical, and moral achievement could produce Catholic/Protestant/Jewish/Muslim/black/white/Asian/Hispanic/Indian United States presidents/cabinet members/senators/generals/admirals/scholars/educators/engineers/scientists/physicians/business leaders/entrepreneurs, and produce them in great numbers. These individuals are needed for a nation to grow and prosper and to preserve democracy.

During their brief periods of existence, democracies have been the greatest success stories in the history of mankind. There is no need for the deterioration or failure of the world's greatest success story to date, democracy in the United States.

r̃lz r̃lz r̃lz ʃh ʃh ʃh

Everyone undoubtedly has a list of political changes he believes would be helpful for the nation's well-being. Although it is tempting to suggest specific political remedies for economic and social predicaments faced by American society, it is not my purpose to address these specifically. I have synthesized information and statistics to present a personal interpretation to the reader in order to stimulate his thinking. It is my hope that each reader will apply the information in this book toward enhancing life for himself, his family, and (if so inclined and capable) society at large.

Individual, group, and national successes are achieved by people with open minds who do not allow themselves to be hemmed in by what has always been done, those who can find practical applications for new ideas. Individuals made the world in its present form, and individuals can change it. This book is for laymen, the doers, the achievers, the people who can make things happen. This book is for the innovators.

If no unnatural changes occur in the dominance levels of the United States citizenry, and this great country follows the same cycle of decline as other powers have before it, there is solace in the thought that people adjust—and they forget.

Bibliography

With Separate Bibliographies on Preliminary Research
and The Mothers of Galton's Eminent Men

Adams, Brooks. 1896. *The Law of Civilization and Decay: An Essay on History*. 2nd ed. Vintage, 1955.

Adams, James Truslow, ed.-in-chf. 1951. *Dictionary of American History, v. l.* 2nd rev. ed. Scribner's.

Advisory Panel on the Scholastic Aptitude Test Score Decline. 1977. *On Further Examination*. CEEB.

Akers, Charles W. 1980. *Abigail Adams: An American Woman*. Little.

Allport, Gordon W. and Henry S. Odbert. 1936. *Trait-Names: A Psycho-lexical Study*. Psychological Review.

An Almanack for the Year of Our Lord 1985. 117th ed. Whitaker.

Andreasen, Nancy C. 1984. *The Broken Brain: The Biological Revolution in Psychiatry*. Harper.

Antonov-Ovseyenko, Anton. 1981. *The Time of Stalin: Portrait of a Tyranny*. Trans. George Saunders. Harper.

Arnold, Magda B. 1960. *Emotion and Personality*. 2 vols. Columbia UP.

Asimov, Isaac. 1982. *Asimov's Biographical Encyclopedia of Science and Technology*. 2nd rev. ed. Doubleday.

——. 1985. *Isaac Asimov On the Human Body and the Human Brain*. Bonanza.

——. 1986. *Foundation and Earth*. Doubleday.

Atrill, Verne. 1981. *The Freedom Manifesto*. Dimensionless Science.

Bachofen, J. J. 1926. *Myth, Religion, and Mother Right*. Trans. Ralph Manheim. Princeton UP, 1967.

Banking and Monetary Statistics 1941-1970. 1976. Bd. of Govs., Fed. Reserve.

Bartlett, John. 1980. *Familiar Quotations*. 15th rev. ed. Little.

Batra, Ravi. 1985. *The Great Depression of 1990*. Venus.

Bell, T. H. 1973. *Your Child's Intellect: A Guide to Home-Based Pre-school Education*. Olympus.

Bettelheim, Bruno. 1969. *The Children of the Dream: Communal Child-Rearing and American Education*. Avon.

Binswanger, Harry, ed. 1986. *The Ayn Rand Lexicon: Objectivism from A to Z*. NAL.

Bloom, Allan. 1987. *The Closing of the American Mind*. Simon.

Bois, J. Samuel. 1966. *The Art of Awareness: A Textbook on General Semantics and Epistemics*. 3rd ed. Brown, 1979.

333

Boorstin, Daniel J. 1987. *Hidden History*. Harper.

Bourne, Geoffrey H. and Maury Cohen. 1975. *The Gentle Giants: The Gorilla Story*. Putnam's.

Bramblett, Claud A. 1976. *Patterns of Primate Behavior*. Mayfield.

Branden, Nathaniel. 1969. *The Psychology of Self-Esteem: A New Concept of Man's Psychological Nature*. Nash.

Briffault, Robert. 1927. *The Mothers*. Abr. ed. Ruskin, 1959.

Brinton, Crane, John B. Christopher, and Robert L. Wolff. 1955. *A History of Civilization*. 2 vols. 4th ed. Prentice, 1971.

Brodie, Fawn M. 1967. *The Devil Drives: A Life of Sir Richard Burton*. Norton.

Brough, James. 1977. *The Ford Dynasty: An American Story*. Doubleday.

Brown, Archie, John Fennell, Michael Kaser, and H. T. Willetts, gen. eds. 1982. *The Cambridge Encyclopedia of Russia and the Soviet Union*. Cambridge UP.

Burns, James MacGregor. 1978. *Leadership*. Harper.

Bury, J. B. and Russell Meiggs. 1900. *A History of Greece to the Death of Alexander the Great*. 4th rev. ed. St. Martin's, 1978.

Carmelli, Dorit, Gary E. Swan, and Ray H. Rosenman. 1985. The Relationship Between Wives' Social and Psychologic Status and Their Husbands' Coronary Heart Disease. *American Jour. of Epidemiology* 122:1.

Carmichael, Joel. 1976. *Stalin's Masterpiece: The Show Trials and Purges of the Thirties—The Consolidation of the Bolshevik Dictatorship*. St. Martin's.

Caro, Robert A. 1974. *The Power Broker: Robert Moses and the Fall of New York*. Vintage.

———. 1982. *The Years of Lyndon Johnson: The Path to Power*. Knopf.

Christian, Shirley. 1985. *Nicaragua: Revolution in the Family*. Random.

Clark, Ronald W. 1984. *The Survival of Charles Darwin: A Biography of a Man and an Idea*. Random.

College Board Score Reports. 1957-1963. CEEB.

College-Bound Seniors: Eleven Years of National Data from the College Board's Admissions Testing Program 1973-83. 1984. CEEB.

College-Bound Seniors: 1988 Profile of SAT and Achievement Test Takers. 1988. CEEB.

Collier, Peter and David Horowitz. 1976. *The Rockefellers: An American Dynasty*. Holt.

Concise Dictionary of American History. 1983. Scribner.

Connolly, Cyril (Palinurus). 1945. *The Unquiet Grave*. Viking.

Council on Environmental Quality and U. S. Dept. of State. 1980. *The Global 2000 Report to the President: Entering the Twenty-First Century, v. 1*. USGPO.

———. 1981. *Global Future: Time to Act. Report to the President on Global Resources, Environment and Population*. USGPO.

Darwin, Charles. 1859 and 1871. *The Origin of Species & The Descent of Man*. Modern Library, n.d.

Davies, Reginald T. 1984. *The Golden Century of Spain: 1501-1521*. AMS.

Descola, Jean. 1970. *The Conquistadors*. Trans. Malcolm Barnes. Kelley.

Diederich, Bernard. 1981. *Somoza and the Legacy of U. S. Involvement in Central America*. Dutton.

Dimont, Max I. 1971. *The Indestructible Jews: An Action-Packed Journey Through 4,000 Years of History*. NAL.

Diner, Helen. 1965. *Mothers and Amazons: The First Feminine History of Culture*. Trans. and Ed. John P. Lundin. Julian.

Dobson, James. 1970. *Dare to Discipline*. Bantam.

Drucker, Peter F. 1973-1974. *Management: Tasks, Responsibilities, Practices*. Harper.

Durant, Will and Ariel. 1935-1975. *The Story of Civilization*. 11 vols. Simon.

———. 1968. *The Lessons of History*. Simon.

Dyer, Henry S. 1953. *College Board Scores No. 1*. CEEB.

The Emergence of Man. 19 vols. 1972-1975. Time-Life.

The New Encyclopaedia Britannica. 30 vols. 15th ed. 1979. Encyclopaedia Britannica.

The New Encyclopaedia Britannica. 32 vols. 1985. Encyclopaedia Britannica.

Encyclopaedia Judaica, v. 13. 1971. Macmillan.

Encyclopaedia Judaica Decennial Book: 1973-1982. 1982. Keter.

The Europa Year Book 1985: A World Survey. 2 vols. 1985. Europa.

The Europa Year Book 1986: A World Survey. 2 vols. 1986. Europa.

Eysenck, H. J. and Leon Kamin. 1981. *The Intelligence Controversy*. Wiley.

Faber, Doris. 1968 and 1978. *The Presidents' Mothers*. St. Martin's.

Fancher, Raymond E. 1985. *The Intelligence Men: Makers of the IQ Controversy*. Norton.

Fast, Howard. 1968. *The Jews: Story of a People*. Dell, 1982.

Fehrenbach, T. R. 1973. *Fire and Blood: A History of Mexico*. Bonanza, 1985.

Fishman, Joshua A. 1957. *1957 Supplement to College Board Scores No. 2*. CEEB.

Flaherty, John E. 1979. *Managing Change: Today's Challenge to Management*. Nellen.

Flexner, James T. 1978. *The Young Hamilton: A Biography*. Little.

The Forbes Four Hundred 1983 Edition. 1983. Forbes. Fall.

The Forbes Four Hundred 1984 Edition. 1984. Forbes. Oct. 1.

The Forbes Four Hundred 1985 Edition. 1985. Forbes. Oct. 28.

Fossey, Dian. 1983. *Gorillas in the Mist*. Houghton.

Foy, Felician A., ed. 1982. *Catholic Almanac 1983*. Our Sunday Visitor.

———. 1984. *Catholic Almanac 1985*. Our Sunday Visitor.

Friday, Nancy. 1977. *My Mother/My Self: The Daughter's Search for Identity*. Delacorte.

Friedman, Meyer and Ray H. Rosenman. 1974. *Type A Behavior and Your Heart*. Fawcett.

Galdi, Theodor W., Caleb Rossiter, and Alfred Reifman. 1982. *Costs and Benefits of U. S. Foreign Aid*. Library of Congress. Oct. 25.

Galton, Sir Francis. 1892. *Hereditary Genius: An Inquiry into Its Laws and Consequences*. 2nd ed. Meridian, 1962.

Garrison, Robert J., V. Elving Anderson, and Sheldon C. Reed. 1968. Assortative Marriage. *Eugen. Quart*. 15:2.

Gibbon, Edward. 1776-1788. *The Decline and Fall of the Roman Empire.* 2 vols. Encyclopaedia Britannica, 1978.

Glubb, John Bagot. 1976. *The Fate of Empires and Search for Survival.* Blackwood, 1981.

———. 1983. *The Changing Scenes of Life: An Autobiography.* Quartet.

Goertzel, Victor and Mildred. 1962. *Cradles of Eminence.* Little.

Goodall, Jane. 1971. *In the Shadow of Man.* Houghton.

———. 1986. *The Chimpanzees of Gombe: Patterns of Behavior.* Belknap.

Gould, Stephen Jay. 1981. *The Mismeasure of Man.* Norton.

Grun, Bernard. 1975. *The Timetables of History: A Horizontal Linkage of People and Events.* Simon, 1982.

Hall, Bernard and Richard Rhodes, eds. 1967. *Living in a Troubled World: Selected Writings of William C. Menninger, M.D.* Hallmark.

Hamburg, David A. and Elizabeth R. McCowen, eds. 1979. *Perspectives on Human Evolution, v. V: The Great Apes.* Benjamin/Cummings.

Hayakawa, S. I. 1939. *Language in Thought and Action.* 3rd ed. Harcourt, 1972.

Herold, J. Christopher, ed. and trans. 1955. *The Mind of Napoleon: A Selection From his Written and Spoken Words.* Columbia UP, 1961.

Heron, eds. 1978. *The Book of Numbers.* A&W.

The Holy Bible: Old and New Testaments in the King James Version. Ref. ed. Nelson, 1976.

Howe, Irving. 1976. *World of Our Fathers: The Journey of the East European Jews to America and the Life They Found and Made.* Harcourt.

Ibn Khaldun. n.d. *The Muqaddimah: An Introduction to History.* Trans. Franz Rosenthal. Abr. and Ed. N. J. Dawood. Princeton UP, 1967.

International Financial Statistics. 1985. IMF. Nov.

Irvine, William. 1955. *Apes, Angles, and Victorians: The Story of Darwin, Huxley, and Evolution.* Time-Life, 1982.

Jacob, Francois. n.d. *The Logic of Life: A History of Heredity.* Trans. Betty E. Spillmann. Pantheon, 1973.

Jacquard, Albert. 1984. *In Praise of Difference: Genetics and Human Affairs.* Trans. Margaret M. Moriarty. Columbia UP.

———. 1985. *Endangered by Science?* Trans. Margaret M. Moriarty. Columbia UP.

Jay, Antony. 1968. *Management and Machiavelli: An Inquiry into the Politics of Corporate Life.* Holt.

Jennings, Eugene E. 1960. *An Anatomy of Leadership: Princes, Heroes, and Supermen.* McGraw, 1972.

Jensen, Arthur R. 1980. *Bias in Mental Testing.* Free.

———. 1981. *Straight Talk About Mental Tests.* Free.

John, Eric, ed. 1964. *The Popes: A Concise Biographical History.* Hawthorn.

Jones, Landon Y. 1980. *Great Expectations: America and the Baby Boom Generation.* Coward.

Kamin, Leon J. 1974. *The Science and Politics of I.Q.* Erlbaum.

Karlsson, Jon L. 1978. *Inheritance of Creative Intelligence.* Nelson.

Katznelson, Ira. 1976. *Black Men, White Cities: Race, Politics, and Migration in the United States, 1900-1930, and Britain, 1948-68*. U of Chicago P.

Kearns, Doris. 1976. *Lyndon Johnson and the American Dream*. Harper.

Kennedy, Paul. 1987. *The Rise and Fall of the Great Powers: Economic Change and Military Conflict from 1500 to 2000*. Random.

King, Jonathan and Steve Rees. 1982. *Poor Ronald's Almanac: Hard Facts for Hard Times*. Foundation for Natl. Progress.

Klauder, Francis J. 1971. *Aspects of the Thought of Teilhard de Chardin*. Christopher.

Kuhn, Thomas S. 1962. *The Structure of Scientific Revolutions*. 2nd ed., enl. U of Chicago P, 1970.

Lawick, Hugo van and Jane van Lawick-Goodall. 1971. *Innocent Killers*. Houghton.

Leakey, Richard E. 1981. *The Making of Mankind*. Dutton.

Leakey, Richard E. and Roger Lewin. 1977. *Origins: What New Discoveries Reveal About the Emergence of our Species and its Possible Future*. Dutton.

Lederer, William J. and Don D. Jackson. 1968. *The Mirages of Marriage*. Norton.

Leopold, Aldo. 1966. *A Sand County Almanac*. Ballantine.

Lerner, Alan C. 1982. Why Supply-Side Economics Is Not Working: A Wall Street Perspective. Address to Conf. Spons. Federal Reserve Bank of Atlanta and Emory University Law and Economics Center. March.

Levinson, Daniel J. 1978. *The Seasons of a Man's Life*. Knopf.

Lewontin, R. C., Steven Rose, and Leon J. Kamin. 1984. *Not In Our Genes: Biology, Ideology, and Human Nature*. Pantheon.

Library of Nations. 20 vols. 1985-1988. Time-Life.

Lingeman, Richard. 1980. *Small Town America: A Narrative History 1620-The Present*. Putnam's.

Lorenz, Konrad. 1966. *On Aggression*. Trans. Marjorie Kerr Wilson. Bantam.

Luther, Martin. n.d. *Luther's Ninety-Five Theses*. Intro. E. G. Schwiebert. Concordia.

McClellan, Grant, ed. 1981. Immigrants, Refugees, and U. S. Policy. *The Reference Shelf* 52:6. Wilson.

McClelland, David C. 1961. *The Achieving Society*. Free.

———. 1975. *Power: The Inner Experience*. Irvington.

———. 1985. *Human Motivation*. Scott.

Macdonald, Julie. 1965. *Almost Human: The Baboon: Wild and Tame—In Fact and In Legend*. Chilton.

McKeon, Richard, ed. 1941. *The Basic Works of Aristotle*. Random.

McMurry, Robert N. 1974. *The Maverick Executive*. AMA.

McNeill, William H. 1976. *Plagues and Peoples*. Doubleday.

Maidens, Melinda, ed. 1981. *Immigration: New Americans, Old Questions*. Facts on File.

Margolis, Maxine L. 1984. *Mothers and Such: Views of American Women and Why They Changed*. U of Calif. P.

Marx, Karl and Friedrich Engels. 1888. *The Communist Manifesto*. Trans. Samuel Moore. Penguin, 1967.

Maslow, Abraham H. 1968. *Toward a Psychology of Being*. 2nd ed. Van Nostrand.

Menninger, Karl. 1938. *Man Against Himself*. Harcourt.

———. 1942. *Love Against Hate*. Harcourt.

———. 1958. *Theory of Psychoanalytic Technique*. Harper.

———. 1973. *Whatever Became of Sin?* Hawthorn.

Meyer, Herbert E. 1979. *The War Against Progress*. Storm King.

Milgram, Stanley. 1974. *Obedience to Authority: An Experimental View*. Harper.

Miller, Richard L. 1986. *Truman: The Rise to Power*. McGraw.

Montagu, Ashley, ed. 1964. *The Concept of Race*. Macmillan.

Morton, Frederic. 1979. *A Nervous Splendor: Vienna 1888/1889*. Weidenfeld.

Moskowitz, Milton, Michael Katz, and Robert Levering, eds. 1980. *Everybody's Business: An Almanac*. Harper.

National Commission on Excellence in Education. 1983. *A Nation at Risk: The Imperative for Educational Reform*. USGPO.

National Report on College-Bound Seniors, 1984. 1984. CEEB.

National Report on College-Bound Seniors, 1985. 1985. CEEB.

Noe, Ronald, Frans de Waal, and Jan van Hooff. 1980. Types of Dominance in a Chimpanzee Colony. *Folia Primatol*. 34.

Ornstein, Robert and Richard F. Thompson. 1984. *The Amazing Brain*. Houghton.

Ortega y Gasset, Jose. 1932. *The Revolt of the Masses*. Trans. Anon. Norton, 1985.

Ouspensky, P. D. 1950. *The Psychology of Man's Possible Evolution*. Knopf, 1971.

Oxford Analytica. 1986. *America In Perspective: Major Trends in the United States Through the 1990s*. Houghton.

Plato. n.d. *The Republic of Plato*. Trans. Francis MacDonald Cornford. Oxford UP, 1941.

Rand, Ayn. 1946-1966. *Capitalism: The Unknown Ideal*. NAL.

———. 1961. *The Virtue of Selfishness: A New Concept of Egoism*. NAL.

Rhodes, Richard. 1986. *The Making of the Atomic Bomb*. Simon.

Riding, Alan. 1985. *Distant Neighbors: A Portrait of the Mexicans*. Knopf.

Riss, David and Jane Goodall. 1977. The Recent Rise to the Alpha-Rank in a Population of Free-Living Chimpanzees. *Folia Primatol*. 27.

Rostow, W. W. 1971. *Politics and the Stages of Growth*. Cambridge UP.

Sampson, Anthony. 1975. *The Seven Sisters: The Great Oil Companies and the World They Shaped*. Bantam.

Santillana, Giorgio de. 1955. *The Crime of Galileo*. Time-Life, 1981.

Schlesinger, Arthur M., Jr. 1986. *The Cycles of American History*. Houghton.

Seagrave, Sterling. 1985. *The Soong Dynasty*. Harper.

Seldes, George, comp. 1985. *The Great Thoughts*. Ballantine.

Shoup, Paul S. 1981. *The East European and Soviet Data Handbook: Political, Social, and Developmental Indicators, 1945-1975*. Hoover Inst.

Skinner, B. F. 1971. *Beyond Freedom & Dignity*. Bantam.

Small, Meredith F., ed. 1984. *Female Primates: Studies by Women Primatologists*. Liss.

Smith, Anthony. 1985. *The Body*. Rev. ed. Allen.

Smith, Huston. 1958. *The Religions of Man*. Harper.

Smith, Liz. 1978. *The Mother Book.* Doubleday.

Solzhenitsyn, Alexander. 1963. *One Day in the Life of Ivan Denisovich.* Trans. Ralph Parker. NAL.

——. 1973. *The Gulag Archipelago 1918-1956: An Experiment in Literary Investigation.* Harper.

Sowell, Thomas. 1980. *Knowledge and Decisions.* Basic.

——. 1981. *Ethnic America: A History.* Basic.

——. 1983. *The Economics and Politics of Race: An International Perspective.* Morrow.

——. 1984. *Civil Rights: Rhetoric or Reality?* Morrow.

Spock, Benjamin. 1945-1946. *The Common Sense Book of Baby and Child Care.* Duell.

Statistical Profile of Golf in the United States: 1983 Annual Review. Natl. Golf Foundation.

Strong, James. *The New Strong's Concordance of the Bible: A Popular Edition of the Exhaustive Concordance.* Nelson, 1985.

Tawney, R. H. 1926. *Religion and the Rise of Capitalism: A Historical Study.* NAL.

Teilhard de Chardin, Pierre. *Writings in Time of War.* Trans. Rene Hague. Harper, 1968.

——. *Christianity and Evolution.* Harcourt, 1971.

Time Frame. 11 vols. 1987-1988. Time-Life.

Toffler, Alvin. 1980. *The Third Wave.* Morrow.

Toland, John. 1976. *Adolph Hitler.* Doubleday.

Toynbee, Arnold J. 1947 and 1957. *A Study of History.* Abr. D. C. Somervell. 2 vols. Oxford UP.

Turnbull, William W. 1985. *Student Change, Program Change: Why the SAT Scores Kept Falling.* CEEB.

Tyler, Leona E. 1965. *The Psychology of Human Differences.* Meredith.

Understanding Human Behavior: An Illustrated Guide to Successful Human Relationships. 24 vols. 1974. BPC.

Urdang, Laurence, ed. 1981. *The Timetables of American History.* Simon.

U.S. Dept. of Commerce, Bureau of the Census. 1975. *Historical Statistics of the United States: Colonial Times to 1970.* Bicentennial ed. USGPO.

——. 1981. *Statistical Abstract of the United States 1982.* 102nd ed. USGPO.

——. 1984. *Statistical Abstract of the United States 1985.* 105th ed. USGPO.

——. 1985. *Money Income and Poverty Statistics of Families and Persons in the United States: 1984.* USGPO. P-60:149.

——. 1989. *Statistical Abstract of the United States 1989.* 109th ed. USGPO.

Utechin, S. V. 1961. *Everyman's Concise Encyclopaedia of Russia.* Dutton.

Vernon, Philip E. 1979. *Intelligence: Heredity and Environment.* Freeman.

Waal, Frans B. M. de. 1984. *Chimpanzee Politics: Power and Sex Among Apes.* Harper.

Weber, Max. 1904-1905. *The Protestant Ethic and the Spirit of Capitalism.* Trans. Talcott Parsons. Allen, 1930.

Weeks, John R. 1981. *Population: An Introduction to Concepts and Issues.* 2nd ed. Wadsworth.

Winterbottom, Marian R. 1953. *The Relation of Childhood Training in Independence to Achievement Motivation.* U of Michigan Ph.D. diss.

Wolf, Josef. 1978. *The Dawn of Man.* Trans. Margot Schierlova. Abrams.

The World Almanac & Book of Facts 1975. 1974. Newspaper Enterprise Assn.

The World Almanac & Book of Facts 1984. 1983. Newspaper Enterprise Assn.

The World Almanac & Book of Facts 1985. 1984. Newspaper Enterprise Assn.

The World Almanac & Book of Facts 1987. 1986. Newspaper Enterprise Assn.

Preliminary Research

Achievement Needs
McClelland, David C. 1961. *The Achieving Society*. Free.

Aggression
Ardrey, Robert. 1976. The Hunting Hypothesis. *Book Digest*. May.
Burke, Charles. 1975. *Aggression in Man*. Stuart.
Effect of Mother on the Development of Aggressive Behavior in Rats. 1975. *Developmental Psychobiology*. Jan.
Harlow, Harry and Margaret. 1962. Social Deprivation in Monkeys. *Scientific American*. Nov.
Lorenz, Konrad. 1966. *On Aggression*. Trans. Marjorie Kerr Wilson. Harcourt.
Tinbergen, Niko. 1965. *Animal Behavior*. Time-Life.

Alexander the Great
Wells, H. G. 1920. *The Outline of History*. Garden City.

Da Vinci, Leonardo: Childhood
Crow, John A. 1965. *Italy: A Journey Through Time*. Harper.

Heraclitus
Adamson, Robert. 1908. *The Development of Greek Philosophy*. Blackwood.
Appleton, R. B. 1922. *Greek Philosophy from Thales to Aristotle*. Methuen.
Armstrong, A. H. 1959. *An Introduction to Ancient Philosophy*. New.
Benn, Alfred W. 1898. *The Philosophy of Greece*. Richards.
Brumbaugh, Robert S. 1964. *The Philosophers of Greece*. Crowell.
Chambers Encyclopaedia. 1967 ed. Heraclitus. Pergamon.
Durant, Will. 1933. *The Story of Philosophy*. Simon.
Encyclopaedia Britannica. 11th ed. Heraclitus. Encyclopaedia Britannica.
Fairbanks, Arthur. 1898. *The First Philosophers of Greece*. Kegan.
Guthrie, W. K. C. 1957. *In the Beginning*. Cornell UP.
Kirk, G. S. 1959. *Heraclitus: The Cosmic Fragments*. Cambridge UP.
Wheelwright, Philip. 1959. *Heraclitus*. Princeton UP.

Hitler's Family and Background
Langer, Walter C. 1972. *The Mind of Adolf Hitler*. Basic.
Roberts, Stephen H. 1937. *The House that Hitler Built*. Methuen.
Van Maltitz, Horst. 1973. *The Evolution of Hitler's Germany*. McGraw.

341

Imprinting

Bateson and Jaeckel. 1974. Imprinting: Correlations Between Activities of Chicks During Training and Testing. *Animal Behaviour 22.*

Bowlby, John. 1955. A Note on the Selection of Love Objects in Man. *British Journ. of Animal Behaviour.* July.

Brown, Robert. 1975. Following and Visual Imprinting in Ducklings Across a Wide Age Range. *Developmental Psychobiology.* Jan.

Eiserer and Hoffman. 1974. Acquisition of Behavioral Control by the Auditory Features of an Imprinting Object. *Animal Learning & Behaviour.* Nov.

——. 1974. Imprinting of Ducklings to a Second Stimulus When a Previously Imprinted Stimulus is Occasionally Presented. *Animal Learning & Behaviour.* May.

Fisher and Hale. Stimulus Determinants of Sexual and Aggressive Behaviour in Male Domestic Fowl. *Animal Behaviour 10.*

Gossop, Michael. 1974. Movement Variables and the Subsequent Following Response of the Domestic Chick. *Animal Behaviour 22.*

Guiton, Philip. 1959. Socialization and Imprinting in Brown Leghorn Chicks. *Animal Behaviour 7.*

Hinde, R. A. 1955. The Following Response of Moorhens and Coots. *British Journ. of Animal Behaviour.* July.

——. 1966. *Animal Behaviour.* McGraw.

International Encyclopedia of the Social Sciences. 1968 ed. Imprinting. Macmillan.

Lorenz, Konrad. 1952. *King Solomon's Ring.* Trans. Marjorie Kerr Wilson. Crowell.

——. 1971. *Studies in Animal and Human Behaviour, v. II.* Harvard UP.

Manning, Aubrey. 1972. *An Introduction to Animal Behaviour.* Cloves.

Moltz and Stettner. 1961. The Influence of Patterned-Light Deprivation on the Critical Period for Imprinting. *Journ. of Comparative and Physiological Psychology.* June.

Shipley, William. 1963. The Demonstration in the Domestic Guinea Pig of a Process Resembling Classical Imprinting. *Animal Behaviour.* Oct.

Sluckin, W. 1965. *Imprinting and Early Learning.* Aldine.

Suomi, Stephen. 1974. Social Interactions of Monkeys Reared in a Nuclear Family Environment Versus Monkeys Reared with Mothers and Peers. *Primates.* Dec.

Surway, H. 1955. The Double Relevance of Imprinting to Taxonomy. *British Journ. of Animal Behaviour.* July.

Syme and Syme. 1974. The Relationship Between the Peck Order and Performance in a Competitive Group Feeding Situation by Two Groups of Cockerel. *Behavioral Biology.* Dec.

Thorpe, W. H. 1955. The Nature and Significance of Imprinting. *British Journ. of Animal Behaviour.* July.

Thorpe and Zangwill. 1961. *Current Problems in Animal Behavior.* Harvard UP.

Tinbergen, Niko. 1965. *Animal Behavior.* Time-Life.

Verplanck, W. S. 1955. An Hypothesis on Imprinting. *British Journ. of Animal Behaviour.* July.

Lot: His Daughters and Sons

The Abingdon Bible Commentary. 1929. Abingdon.

Catholic Biblical Encyclopedia: Old Testament. 1959 ed. Lot I, Moab. Catholic UP.

Harper's Bible Dictionary. 1961 ed. Benjamin, Judah, Lot. Harper.

The Interpreter's Bible, v. I. 1952. Abingdon.

The Jerome Biblical Commentary, v. I. 1968. Prentice.

The Oxford Self Pronouncing Bible. Teacher's ed. 1901. Oxford UP.

Mothers

Aretz, Gertrude. 1927. *Napoleon and His Women Friends.* Lippincott.

Baker, Timothy. 1966. *The Normans.* Macmillan.

Barlow, Frank. 1965. *William I and the Norman Conquest.* English UP.

Bowers, Claude G. 1925. *Jefferson and Hamilton.* Houghton.

Canning, John. 1967. *100 Great Kings, Queens and Rulers of the World.* Taplinger.

The Columbia Encyclopedia. 1963 ed. Cesare Borgia. Columbia UP.

Cooke, Jacob E. 1967. *Alexander Hamilton: A Profile.* Hill.

Corvo, Frederick B. 1931. *A History of the Borgias.* Modern Library.

Davies, Margaret. 1964. *Apollinaire.* Oliver.

Hamilton, Allan M. 1910. *The Intimate Life of Alexander Hamilton.* Duckworth.

Hopkins, Tighe. 1910. *The Women Napoleon Loved.* Little.

Leonard, Irving A. 1964. *Books of the Brave.* Gordian.

Markham, Felix. 1963. *Napoleon.* NAL.

Morris, William O. 1901. *Napoleon.* Putnam's.

Ripley, Dr. S. Dillon. 1964. *The Smithsonian Institution.* Crown.

Verrill, A. Hyatt. 1929. *Great Conquerors of South and Central America.* New York Home Library.

Wallechinsky, David and Irving Wallace. 1975. *The People's Almanac.* Doubleday.

Nazi Plans for Families, Women, and Children

Dill, Marshall, Jr. 1961. *Germany: A Modern History.* U of Michigan P.

Grunberger, Richard. 1971. *The 12-Year Reich.* Holt.

Haffner, Sebastian. 1941. *Germany: Jekyll and Hyde.* Dutton.

Hitler's Secret Conversations: 1941-1944. 1953. Farrar.

Hitler's Words. 1944. American Council on Public Affairs.

Langer, Walter C. 1972. *The Mind of Adolph Hitler.* Basic.

Maltitz, Horst von. 1973. *The Evolution of Hitler's Germany.* McGraw.

Palmer and Colton. 1950. *A History of the Modern World.* 3rd ed. Knopf.

Roberts, Stephen H. 1937. *The House That Hitler Built.* Methuen.

Sales, Raoul de Roussy de. 1941. *Adolph Hitler: My New Order.* Reynal.

Stachura, Peter D. 1975. *Nazi Youth in the Weimar Republic.* Clio.

Waln, Nora. 1939. *Reaching For The Stars.* Little.

Origins of Socrates, Plato, and Aristotle

Appleton, R. B. 1922. *Greek Philosophy.* Methuen.

Benn, Alfred W. 1914. *The Greek Philosophers*. Smith.

Bluck, R. S. 1949. *Plato's Life and Thought*. Beacon.

Chroust, Anton-Hermann. 1957. *Socrates: Man & Myth*. Routledge.

Costelloe, B. F. C. and J. H. Muirhead. 1967. *Aristotle and the Earlier Peripatetics, v. I*. Macmillan.

Cross, Nicol R. 1914. *Socrates: The Man and His Mission*. Methuen.

Downey, Glanville. 1962. *Aristotle: Dean of Early Science*. Watts.

Drake, Henry L. 1958. *The People's Plato*. Philosophical Library.

The Encyclopedia of Philosophy. 1967 ed. Aristotle. Macmillan.

Field, G. C. 1930. *Plato and His Contemporaries*. Methuen.

Fite, Warner. 1934. *The Platonic Legend*. Scribner's.

Forbes, J. T. 1905. *Socrates*. Clark.

Fox, Adam. 1945. *Plato For Pleasure*. Westhouse.

Hammond, William A. 1902. *Aristotle's Psychology*. Sonnenschein.

Hardie, W. F. R. 1936. *A Study in Plato*. Clarendon.

Havelock, Eric A. 1963. *Preface to Plato*. Harvard UP.

Jaeger, Werner. 1948. *Aristotle*. Clarendon.

Leonard, William E. 1915. *Socrates: Master of Life*. Open Court.

Livingstone, R. W. 1938. *Portrait of Socrates*. Clarendon.

McKeon, Richard. 1947. *Introduction to Aristotle*. U of Chicago P.

Mure, G. R. G. 1932. *Aristotle*. Benn.

Plato. Black, 1942.

Plato: The Sophist & The Statesman. Trans. A. E. Taylor. Nelson, 1961.

The Portable Plato. Viking, 1948.

Randall, John H., Jr. 1970. *Plato: Dramatist of the Life of Reason*. Columbia UP.

Robinson, T. M. 1970. *Plato's Psychology*. U of Toronto P.

Silverburg, Tom and Alban Winspear. 1939. *Who Was Socrates?* Cordon.

Taylor, A. E. 1926. *Plato: The Man and His Work*. Methuen.

———. 1933. *Socrates*. Davies.

Veatch, Henry B. 1974. *Aristotle*. Indiana UP.

The Ottoman Empire

Barber, Noel. 1973. *The Sultans*. Simon.

Creasy, Sir Edward S. 1878. *History of the Ottoman Turks*. Bentley.

Davison, Roderic H. 1968. *Turkey*. Prentice.

Ducas. *Decline and Fall of Byzantium to the Ottoman Turks*. Trans. Harry J. Magoulias. Wayne State UP, 1975.

Easton, Stewart C. 1961. *The Western Heritage*. Holt.

Gibbons, Herbert A. 1968. *The Foundation of the Ottoman Empire*. Cass.

Hitti, Philip K. 1961. *The Near East in History*. Van Nostrand.

———. 1966. *A Short History of the Near East*. Van Nostrand.

Inalcik, Halil. 1973. *The Ottoman Empire*. Weidenfeld.

Kortepeter, Carl M. 1972. *Ottoman Imperialism During the Reformation: Europe and the Caucasus.* New York UP.

Lewis, Raphaela. 1971. *Everyday Life in Ottoman Turkey.* Putnam.

Muller, Herbert J. 1958. *The Loom of History.* Harper.

Nichols, Marianne. 1975. *Man, Myth, and Monument.* Morrow.

Palmer and Colton. 1950. *A History of the Modern World.* Knopf.

Wells, H. G. 1920. *The Outline of History.* Garden City.

Raising Children

Spock, Benjamin. 1974. *Raising Children In A Difficult Time.* Norton.

Spartan Women and Children

Michell, H. 1952. *Sparta.* Harvard UP.

Unmarried Mothers

Werner, Oscar H. 1966. *Unmarried Mother in German Literature.* AMS.

Young, Leontine. 1954. *Out of Wedlock.* McGraw.

Mothers of Galton's
Eminent Men

George Canning
Petrie, Sir Charles. 1946. *George Canning*. Eyre.

Charlemagne
Boussard, Jacques. 1968. *The Civilization of Charlemagne*. World University Library.
Cabaniss, Allen. 1972. *Charlemagne*. Twayne.
Einhard. *The Life of Charlemagne*. Trans. Samuel E. Turner. U of Michigan P, 1960.
Einhard and The Monk of St. Gall. *Early Lives of Charlemagne*. Trans. Arthur J. Grant. Cooper Square, 1967.
Halphen, Louis. 1977. *Charlemagne and the Carolingian Empire*. North.
Heer, Friedrich. 1975. *Charlemagne and His World*. MacMillan.
Hodgkin, Thomas. 1897. *Charles the Great*. MacMillan.
Loyn, H. R. and John Percival. 1975. *The Reign of Charlemagne: Documents on Carolingian Government and Administration*. St. Martin's.
Russell, Charles E. 1930. *Charlemagne: First of the Moderns*. Houghton.
Sullivan, Richard. 1959. *The Coronation of Charlemagne: What Did It Signify?* Heath.
———. 1963. *In the Age of Charlemagne*. U of Oklahoma P.
Winston, Richard. 1956. *Charlemagne: From the Hammer to the Cross*. Eyre.

John Churchill, Duke of Marlborough
Churchill, Winston. 1958. *Marlborough: His Life and Times*. Harrap.
Foot, Michael. 1967. *The Pen & The Sword*. Monthly Review.

Oliver Cromwell
Ashley, Maurice. 1958. *The Greatness of Oliver Cromwell*. MacMillan.
Belloc, Hilaire. 1936. *Cromwell*. Cassell.
Blauvelt, Mary. 1937. *Oliver Cromwell: A Dictator's Tragedy*. Putnam's.
Carlyle, Thomas. n.d. *Oliver Cromwell's Letters and Speeches*. Estes.
Firth, Charles. 1900. *Oliver Cromwell and the Rule of the Puritans in England*. Putnam's.
Gardiner, Samuel. 1901. *Oliver Cromwell*. Longmans.
Hayward, F. H. 1934. *The Unknown Cromwell*. Allen.
Hill, Christopher. 1970. *God's Englishman: Oliver Cromwell and the English Revolution*. Dial.
Johnstone, Hilda. n.d. *Oliver Cromwell and His Times*. Dodge.
Morley, John. 1936. *Oliver Cromwell*. Cassell.

Benjamin Disraeli

Blake, Robert. 1967. *Disraeli*. St. Martin's.

Bradford, Sarah. 1983. *Disraeli*. Stein.

Clarke, Sir Edward. 1926. *Benjamin Disraeli: The Romance of a Great Career*. MacMillan.

Derieux, Mary. *One Hundred Great Lives*. 1944. Disraeli, Greystone. World.

Benjamin Disraeli's Letters: 1815-1834. U of Toronto P, 1982.

Hibbert, Christopher. 1978. *Disraeli and His World*. Scribner's.

Maurois, Andre. 1928. *Disraeli: A Picture of the Victorian Age*. Time.

Pearson, Hesketh. 1951. *Dizzy: The Life & Personality of Benjamin Disraeli, Earl of Beaconsfield*. Harper.

Johann Wolfgang Von Goethe

Brandes, Georg. 1924. *Wolfgang Goethe*. Frank.

Fairley, Barker. 1947. *A Study of Goethe*. Clarendon.

Friedenthal, Richard. 1965. *Goethe: His Life and Times*. World.

Lewes, George H. 1885. *The Story of Goethe's Life*. Houghton.

Ludwig, Emil. 1928. *Goethe: The History of a Man, 1749-1832*. Putnam's.

Nevinson, Henry W. 1932. *Goethe: Man and Poet*. Nisbet.

George Herbert

Charles, Amy. 1977. *A Life of George Herbert*. Cornell UP.

Fish, Stanley. 1978. *The Living Temple*. U of California P.

Freer, Coburn. 1972. *Music for a King*. Johns Hopkins UP.

Harmon, Barbara. 1982. *Costly Monuments*. Harvard UP.

The Poetical Works of George Herbert. 1854. Appleton.

The Works of George Herbert. 1972. Clarendon.

Alexander von Humboldt

Hagan, Victor von. 1945. *South America Called Them*. Knopf.

Kellner, L. 1963. *Alexander von Humboldt*. Oxford UP.

Terra, Helmut de. 1955. *Humboldt: The Life and Times of Alexander von Humboldt*. Knopf.

Thomas, M. Z. 1960. *Alexander von Humboldt: Scientist, Explorer, Adventurer*. Pantheon.

Washington Irving

Bowden, Mary. 1981. *Washington Irving*. Twayne.

Dudleywarner, Charles. 1909. *Irving*. Houghton.

McFarland, Philip. 1979. *Sojourners*. Atheneum.

Wagenknecht, Edward. 1962. *Washington Irving: Moderation Displayed*. Oxford UP.

Williams, Stanley. 1971. *The Life of Washington Irving*. Octagon.

John Keats

Bate, Walter J. 1963. *John Keats*. Harvard UP.

Bush, Douglas. 1966. *John Keats: His Life and Writings*. MacMillan.

Colvin, Sidney. 1917. *John Keats: His Life and Poetry, His Friends, Critics and After-Fame*. MacMillan.

Gittings, Robert. 1968. *John Keats*. Little.

The Letters of John Keats. Oxford UP, 1952.

Lowell, Amy. 1925. *John Keats*. Houghton.

Peare, Catherine O. 1960. *John Keats: A Portrait In Words*. Dodd.

Ward, Aileen. 1963. *John Keats: The Making of a Poet*. Viking.

William Lamb

Cecil, David. 1954. *Melbourne*. Bobbs.

Martin Luther

Atkinson, James. 1968. *Martin Luther and the Birth of Protestantism*. Knox.

Bainton, Roland H. 1950. *Here I Stand: A Life of Martin Luther*. Abingdon.

Benson, Kathleen. 1980. *A Man Called Martin Luther*. Concordia.

Clayton, Joseph. 1937. *Luther and His Work*. Bruce.

Dickens, A. G. 1977. *Martin Luther and the Reformation*. Hodder.

Erikson, Erik. 1962. *Young Man Luther: A Study in Psychoanalysis and History*. Norton.

Grisar, Hartmann. 1930. *Martin Luther: His Life and Work*. Herder.

Kooiman, W. J. n.d. *By Faith Alone: The Life of Martin Luther*. Philosophical Library.

Marius, Richard. 1974. *Luther*. Lippincott.

Nestingen, James A. 1959. *Martin Luther: His Life and Teachings*. Fortress.

Ritter, Gerhard. 1963. *Luther*. Greenwood.

Simon, Edith. 1968. *Luther Alive: Martin Luther and the Making of the Reformation*. Doubleday.

Smith, Preserved. 1911. *The Life and Letters of Martin Luther*. Houghton.

Todd, John. 1965. *Martin Luther: A Biographical Study*. Newman.

Thomas Babington Macaulay

Bryant, Arthur. 1979. *Macaulay*. Harper.

Clive, John. 1975. *Macaulay: The Shaping of the Historian*. Vintage.

Trevelyan, George. 1978. *The Life and Letters of Lord Macaulay*. Oxford UP.

Felix Mendelssohn

Blunt, Wilfred. 1974. *On Wings of Song: A Biography of Felix Mendelssohn*. Scribner's.

Erskine, John. 1941. *Song Without Words: The Story of Felix Mendelssohn*. Messner.

Marek, George R. 1972. *Gentle Genius: The Story of Felix Mendelssohn*. Funk.

Moscheles, Ignetz. 1874. *Recent Music and Musicians*. Holt.

Werner, Eric. 1963. *Mendelssohn: A New Image of the Composer and His Age*. MacMillan.

Alexander Pope

Fraser, George. 1978. *Alexander Pope*. Routledge.

Griffin, Dustin. 1978. *Alexander Pope: The Poet in the Poems*. Princeton UP.

Mack, Maynard. 1982. *Collected in Himself*. U of Delaware P.

Nicolson, M. and G. Rousseau. 1968. *This Long Disease, My Life*. Princeton UP.

Quennell, Peter. 1968. *Alexander Pope: The Education of Genius*. Stein.

Russo, John. 1972. *Alexander Pope: Tradition and Identity*. Harvard UP.

Sherburn, George. 1963. *The Early Career of Alexander Pope*. Russell.

Sitwell, Edith. 1930. *Alexander Pope*. Faber.

Armand-Jean du Plessis Richelieu

Auchincloss, Louis. 1972. *Richelieu*. Viking.

Belloc, Hilaire. 1929. *Richelieu: A Study*. Lippincott.

Burckhardt, Carl J. 1967. *Richelieu and His Age: His Rise to Power*. Harcourt.

Erlanger, Phillipe. 1968. *Richelieu: The Thrust For Power*. Stein.

Lodge, Richard. 1896. *Richelieu*. MacMillan.

O'Connell, D. P. 1968. *Richelieu*. World.

Lucius Annaeus Seneca

Griffin, Miriam. 1974. *Seneca*. Routledge.

Gummere, Richard. 1963. *Seneca the Philosopher and His Modern Message*. Cooper Square.

Seneca: His Tenne Tragedies. Indiana UP, 1964.

Seneca's Tragedies. MacMillan, 1969.

Sorenson, Villy. 1984. *Seneca: The Humanist at the Court of Nero*. U of Chicago P.

Sir Philip Sidney

Bill, Alfred. 1937. *Astrophel or The Life and Death of the Renowned Sir Philip Sidney*. Farrar.

Connell, Dorothy. 1977. *Sir Philip Sidney: The Maker's Mind*. Clarendon.

Weiner, Andrew. 1977. *Sir Philip Sidney and the Poetics of Protestantism*. U of Minnesota P.

Sir Robert Walpole

Oliver, F. S. 1931. *The Endless Adventure*. MacMillan.

Plumb, J. H. 1956. *Sir Robert Walpole: The Making of a Statesman*. Houghton.

———. 1973. *Sir Robert Walpole: The King's Minister, v. II*. Kelley.

Arthur Wellesley, Duke of Wellington

Guedalla, Philip. 1931. *Wellington*. Literary Guild.

Longford, Elizabeth. 1969. *Wellington: The Years of the Sword*. Harper.

Petrie, Sir Charles. 1956. *Wellington: A Reassessment*. Barrie.

rle rle rle sh sh sh

The following research on Francis Galton and John Stuart Mill is in addition to the backgrounds of Galton's eminent men.

Francis Galton

Forrest, D. W. 1974. *Francis Galton: The Life and Work of a Victorian Genius*. Taplinger.

Galton, Francis. 1908. *Memories of My Life*. Methuen.

John Stuart Mill

Autobiography of John Stuart Mill. Columbia UP, 1927.

Cowling, Maurice. 1963. *Mill and Liberalism.* Harvard UP.

Ellery, John B. 1964. *John Stuart Mill.* Twayne.

Kamm, Josephine. 1977. *John Stuart Mill in Love.* Gordon.

John Mill's Boyhood Visit to France. U of Toronto P, 1960.

Packe, Michael. 1954. *The Life of John Stuart Mill.* MacMillan.

Ryan, Alan. 1974. *J. S. Mill.* Routledge.

Smith, Robert M., ed. 1930. *A Book of Biography.* Autobiography of John Stuart Mill. Doubleday.

Index

Abortion, 55, 84-85, 130-131
Achievement levels of countries, ways to measure, 160
Acton, Lord, 160-161
Adams, Abigail, and family, 51
Adams, Brooks, 185-186
Adoption programs, 127, 302, 315-316
Adult education, 275, 276-277
Affirmative action, 138
Affluence: decadence and, 198, 285-286; decline in U.S., 232, 234-236, 243, 245-247; decline in U.S. (future), 247-249; discussion by Glubb, 188-189, 192-193; higher education and, 273-277; illusion of, 300; indicators of, 226-231; intellectual pursuits and, 259; military action and, 189, 193-194, 291-292; of U.S. birth generations, 260; U.S. government policies and, 236-237, 239-240, 243, 244-246, 247-249; witholding of children by dominant women and, 107, 130-131, 133-134, 174
Africa: baby boom in, 283; origin of human species in, 143-144
Alaska, purchase of, 206
Alexander the Great, 175-176, 316
Algiers, 208
Allport, Gordon W., 12-13
Animal behavior, 25-26
Anti-Semitism, see Jews, discrimination against
Arabs, empire of, 188-191
Argentina, Great Britain and, 300
Aristotle, 30, 316
Armenians, massacred by Turks, 161
Arnold, Benedict, 294
Artificial insemination, 117-118
Asimov, Isaac, 178
Assortative mating, defined, 110
Attica Prison riots, 295
Attorneys, 230-231

Austria, 125
Aztecs, 147-148, 150

Baby boom, 260-261, 270, 274, 283
Balance of trade, 215-221, 223-224, 246-247
Barnes, Edward, 295
Bayme, Steven, 122
Beirut, Lebanon, attack on Marines in, 292
Bell, Terrel H., 267
Biafra, 161
Bible, The: evolution and, 98-99; spread of literacy in order to study, 212
Binet, Alfred, 96
Biological determinism, 25-27, 95-118, 137-138, 312-313, 321
Birth control, 55, 84, 130-131
Birth order, 36
Birth rate: in Africa, 283; in China, 329; in Japan, 266; of Jewish women, 127, 213; of Protestant women, 213; system of government and, 169-171; U.S. nadir, 302
Birth rate, declining, among dominant women: affluence and, 107, 130-131, 133-134, 174, 233; contrasted with nondominant women, 84-85, 233, 283; in U.S., 55, 88, 133-134, 233, 283
Blacks: discrimination against, 136-141, 286; intellectual achievement and, 116-117, 137-138; U.S. population of, 137
Boxer Rebellion, 207
Brain, size and capacity of, 97, 103-104
Bramblett, Claud, 26
British Proclamation of 1763, 202
Burns, Robert, 54, 124
Burt, Sir Cyril, 115-116

Cabet, Etienne, 285, 288
Calvinism, 212-213

351

Cambodia, 153-155
Cannata, Sam, 290
Capitalism, 167, 212-213
Careers, see Occupations
Carmelli, Dorit, 56-57
Carnegie, Andrew, 69; and family, 30-31
Caro, Robert A., 46-50
Carter, E. Graydon, 295
Céline, Louis Ferdinand, 184
Central America, migration and immigration, 146-150, 153-155. See also names of individual countries
Child-rearing methods: day-care centers and, 317; Dr. Spock and, 283-285; transmitted from mother to daughter, 27, 36, 61, 64; transmitted from mother to son, 50-51, 64, 91; transmitted through books, 64, 285
Child-rearing schools, proposed, 324-326, 328, 329-330
Children: physical development of, 27-28; psychological development of, 28-30
China: birth rate of, 329; Boxer Rebellion, 207; currency inflation, 248; dominance and communism in, 163, 171; dynastic cycles, 195, 207; foreign investment allowed in, 172; peasant population of, 171, 329; Taiwan, 171; U.S. intervention in, 207
Christianity, evolution and, 98-99
Civil War: dominance and, 173-174; foreign trade during, 216
Civilizations, stages of: defined by Sir John Glubb, 186-193; events marking, 198-200. See also Cycles of history
Class systems, 105-108, 119, 166-167
Collective attitude, of country, 159, 175, 177, 249, 292
Colleges, junior and community, 273-275
Colleges and universities, U.S.: funding for, 251-252, 273-274, 275, 279, 316, 325; future of, 279; increased expectations about, 274-279; numerical growth of, 251-252, 273-275, 276-277
Comaneci, Nadia, 329
Communal living, 285, 288, 322-323
Communism, 163-172
Connolly, Cyril, 124

Consultants, 232
Corporations, funds for education from, 325
Counterculture, 285, 286
Creation, date of, 98-99
Credit, consumer, 235
Crete, 214
Crime: decadence and increases in, 287, 293, 294-297, 298-299; dictatorships and, 170, 298; intolerance of, in U.S., 226; vigilante reactions to, 299
Criticalness, confused with dominance, 17, 137
Cro-Magnon man, 103
Cuba, 153-155, 163, 171, 172, 207
Cults, 290-291
Culture: defined, 27; evolution and, 102
Currency debasement, 238-239, 248
Cycles of history: analyses of specific, 184-197; concept of, 175-178, 183-186, 198. See also Civilizations, stages of

Darwin, Charles, 98-99, 101, 105, 117, 161-162
Day care, 31, 317
Debt: consumer, 235; international, 247; national, 224-225, 245-246, 247-248, 293, 301-302
Decadence: affluence and, 285-286; crime and, 287, 293, 294-297, 298-299; defined, 192, 281-282, 287
Deference, dominance and, 16-17
Deferred adjudication, 226, 293, 295
Deficit spending, see Debt, national
Demands, see Child-rearing methods; Discipline; Expectations
Democracy: Athenian, 184; dominance required for, 162-163, 168, 173-174, 177-178, 314, 329; foreign investment and, 172; future of U.S., 314-315; nondominant citizens and, 165, 174-175, 314; U.S.S.R. and, 175, 177-178, 329
Depressions, U.S., 217, 218, 224, 263
Devsirme, 319-321, 323-324, 330
Diaspora, 123
Dictatorships: potential for U.S., 297-301; predicted by Plato, 184; steps in establishing, 169-171; U.S.S.R. compared to Tsarist Russia, 165-166

Dignity, 278-279
Discipline, defined, 29
Discrimination: against blacks, 136-141, 286; against dominant groups, 123-126, 128, 161, 313-314; against Hispanics, 141; against Jews, 120, 123-128, 161, 167, 177-178; against non-dominant groups, 161-162, 313; against women, 73, 78-79, 129-136, 139, 141, 263-264, 266; defined, 119-120
Divorce: changing attitudes toward, 89, 90, 233, 288; dominance combinations and, 60, 72, 82, 90; economic status and, 82-84, 134-136
Dobson, James, 285
Dominance: confused with criticalness, 17, 137; confused with unfriendliness, 17-18, 137; deference and, 16-17; defined, 11-12, 14-18, 308-309; underlying motivations for, defined, 28-30, 32-33
Dominance ratios: in China, 171; in communist countries, 163-165; in East Germany, 164-165; in eastern and western U.S., 151-153; in Ireland, 165; in Mexico, 147-148, 155-156; national success and, 209-210, 313; in Poland, 165; political systems and, 160, 162-175, 313-315; in U.S.S.R., 163-164, 177-178. See also Immigration
Dominican Republic, 207
Dropouts, 84, 316-317
Drug abuse, 294-295
Duke, Paul, Jr., 220
Durant, Will and Ariel: on equality and freedom, 149, 163; on the Huguenots, 176; on intellectual achievement and decadence, 279; on population control, 157; works authored by, 186

Early man, 101-103, 143-147
Economic status: divorce and, 82-84, 134-136; political systems and, 163-168
Education: change in minimum expected level of, U.S., 274-278; effect of teachers on, 261, 263-266, 272-273; funding for, 251-252, 273-274, 275, 279, 316-317, 325-326; growth of

higher, in U.S., 251-252, 273-275, 276-277; inadequacies in U.S., 261-263, 264, 265, 267-273, 276; intelligence and, 265; in Japan, 265-267; kibbutz, 321-324, 330; in Ottoman Empire, 319-321, 323-324, 330; parental demands and, 31, 62, 63-66, 68, 265, 266; Plato's theories of, 318-319, 321, 323; in U.S.S.R., 329
Educational testing, 269-272
El Salvador, 170
Emigration, see Immigration
Emotional stability, 20-21
Employee theft, 293
Employment, guaranteed, 140, 166, 167-169
Energy and success, 18-20, 109, 115
Engels, Friedrich, 195
England, see Great Britain
Entrepreneurs, 35, 75
Environment versus heredity, 25-27, 95-118, 312-313, 321
Equality, 55-56, 149, 163, 166, 170, 174
Etruscans, 194
Evolution: biological versus cultural, 101-102; of early man, 101-103, 145; intelligence and, 101, 103-104, 115, 117; religious controversy over, 98-99, 117
Expectations: of father, 51, 63-68, 75-76, 315; of mother, 27-35, 36-37, 54, 61-63, 73-75, 97-98, 309-310, 315; societal, 66, 67, 77, 78, 274, 278-279; and success, 19-20, 22-23, 66-67, 74-75, 275, 278; of teachers, 263-265
Eysenck, H. J., 95-96, 111

Failure, fear of, 34-36, 63, 312
Failure rate, of businesses, 225-226
Falkland Islands, 300
Family size, 260, 270, 329. See also Birth rate
Fancher, Raymond, 108
Farmers, 235-236
Fatalism, 261-262
Federal Deposit Insurance Corporation (FDIC), 249
Federal Home Loan Bank Board, 248
Federal Savings and Loan Insurance Corporation (FSLIC), 248-249

Fertility, *see* Birth rate; Birth control
Fiat money, 239, 243, 244-245
Financial advisers, 232
Fiscal responsibility, of countries, 242-245
Flexner, James Thomas, 120-121
Florida, acquisition of, 205-206
Forbes 400, 288-289
Ford, Henry, 184; and family, 112
Foreign aid, 236-237
Foreign investment, 172
Foreign trade, 215-221, 223-224, 246-247
Fourier, Charles, 285, 288
France: historical cycles of, 195, 299; Huguenots, 161, 176-177; lotteries in, 292; North America and, 202, 205; political system, 169; work week in, 232
Frank, Leonard Roy, 159
Freedom: decadence and, 287-288, 297-298; dominance in U.S. and, 173; equality and, 149, 163; immigration to U.S. and, 149; socialism and, 169; in U.S.S.R., 177-178
French and Indian War, 202
Freud, Sigmund, 27, 34, 129, 161, 185, 323
Friedman, Meyer, 56
Fuchs, Klaus, 294

Galdi, Theodor W., 236-237
Galton, Sir Francis: Charles Darwin and, 101, 104-105; class system and, 105-108; selection of eminent individuals by, 111-112, 114; theories of, 96, 108-111, 115, 117
Gardner, David P., 267
Gender and dominance, 43-44, 51, 63, 67, 75, 77, 91
Generations: accomplishing, 197-198, 202-204, 259; birth, 197, 202-203; birth, actions of U.S., 301-302; birth, affluence and U.S., 260; defined, 187, 197-198; political rights of, 301
Genetics and intelligence, 95-118, 137-138, 312-313, 321
Germany: East, 164-165; Jews in, 124-125, 126; Third Reich, 194-196, 221, 248, 299; Weimar Republic, 126;

West, 214, 230; World War II population losses, 221
Gibbon, Edward, 185
Glubb, Sir John, 186-193, 260
Goertzel, Victor and Mildred G., 42, 79
Gold, 225, 239-245, 289
Golf, 226-229
Good, I. J., 157
Goodall, Jane, 26
Government spending: deficit, 225, 245-246, 248, 293, 301-302; waste in, 293
Grace, J. Peter, 293
Great Britain: Age of Affluence in, 227, 230-231; currency debasement in, 238; decline in world status of, 300-301; trade and production in, 214, 217
Greece, 184-185, 214. *See also* Alexander; Democracy
Guam, 207

Haiti, 153-154, 207
Harter, Carl, 260
Head Start, Project, 317
Heidrick and Struggles, 133
Heredity and personality, 25-27
Heritability of intelligence, 95-118, 137-138, 312-313, 321
Hippies, *see* Counterculture
Hispanics, discrimination against, 141
Hitler, Adolf, 124-125, 194-196, 299
Home ownership, 234-235
Homo erectus, 101-103
Homo habilis, 101
Honduras, 170
Huguenots, 161, 176-177
Human nature, lack of change in, 185, 210
Hume, David, 54
Hungerford, Margaret Wolfe, 54

Ibn Khaldun, 300
Illegal immigrants, 140, 153-154
Illegitimate children, 324
Illiteracy, 212, 267, 276
Immigration: Central American and Caribbean to U.S., 153-155; Chinese to U.S., 171; colonization of U.S., 149-150; Cuban to U.S., 153-155;

dominant women, 149; European to U.S., 150-151; Huguenot, 176-177; illegal, 140, 153-154; Indians of North and South America, 146-150; Indochinese to U.S., 153-155, 171; Irish to U.S., 153-154; marriage patterns and, 88-89, 90, 123; Mexico to U.S., 153-155; slaves brought to U.S., 137; Spanish conquests in New World, 149-150; U.S. laws and, 174; western areas of U.S., 151-153; world limits reached, 156-158

Import and export ratios, see Balance of trade

Incas, 147-150

Income: factors obscuring decline in U.S., 234-235; U.S. statistics, 61, 234

Income tax, 288

Indians, North American: migration patterns of, 146-148; population, 149-150; wars with, 150, 202, 206, 209

Indians, South and Central American, 146-150

Indochina, 153-155, 163, 171, 294

Inherited wealth, 22, 69, 75-76, 91, 105-107

Intellectual achievement, related to cultural decline, 260, 279

Intelligence: definitions of, 265; and early stimulus, 31, 34, 62, 97-98, 110; heritability of, 95-118, 137-138, 312-313, 321; success and, 18-20, 109, 115

Intelligence tests, author's experience with, 2-5

International commerce: relation to dominance of, 215, 221-222. See also Foreign trade

Ireland, 153-154, 165

Islas Malvina, Las, 300

Isolation, of low-income groups, 69-70, 85

Israel, 125, 296-297, 321-324, 330

Jacquard, Albert, 98

Janissaries, 319-321, 323-324, 330

Japan: affluence in, 228, 230, 232, 249; childhood demands in, 62; Commodore Perry and, 207; education in,

265-267; gold reserves of, 242-243; historical cycles of, 196-197; intellectual achievement in, 259; postwar commercial success of, 214, 221; status recognition in, 16-17; work ethic in, 213, 232; World War II population losses of, 221

Jefferson, Thomas, 292, 301

Jensen, Arthur R., 115-117

Jesuits, 327-328

Jews: discrimination against, 120-128, 161, 167, 177-178; intellectual achievement and, 111, 121, 123; marriage patterns of, 90, 121-123; matrilineal descent and, 121-123; U.S. population of, 127-128. See also Israel

Johnson, Lyndon, and family, 44-46, 50-51

Jones, Landon Y., 260

Jones, Syl, 117

Kamin, Leon, 115-116, 118

Kearns, Doris, 44-46

Kennedy, Joseph P., and family, 113

Kibbutz, 321-324, 330

Kipling, Rudyard, 195

Korea, 165

Labor unions, 225, 232

Lancaster, Jane B., 25

Laos, 153-155

Larsen, Yvonne W., 267

Lawick-Goodall, Hugo and Jane van, 26

Lazarus, Emma, 151

Leadership, relation to dominance defined, 15-16

Leopold, Aldo, 184

Liberia, 156

Literacy, 212, 267, 276

Livy, 194

Lotteries, 292

Louisiana Purchase, 205

Loyola, Ignatius of, 327

Lueger, Karl, 125

Luther, Martin, 211-212

Macdonald, Julie, 25

Macedon, 175-176, 184

Machiavelli, Niccolo, 185

Maine, attack on the, 207, 291-292

Marriage: arranged, 88; second, 82-83, 90

Marriage patterns: in class systems, 105-108; dominance and, 56-91; of immigrants, 88-89, 90; Jewish, 90, 121-123

Marx, Karl, 195, 322

Maslow, Abraham, 22

Mayas, 147-150

McClelland, David C., 33, 35, 160

Medical discoveries, 255

Medical professions, 132-133, 231

Meiji restoration, 197

Menninger, Karl, 124, 210

"Mental age," 96

Mexican War, 206-207

Mexico: dominance levels in, 147-150, 170; foreign investment, 155-156, 172; gold ownership of, 244; U.S. military actions in, 206-207

Migrations, of early man, 145-146. *See also* Immigration

Military personnel, children of, 72-73

Mill, John Stuart, 330; and family, 51, 315

Minimum wage laws, 139-140

Minoans, 214

Mizuno Tadakuni, 196-197

Montagu, Ashley, 100

Moses, Robert, and family, 46-51

Moshav, 322

Mozart, Wolfgang Amadeus, and family, 315

Muromachi shogunate, 196

Mycenae, 214

Napoleon Bonaparte, 175, 195, 299

Nation at Risk, A, 267-268

National Commission on Excellence in Education, 267

National debt, 224-225, 245-246, 247-248, 293, 301-302

Nicaragua: communism and, 163, 171; immigration to U.S. from, 154-155; U.S. intervention in, 207-208

Ninety-Five Theses, 211-212

Nobel prize, 255-259

Nomads, 193-194

Nondominance: defined, 16; self-confidence and, 63; tolerance and, 11, 309

O'Sullivan, John Louis, 195

Obedience, 162, 170

Obesity, 231

Occupational level, educational level and, 275-276, 277-278

Occupations, and personality traits, 19-21, 72-73, 210, 311-312

Odbert, Henry S., 12-13

Olympic Games, 164, 329

Oneida Community, 285

Ottoman Empire, 319-321, 323-324, 330

Overpopulation, 157-158

Parthia, 127-128

Patriarchal attitudes, *see* Women, discrimination against

Patriotism, 294, 315

"Peer pressure," 31-32

Perceptions: distorted by expectations, 22-23; distorted by personality traits, 53-57; variance with age, 310

Permissiveness, 283-285

Perry, Commodore Matthew C., 207

Perry, Nancy J., 325

Persecution, *see* Discrimination

Personality and heredity, 25-27

Personality and personality traits, definition of, 12-14

Personality surveys, author's experience with, 2-5

"Pet rock," 229-230

Pets, 229

Philippines, 171, 207

Phoenicia, 214

Plato, 184, 318-319, 321, 323-324

Poland, 165

Political asylum, 155

Political systems, influence of national dominance levels on, 160, 162-175, 313-314

Pollution, 236, 293

Polybius, 131, 184-185

Population: American Indian, 149-150; black, in U.S., 136-137; European immigrant, in U.S., 151; Jewish, in U.S., 127-128; peasant, in China, 171, 329; urban, in U.S.S.R., 166; world growth, 102-103, 156-158

Prison, 295-296